Talking with Nature
Journey into Nature

A Michael Roads Reader

Michael J. Roads

NEW WORLD LIBRARY
NOVATO, CALIFORNIA

An H J Kramer Book

published in a joint venture with

New World Library

Editorial office: Administrative office:
P.O. Box 1082   14 Pamaron Way
Tiburon, California 94920   Novato, California 94949

Talking with Nature © 1985, 1987 Michael J. Roads
Journey into Nature © 1990 Michael J. Roads

Cover Design: Cathey Flickinger
Interior Illustrations for *Talking with Nature:* Genevieve Wilson
Typography: Cathey Flickinger

Library of Congress Cataloging-in-Publication Data
Roads, Michael J.
Talking with Nature and Journey into Nature / by Michael Roads
p.   cm.
ISBN 1-932073-05-1 (pbk.   :   alk. paper)
1. New Age Movement.   2. Nature—Religious Aspects
3. Consciousness—Religious aspects.   4. Pan (Greek deity).
I. Title
BP605.N48R615   2003   88-80727
219.2'12—dc   CIP

First Omnibus Edition, July 2003
ISBN 1-932073-05-1
Printed in Canada on acid-free, partially recycled paper
Distributed to the trade by Publishers Group West

10 9 8 7 6 5 4 3 2 1

Contents

Publishers' Preface

Talking with Nature is a book that cries out for special attention. It is the story of a man who discovered he possessed the ability to commune intelligently and articulately with the souls of plants, animals, and even rocks and rivers. It evokes the same sense of contact with the miraculous that distinguished Carlos Castaneda's early work.

At first, Michael Roads found himself disturbed by his strange new power. He questioned it relentlessly. Finally, when he could no longer deny his experience, he allowed Nature to nourish and heal him. Nature spoke to him of her deep concern with the role of man in determining the fate of the Earth. With patience, compassion, and even humor, she taught him how to become one with the whole of creation.

Talking with Nature is an important book because it offers a new way for those who want to heal the wounds of alienation and become reunited in loving awareness with the natural world.

When Michael Roads went on to write *Journey into Nature,* we felt privileged to publish this second book as well. Michael had learned to merge his consciousness with Nature. Rather than merely communicating, he became one with water, plant, mineral, animal, and even the terrifying fury of a raging storm. He writes of these experiences with chilling veracity, telling us what Nature is longing for all of us to hear.

The message of these books is one of hope. A solution is in sight. Like Michael Roads, humanity can learn to accept and listen to the voices of Nature. We can learn to reconnect ourselves with the spiritual essence of the universe.

Michael Roads has taken a giant step. The nourishment of the soul, body, and spirit which Nature offered to him is available to us all. He speaks to us of the gift of joyful reconciliation. Nature can be our friend instead of our adversary. She can instruct us in finding our way back to the true path. The birds, plants, rivers, winds are praying for us. Will we listen to them before it is too late? Can we learn to hear in time?

We believe we can. That is why we publish this book with such special enthusiasm.

Harold and Linda Kramer, Publishers

Talking with Nature

To my darling Treenie, with love.
The fairy ring is growing!

Foreword

This is a lovely, extraordinary book. For many, it will open the way to a new connection with Nature.

Nature is a great work of art and design, a fantastic, intricate, ever-flowing Oneness, of which we are an integral part. We of the civilized world now feel separate from Nature because in the last centuries we have become onlookers and seek only to control Nature for power and profit. We, the rightful stewards of the planet, have failed lamentably and culpably in our stewardship and are rapidly turning this beautiful world into a desert.

In the past centuries, the sensitive feminine faculties of the right hemisphere of the brain have largely gone dormant and become atrophied. These poetical and imaginative powers can apprehend the Living Whole. We must now renew our awareness that visible Nature is the form; the heart is the living Idea. The human being, that crown of evolution, has been so designed that he or she can blend in thought with these Ideas.

Realize the great truth that each of us is a droplet of divinity, a spiritual being housed in a temple, the body, which enables us to operate

3

Talking with Nature

in the heavy density of the material world. We have become so imbued with the "onlooker consciousness" that we too easily assume that God or our guides will speak to us from outside. But the great truth is that the beings of the higher worlds speak to us *within our own thinking.* All is Thought; in thinking we blend with higher beings.

God speaks to us within our thinking. God is within every flower and tree, animal and bird, crystal and cloud and ocean wave. Therefore, it follows that humanity, once over the barrier of conceptual separation, can blend and unite *in thinking* with the higher worlds.

Now we are offered this remarkable book describing one man's experience. If the author can achieve this "talking with nature" then all of us can potentially do the same. The manner of approach and attitude of mind are what matter. Approach the natural form — tree or hill, river or blossom — and speak inwardly with the elemental being within it. Then watch the response in your mind and heart and give back love. Let the flow begin. This form of meditation is awakening the "eye of the mind."

This book is a beautiful statement of this experience, which is open to us all. Those who achieve it are part of the awakening of Planet Earth, for humanity now stands at the threshold of a birth into wider consciousness of the great Oneness of all life.

Of course, this is the knowledge of the mystics and initiates of all ages. It has in our time been well demonstrated in such centers as Findhorn in Scotland, where Peter Caddy, through his sensitive friend Dorothy Maclean, established direct telepathic contact with elemental beings. The result was a fabulous garden of vegetables, fruits, and flowers grown in arid sand dunes. The desert can indeed blossom like the rose when man contacts and works with the nature spirits and devas.

This, Michael Roads's experience and achievement, is a wonderful step and an inspiring example. Read this book and learn how each of us can make this approach. It is an aspect of the great awakening of humanity now taking place on the threshold of the Aquarian Age.

Sir George Trevelyan
Badminton, Avon
May 15, 1987

4

Acknowledgments

First and foremost, I wish to thank Treenie, for "believing" in me. Without her support and encouragement this book would never have been written. Togetherness is the key which helped unlock the hidden.

To Richard Bach, who has proved that words can bridge time and distance, I offer my special thanks for the comment on the cover and for his loving support and inspiration.

To Hal Kramer, a publisher who not only believes in changing lives, but actually makes it happen, my deepest gratitude.

My thanks to the universe for sending Linda Tellington-Jones to visit with such perfect timing.

Thanks also to my editor, Greg Armstrong, who edited my manuscript with great sensitivity and caring.

Every writer needs to be discovered by a person sensitive to their potential. My special thanks to Linda Lutzkendorf who recognized the potential of this book and helped to make it possible.

Jack Igguldon, who was my first literary critic, advisor, and mentor — thank you.

Various people throughout my life have been important catalysts. With perfect timing they have revealed my life's path, and always in accordance with my faltering stumble. To these people, whom I count as very special friends, thank you.

1 September

The Platypus disappeared underwater as though sucked downward, so effortless was its passing. Not far away, wind whistled through the long, thin needles of a solitary River Oak, a high melody of sound invoking a feeling of coolness despite the warmth of the spring sun. A slight breeze moved the leaves near where I was sitting on the river bank. The water flowed cool and clear, sparkling in the sun from endless flickering points of light.

"Help me," I asked.

I spoke to the river, to the rocks, to all the different plants which grew in a semitropical profusion around me. I spoke to Nature. Inside, I felt it was smiling at me.

Help yourself. If you wish to tell the story of our connection, then write from the point of contact which you are.

This was not going to be easy. I tried again.

"What I need is help to explain in a concise and simple way the human connection with Nature. I need something that people can relate to. Something which is easy to understand and accept."

The smile became more pronounced.

You are suggesting some written material which does not stretch the imagination, something simple enough for the mind to comprehend.

"That's it," I said triumphantly. "Just the thing."

The smile vanished.

Forget it. How can we write of unseen realities, hint of unheard concepts, or even demonstrate the practicality of inner truths, without disturbing the slumbering Self within?

A long, deep sigh.

We have a choice, my friend. Either you write it as it happens, as it is revealed, or forget the whole project. I can offer no compromise. Accept it. This will be written as a synthesis of man and Nature.

For a long time I stared across the river, trying to pretend it was not happening this way. Surely I could write my book the way I wanted. It was mine to control. The rock beneath me was very patient. In a physical sense it had not moved in a very long time, but I could feel a surge of conscious activity. I was plagued with a cross-section of thoughts. Who will believe me if I present it the way it is happening? Surely the best plan is to disguise the issue and make a story of it? The thought of *Jonathan Livingston Seagull* crossed my mind. Problem is, that's already been done. This is ridiculous. I cannot just write that I listen to trees and rocks and rivers, that I talk to them and they talk back into my mind. I squirmed and fidgeted, pretending I could not hear the river chuckling as it flowed smoothly past my rock.

I could feel an expectancy around me. The trees all looked their normal, majestic, indifferent selves, while the rocks maintained a solid silence. A Heron swooped down, bright eyed and alert. Deciding I was no threat, it carefully alighted on the gravel on the opposite side of the river and, cocking its head to one side, held me with a fixed stare.

"Okay," I said. "If you have an opinion we might as well hear it."

There was a powerful feeling of bird energy moving into the more subtle areas of awareness.

We would also like to be involved. If you are going to write of our connection, then we will represent our own point of view.

I stared at the Heron.

"Do you represent all birds or just your own species?"

The Heron stabbed into the shallows, its rapier beak flashing downward in an action defying the eye. Thrusting itself into the air, it winged slowly away.

We represent ourselves only. We will contact you when the time is right.

The consciousness of Heron was curling in upon itself, becoming smaller and fading swiftly. It was interesting to realize that in no way was it a single, solitary bird which spoke into my mind. Rather the bird was no more than a trigger for my slowly developing awareness. It was the point of focus which allowed me to be aware that the Heron consciousness waited for me, not wishing to impose on my mind unannounced. I stared at the words I had written.

"Nobody's going to believe this."

I spoke to the river flowing past my feet. For a while there was silence. I became aware of a surge of power from the river as though there was a gathering of force.

You have already reached your decision. It was made long before you came here. I suggest you now allow the clarity of a higher truth to move through you. The fear you have established is a real one and it can cause problems. You will now need to act in trust, knowing that the timing is right. Only the few will mock you. Those who are attracted to this book will have an inner hunger which seeks appeasement.

Your words will not be easy to digest. Questions will be asked and much inner dialogue will be worked through. This, however, is not your concern.

A favorite quotation by Victor Hugo moved swiftly across my mind: "Nothing has greater power than an idea whose time has arrived." It was a flash of illumination. The time "has" arrived. More and more people are looking for a higher truth and meaning in life, and what better starting place than our connection with Nature?

I smiled into the water.

"Okay, I'll do it your way, but if I am trying to present something which seems incredible, please help it to become credible."

The energy of river, coiled in an almost serpentine formlessness around me, was suddenly in motion. I had the fleeting sense of being in the center of a vast whirlpool, expanding outward with an exultant joy.

Go now. With acceptance comes expansion. If you can capture the experience on paper, this will be our mutual presentation to the people with whom you seek to communicate.

Several days elapsed while I digested the first encounter and prepared to commit myself to paper. I read and reread my words.

Nobody was going to believe this.

Gradually I was forced to accept that it was I who found it most difficult to believe. I realized that I had yet to conquer my fears.

Just as Nature was my challenge, it was also my guide, so one sunny morning I returned to my favorite place by the river.

It was cold, but crystal clear. A yard below the water surface, a shoal of tiny fish faced into the current, floating effortlessly in their fluid environment. On the smooth stones beneath them, a large, solitary shrimp made its way slowly and carefully to an unknown destination, its antennae waving methodically around it. A catfish drifted slowly past, vanishing beneath an overhanging rock.

It was a tranquil scene, and I felt encouraged by the sense of peace around me. I greeted the river. "Well, I'm back and I'm keen to continue the book."

September

A feeling of coiled power was once more present.

Oh, it's THE book now, is it? Quite an improvement on your previous MY book. If you can retain such an unattached attitude we should have little difficulty.

I felt rather put down.

"You seem to imply that I'm the only one who could be wrong, or is likely to be difficult."

I paused, hoping for some verbal comfort.

While you sit comfortably wrapped in a pitying ego, we have nothing, nothing at all.

For the next ten minutes I gazed in hurt silence across the river. My feeling of resentment slowly faded as I watched the antics of an Eastern Water Dragon trying hard to reach a succulent insect at the end of a long, very thin branch overhanging the water. I could see a connection between the dragon's laborious efforts to reach the end of the branch and acquire his prize, and my own efforts to approach communication with Nature from a clear, uncluttered mind. The dragon was not equipped for stealth on a long, bending, waving branch, but on a riverside tree stump or rock it could be patience itself, leaping like an uncoiled spring when it was sure of its prey. The branch denied this, so it had to change style. A plop as the dragon dropped into the water indicated its lack of success. Swimming with head held high, the dragon disappeared under the branches of an overhanging shrub. I also was out on a limb. This limb was of my own making, supported by my old belief system, and sustained by my self-image to the world.

Words moved from the source of power.

Do as the dragon did. Let go and fall into the river Let the river of life sweep you beyond all aid from old and worn concepts. I will support you. Trust me. As you swim from an old consciousness, blind to higher realities beyond your physical world, trust that I will guide you with care and love into a new stream of consciousness. I will open

13

a new world before you. Can you trust me enough to let go of the known, and swim in an unknown current?

Even as I stared into the river, a dark cloud moved across the sun. The water was no longer clear. Suddenly it was dark and opaque, clouded with mystery and, to my reasoning mind, loaded with threat. I knew this was the way it must be. If the way before me was an old familiar scene, then I traveled the known path.

"I accept. I will cast myself as fully as I can into the stream you offer, and I am grateful. I ask only that you are patient with me, for I have many old fears, and like the dragon, I cling from long habit."

The cloud swept away and the river was again clear, sparkling with invitation. The power surged, slowly uncoiling with an inner sigh. I felt a sense of peace and joy sweep over me.

My commitment was made.

My COMMITMENT to the task hadn't happened all at once. It had unfolded like fate over the years during my life as a farmer. I can look back now and recognize the stages.

It began with my wife, Treenie.

One evening, while sitting relaxed in our living room, she glanced at me. "The cows want moving," she suddenly announced.

I snorted with indignation. Her statement seemed a challenge, and I responded.

"Right! Just to prove you're wrong, we'll drive up there tomorrow at nine o'clock, and you can see for yourself all the contented cows on plenty of pasture."

In my smug satisfaction, I burrowed back into my book.

Next morning at nine o'clock, Treenie and I drove up to the back paddock. Shock! Practically the entire herd of cows was standing impatiently at the gate, waiting to be let out. I gaped at them, not willing to meet Treenie's eyes. You can imagine her next comment!

This was not to be an isolated incident. Over the next few months Treenie often became aware of the herd's need to change paddocks, regardless of the amount of pasture available. It occurred to me that since Treenie could receive their "move" messages, we could influence them with our thoughts. One evening we combined our thoughts to reach them. *We will move you cattle at nine o'clock tomorrow morning.* Smile if you like, but next morning at nine o'clock the cattle were all waiting to be moved. Now, I am not suggesting cattle can tell the time, because we eventually proved that they would begin to congregate well before the chosen hour; but the method worked, consistently, showing a stunning disregard for logic or reason.

During this time an area of land we had bought from the Forestry Commission had been cleared, developed and sown down to improved pasture. This land, known as Carvilla, lay at a 2,000-foot altitude, offering splendid views of the ocean along the north coast in one direction, while towering, rugged mountains dominated the other. Apart from where Carvilla joined our main farm at one end, the pasture was completely surrounded by unfenced forest, stretching as far as the eye could see over thousands of wild acres. Carvilla jutted as an elongated spur into the forest, possessing a long boundary. Not unnaturally, the wildlife were partial to a nibble of improved pasture and were lured in considerable numbers to our land.

With the organic development and improvement of the soil, Carvilla did not respond with growth the way I anticipated. I slowly realized that the forest wildlife was extracting a heavy toll from the new pasture.

After a few night visits, to my consternation, I found large numbers of Bennett's Wallaby (quite big fellows) and Scrub Wallabies and Pademelons in profusion. In the only way I knew to defend my pasture, I began to spend two nights a week shooting them. I quickly found it extremely distasteful, and rather than continue such a heartless task I contacted a few locals, offering them the opportunity to shoot for sport and meat — an offer quickly accepted. It seemed, however, to make little difference. The pasture which was carrying only thirty cows and calves made little extra growth.

To tip the balance in my favor, I decided I would have to become involved again; so once more I began night shooting. One night, after spotting a large wallaby in the headlights, I jumped out, rifle ready. The wallaby was only a few yards away as I raised my rifle. Suddenly the animal's head swung toward me, the shaft of light catching its eyes. Transformed to glowing red jewels, the eyes met mine, and I gazed spellbound into the soul of a wild and wonderful Nature. For long moments our eyes held, locked. Slowly and calmly the animal looked away and quietly grazed the pasture.

I stood silent, shocked to the core. Compassion, a comparative stranger to farmers saturated in death, surged powerfully from somewhere deep inside. I lowered my rifle and turned to walk back to the Land Rover. There had to be a different way. Violence could not be the answer. Violence begets violence. I knew I could not reach my objective in this manner.

I had twice used 10-80 poison, but this was no solution. It is a shocking form of subtle violence, insidious by the absence of the poisoner to witness the agony of death. By its very involvement, a rifle at least places you in a position where you witness your action, demanding a clean kill as a code of ethics.

I talked the problem over with Treenie, and together we reached the only solution possible. If we could "think"-communicate with our cattle, why not try and "think"-communicate with the wallabies.

Making such a decision was one thing, but carrying it out was another. We decided I should be the one to initiate the move owing to my current involvement, but how should I instigate such a thing? One morning, driving up to the wild hills of Carvilla, I stopped near a group of trees in the center of the paddock and, feeling rather self-conscious, prepared myself for an attempted communication.

I held the required agreement clearly in my thoughts, but so silent and remote was the act that I began to verbalize my request. Despite feeling foolish, I felt more positive and comfortable. Warming to my task, I fairly yelled my message to all the wallabies that might listen. It sounded something like this:

"I don't know if you wallabies can hear me, but I am offering an agreement with you by which we each meet our own needs. I am asking you to stop eating our pasture, and in exchange for this I will see to it that nobody shoots you again. However, because I realize I must share this land with you, I will allow you to graze around the outside of the paddock. Please don't take more than twenty yards."

Following this announcement, I paused expectantly. Nothing! Nothing except the mental echo of my own words. I was in no way convinced that anything would happen, but to keep my side of the agreement I chained and padlocked the entrance gate and told the shooters that I wanted no more shooting on my land. Eyeing me as though I were nutty, they agreed. I felt glad I did not tell them the reason!

Within only a few weeks, the pasture was thickening so rapidly that I was able to introduce an extra ten cows and calves. It continued to improve. Soon I had ninety cows and calves grazing over Carvilla, while the white clover grew in abundance. For three years we maintained this tenuous agreement, the pastures continuing to thrive and flourish. When the pasture was knee-high it was crisscrossed with wallaby trails, but their grazing was concentrated at the boundary. I confess, whoever they chose to measure the twenty yards took mighty strides. . . or bounds! In some areas, pasture grew right to the forest edge, while in other places they fed a long way into the paddock. On average I estimated they grazed about forty yards into the field.

One fact which emerged was obvious. We were able to communicate our wishes to the wildlife and reach an agreement for our mutual benefit. We recognized their divine right to life, realizing that cooperation with Nature offers unlimited potential.

There is a follow-up to this story. When we eventually decided to sell our farm, we sold it under separate titles. When the new occupants moved into Highfields, we retained ownership of Carvilla for another two years before selling it to the original buyer. During this time shooters broke the padlocks and, without our knowing, began shooting wallabies once more. When I visited the area three years after selling the farm, the owner asked me if pasture had ever grown on Carvilla. I stared at him in surprise.

"When I last walked Carvilla, white clover was knee-high," I said. He looked dour.

"Well, mate, I can assure you there's none there now," he replied.

He went on to tell me how he had found the place crawling with wallabies. They shot six thousand wallabies in two years! I was stunned. I realized immediately that such a number could not have been bred in such a short time. Considering the huge amount of forest, I had suspected there were large numbers in the area when we made our agreement, but I had no idea I was dealing with such numbers. It was only then I fully understood the extent to which our agreement had been kept. Apparently, as soon as the shooting began, the wallabies swarmed in, and, despite six thousand shot, they literally wiped out the pasture. I felt shocked, guilty, and angry.

But what could I say? I had never told him about the agreement — who would believe such a thing?

WE HAD BEEN MILKING for about eight years when dairying slid into economic decline. It was the perfect moment to merge the Friesian dairy herd into the Friesian/Hereford herd we had been breeding for several years and turn to beef farming.

One happy morning, I began the long-awaited task of demolishing the despised milking yards. It was blissful, but it proved to be a much tougher job than I anticipated. The rails were solidly welded water pipes. Swinging a fourteen-pound sledgehammer, I attacked each joint with eight years of pent-up ferocity, and it did not take long to raise some large blisters on my already-calloused hands. By using around twenty blows per joint, the yard slowly and painfully succumbed. Halfway through I was wiped out. As I sat quietly resting, a change of attitude moved through me, precipitated by an incredible thought. *If all life is connected, then the animal, mineral, and vegetable kingdoms are interconnected. Knowing the cooperation I have experienced with plants and animals, why should metal be so different?*

Gradually I surrendered to an inner peace, feeling some oh-so-subtle shift take place within. Refreshed, I stood up and, grasping the sledgehammer, prepared for another onslaught! Subtly, so subtly, the words moved easily into my mind.

Change your attitude. See the metal as living. Respect the material, the form of life. Approach the task with humility.

It all fit. I felt comfortable with this odd thought, even if I had no more than a surface understanding. I swung the sledgehammer with little force, my mind on the metal, once — twice — the third blow, and the end of the rail fell away. Rapidly I moved to the other end and repeated it. Two hours later, the yard was dismantled. Only then did I feel stunned . . . and frustrated. I mean, who would ever believe such a thing?

WE REACHED A STAGE where we were committed to selling the farm. We had several reasons. I had a chronic back injury, and we were fed up with the financial pressure. But, above and beyond all the normal, mundane reasons, something else beckoned. I cannot give it a name, or easily identify it, but within Nature I had become aware of another dimension. A dimension which, when explored, promised to vastly enrich our lives. A different truth was calling to us, for we were no longer the same people who had commenced farming a decade earlier in Australia.

I had become deeply involved with the organic farming movement in Tasmania. When Treenie and I were workers at a weekend

Organic Field Demonstration, I was introduced to a tall, bearded American with a Florida drawl. Hunter Lilly, a man in his late twenties, strolled into our lives as though he were a long-lost wayward son. It seemed natural that he would return home with us, becoming part of the family until we left Tasmania. The farm was sold and we were in the last few weeks of selling stock, tidying our affairs, farewelling friends, and attending to all the numerous things that need attention when a family of six decides to go nomadic for a lengthy period. The situation was practically under control when Hunter suggested he and I walk the South Coast Track. The reference did not mean much to me, but when he pointed it out on a map, I realized it was a walk of approximately 110 miles, with a small proportion on the remote, isolated, south coast beaches.

After some misgivings I agreed to accompany him. We made our preparations, and Treenie drove us on the six-hour journey down to Cockles Creek, south of Hobart. As she drove away, leaving us to face the wilderness, my misgivings once again bubbled to the surface. The night before we left home I had a very powerful dream. I dreamed that I had died. The dream was not frightening, but the experience was unusually strong. I stood with an angel in a cathedral-like valley, surrounded by people who were close and dear to me. I was overwhelmed. I knew these people, yet I didn't know them! But I knew, clearly, that I was dead. Anyway, I had been walking only an hour when the first blister emerged on one heel, and the ill-fitting, sixty-pound pack began to make its presence known. I wondered then if I might die on this walk, so powerful was the dream experience.

By the end of the first day of the ten-day walk, I had developed blisters on the heels of both feet. I had learned too late of the need for proper, thorough preparation for serious bush walks in a kind of wilderness from which some unfortunate people never emerge.

We walked — correction, Hunter walked, I limped — day after day through some of the world's most rugged and beautiful country. After eight days' walking filled with adventure and danger, some grim moments and some hilarious ones, we decided to rest for three days in a bush-walker's hut at Melaleuca, a remote, lonely tin-miner's retreat, miles from anywhere. There I attempted to heal my wounded heels. The blisters had long since turned into holes gouged into the flesh, which bled freely as I walked.

The attempt was futile. When we set off on our last two days of walking, it took only an hour for the wounds to reopen. I continued to our destination, Lake Pedder, in a blur of pain. Tormented shoulders met and merged with the pain lancing up from ravaged heels.

We started off on our last day at seven o'clock in the morning, determined that it would indeed be the last day. It was about four o'clock in the afternoon, and walking at the pace we had set had become an automatic process. We were already long overdue, and I knew Treenie would be getting really worried. We had walked hard for nine hours on the last day, and by four o'clock I had reached a stage where my fatigue was so dominant that toes squishing in my own blood were no longer important. I had become a walking-machine, lost in a blur of pain. We were heavily laden because of the extreme weather conditions — especially the wind which swept the southern land mass of this area, which is not terribly far from the Antarctic. Within my pain I was completely isolated from any outer reality. My environment had shrunk to one of pain — walk — pain — walk — keep on keeping on. We had at least three hours' walking ahead of us, and we were now not only racing time, but also a colossal storm which had been building up all day. Repeatedly I told myself I would collapse after the next fifty paces — another fifty — pain and walk. My mind was dazed, my body numb as I thought, "God, I can't keep going. What do I do?" Without doubt my exhaustion erased all resistance, for into my mind, powerfully, came a flow of words.

Why do you choose to walk this way, alone and alienated from the surrounding abundance of energy? The plants around you are filled with energy; all life is energy. This is yours if only you can be aware that you are not separate; you are part of a Whole. Be open, be loving. Become All in One, the One in All.

Exhaustion erased resistance. I do not know how, but in a blaze of inner realization came "knowing," and with this "knowing" came energy. In moments I was a powerhouse — vital, alive, and aware — while the pain receded to no more than a background murmur, unimportant in the overall act of life. I became "one" with my environment. Suddenly I was alive in a way never before experienced. I related to every twig, every leaf, each blade of grass, the living soil, the fading, watery sun. All became part of myself, and I in turn became part of the Whole. Hunter, who was leading the way, was also nearly out on his feet, and, as I watched him stumbling along, I felt such a love for him — for all he was as a person — that my "knowing" also encompassed him. I called out, "Hunter. Let love embrace you in its power. Love, Hunter. Love your environment." As I had been, he was too exhausted to question my sanity, or resist my words, and the same energy which had entered me swept him up also, our pace doubling and trebling as we strode along. Two hours later when we sat in the only other shelter of the walk, with the storm raging around us, Hunter looked at me, paused, and with awe in his voice asked, "Wow, what happened back there?"

What indeed?

It was as though the incredible culmination of this journey highlighted a series of connections with Nature dating back to my childhood. With this experience fresh in my mind, all previous experiences fused into "one," standing on the edge of some other, unknown dimension, and offering a journey into states of consciousness requiring courage...and surrender. I needed to surrender fear, fear of the unknown. For, strangely, the deeper this inner journey went, the stronger grew a mysterious, inexplicable fear.

September

One night I had a dream of such clarity and depth, of such color and feeling that it is forever imprinted in my memory. In my dream it was late evening on a sultry night. High in the sky a full moon lit up the beach on which I was standing, while each gentle wave reflected a million rippling stars. The sand was white, reflecting and highlighting the pearly moon glow; the sea murmured quietly as it caressed the beach. I stood alone, my head back, gazing at the stars. I was not surprised when a falling star streaked across the sky, seeming to land almost on the beach before it flickered out. A few minutes passed, and giving a deep, contented sigh I began to walk away from the sea toward a distant cottage — my home.

Only then did I notice a figure walking toward me from the direction of the falling star. Somehow I knew this person was looking for me, so I stopped, waiting quietly. As the figure approached, I realized it was a man, his face shadowed. He was only yards from me when the moonlight caught his face, illuminating his features.

I gazed at myself! Shock numbed and paralyzed me. I could only raise my arms, feebly trying to hold this other me away, but with a smile he/I walked right into me — and we merged.

Instantly, everything changed! The way I had experienced the whole world ceased — and a new reality emerged. I "knew" deeply and intimately every grain of sand on the beach. Each grain was as individual as you and I. Each had an identity. Each had a sound. I listened to a celestial sound which is quite indescribable. Cosmic song, music of the spheres, song of the universe — none can describe that sound of immeasurable richness. Sound which I could not only hear, but also feel and see. Sound which I became, for only in becoming could it be experienced. Each molecule of water in the ocean became "known." No other words can describe it. I "knew." Every star in the sky became "known."

Closer than a loved one in normal life, I was as close to the universe as life itself. I was whole, complete, vibrant — the All in All — the One in All — the All in One. I watched colors which have neither name nor meaning swirling and merging all around me. Color and sound, visual and auditory, became "One" within me.

How long this all lasted I do not know, but there came a moment when this other I stepped away from me and walked slowly away. The effect was devastating. To say I felt as though I was cast into the densest, blackest hole in existence, blind, deaf, dumb, and drugged beyond feeling, would not be an exaggeration. Desperately I called out to the departing me, "Please . . . help me . . . don't leave me like this."

The figure turned around, pity on his/my face, walked toward me and embraced me. Normality returned, my normal world . . . and I woke up.

I lay for a while, shocked and distressed. It had ended, but I had not been asleep. I knew I had experienced a peak reality. I was not awakening from a dream, I was falling asleep after experiencing heightened awareness.

My dull and cluttered normal senses defied an intimate relationship with Nature. I could not deny the experience by saying, "Just a dream." Inside my heart I was aware I had been involved in life's movement in a way denied to normal physical reality. I was deeply grateful, yet I suffered an overwhelming sense of loss. The song was no more. Not a song of a physical world, but of the realms of Spirit. It was a song of life, of promise.

The tiny flame which had ignited in me during the times of isolation as a youth was renewed, revived; yet at the same time, a vague fear which haunted the back of my mind, moving as a ghost through ancient memories, was also fanned into life.

Simultaneously there moved into my life a deep inner conviction of the dream being a reality I wanted to consciously experience and a fear which was to try every conceivable way to make me undermine such a conviction. This fear carried the power of a death threat. I could not understand it, yet it was an energy which was to put me through years of self-doubt and mental anguish.

September

VERY EARLY ONE MORNING a friend and I were driving at a steady eighty miles per hour in his rather beat-up panel van, when in front of us a huge Old Man Kangaroo moved his mob off the road, bounding into the scrub with deceptive ease. A fawn-colored doe paused after a couple of bounds, staring at us in the characteristic stance of an alert kangaroo. She had an ethereal quality as the early morning sun caught her hide, turning her in the instant into burnished gold. Her beauty in that frozen moment was so complete that a sob of emotion forced the question into my mind: "Why? Why does man kill such beauty for so little gain?" The moment was magic. As I craned my neck to watch the kangaroo, she lost the shaft of sun, becoming mortal again. In that still frozen reality I heard a whisper of thought in the silence of my mind.

Our pain is the sickness of man. This will only end when man heals himself. He is sick, for he has no knowing of himself or the part he plays in life. Man stands alone — and very afraid.

The voices of Nature, which had slowly been entering my conscious awareness, deepened and strengthened, and with them grew the deep, subconscious, unreasonable fear. Nature began speaking from trees, from rocks, from the ocean, and from the river, particularly the river. The dream had triggered an upsurge of thought, far deeper and more profound than my own, which moved into my mind with immense power and clarity, yet — paradoxically — with silence and subtlety.

I both welcomed this movement and cringed from it in fear. My logic told me I was going insane, while my intuition suggested that, indeed, it was total sanity. I was caught in the powerful grasp of two opposing aspects of myself, with neither side relenting.

In 1982 I was a speaker at the One Earth Conference in Australia where Treenie and I met Linda Tellington-Jones, and, when she called to see us after the conference was over, she became an important catalyst in my life. During our conversation she talked of the most outrageous things — UFO's, space visitors, Nature, talking trees, inner guidance. You name it, and Linda could embrace it with her own brand of discretion.

Under her inspiration I found myself sharing dreams, experiences, and strange happenings that I had kept locked away inside myself for a long time. Just talking about the voices of Nature which persisted in calling for my attention, and finding myself totally accepted by a stranger, was an incredible release. Linda was an ideal catalyst. She precipitated a change which resulted in an incredible happening three days after her departure. It began following another special dream. I had dreamed this particular dream week after week for a long time. It was powerful in its symbolism, but each time I awoke, the dream was gone, erased from my memory without trace or recall. I was only left with a sense of despair.

The third night after Linda's departure, I once again dreamed my recurring dream, but on awakening I remembered it all in clear and exact detail. While I lay awake feeling disturbed, the dream strong upon my mind, I gradually became aware of a presence in our bedroom. Treenie was asleep, breathing softly and easily, while the room around me became increasingly vibrant with energy. Peering into the darkness I could see nothing, but the presence was electric with intensity and power. Calmness and trust flowed over me, quelling all fear. Stilling my probing mind, I framed a question in my thoughts: "Who, or what, are you?" Immediately these words flowed into my receptive mind.

If you need to identify me, know me as the Spirit of Change. You are aware now of having this dream many times, yet never have you retained or understood its meaning.

Relaxed, I lay quietly accepting the experience. An instant comprehension of the recurring dream was impressed in my mind. I understood with total clarity. The voice from the Silence continued.

A long time ago, six lifetimes to be exact, you were a botanist. While your talents for the physical aspects were only average, you were blessed with a unique rapport with the plant kingdom.

Time elapsed and your studies deepened until you reached a stage where you began to experience a spiritual bonding with your plant subjects. Into your mind would flow ideas and images, projecting you into realms of thought quite unexplored. Later, as you deepened in your love and trust of Nature, you began to hear a flow of words in your mind, and you realized that there was an Intelligence which could communicate through the kingdom of Nature. You took copious notes on this, and for the first time you began to tell your friends. At first you talked with discretion, but gradually, flushed with their admiration, you spoke to others, and word went around to all who would listen. This led to your downfall, for some who listened considered your words blasphemous. Soon you were exposed to ridicule, and, when opinion went against you, you were subject to more persecution, finally seized, and you died under torture.

Your name of that time is not important; it died with you, and your papers were destroyed. Before you died, however, the pain of suffering induced a change in you, and you died blaming a divine gift for your torment. Thus, a block was imposed in your unconscious mind, and through the following four incarnations it has remained, unrealized and unchallenged. In this life, you have chosen to remove that mental block and once again allow the spiritual union with Nature to reestablish and develop. You are now aware of why you could not remember a recurring dream which your Soul-Self projected forward, hoping to cause you to remember. The unconscious block was too strong, the fear too great. This fear has been the spur behind your doubts, causing you to question beyond reason, for fear of more torment and an ongoing agony.

You are now ready to know the truth. In your dream six years ago, the sound of a joyous universe echoed in your ears and spun before your eyes. You experienced a divine truth. Buried and hidden beyond the five senses of man, truth beckons eternally to the human spirit. No longer need you fear persecution or torture. Humanity now enters a period of transition and those who seek to "know" must have that chance. No matter how humble the offering, it must be laid on the altar of truth. All you need will be revealed as you move to deepen the bonding, and only by your efforts will it be so.

The presence was gone, instantly departed, yet an energy lingered in the room as I lay in awe of things unseen and of unknown power. For the first time I understood my fear. The death-threat feeling was based on reality. I had once died, not because of communicating with Nature's inner reality, but because I lived in a time when such an action was sorcery, for which the penalty was death.

The Being had also referred to my earlier dream, and, as I suspected, my dream was of reality. Lying awake, I was aware that only by action could I resolve the fear and end the doubts. As before, understanding a cause does not immediately change the effect. I would face the fear by deepening my link with an inner Nature.

For a time I had floundered, at a loss to find a way to present the voices of Nature. But then, that day, I had followed Treenie's suggestion and gone to the river flowing past our house and asked for help, and help had been given.

The day after my visit to the river I took our rubbish to the local dump, which was filled with tons of junk from our throw-away world. Having disposed of the garbage, I strolled into the surrounding bush — so different from the vegetation around our home. Huge gum trees sucked all the moisture from the soil and only sparse undergrowth scattered the deep, acid leaf litter. I walked slowly on through the open bushland. It was a dull day, and the small flock of birds passing noisily and swiftly overhead made a brief splash of sound and color against the overcast sky. My eyes followed them, while I called out in my thoughts: "Hello, you lucky birds. I rejoice in your freedom of flight."

They were gone in moments, but I remained powerfully aware of a sensation of many birds filling the air.

We greet you. We rejoice in your inner freedom. We rejoice in your new flight path. Remember, however, every freedom has its price to pay. Only the Swift can fly high and at immense speeds, united with the air. Yet the Swift cannot play with the Sparrow. The carefree, tumbling, bumbling play of the Sparrow is lost.

Thus also, for you, the challenge will be that as you soar with the Eagle on higher thermals, with wider vision, so will you lose the companionship of those who seek lower zones. This you must realize and with understanding allow to happen. Any pattern of thought which knows not the freedom of space will become a burden. There will be those who fly even higher. Be aware of your own flight path and let the winds of change be ever fresh on your face.

Despite the cloud-laden sky, the day became brighter as I stood listening to those subtle words. The bird energy slowly dissipated, while a breeze stirred the foliage of a wattle further along on my path.

The wattles were in full bloom. It was as though the sun itself had come to earth to dwell in the deep, golden blossoms smothering the small trees with light and beauty. Fragrance hung heavy in the softly stirring air, and, while inhaling the scent, thoughts of gratitude and love moved through my mind.

"How beautiful you are, my friend wattles, yet I could have walked past without noticing you had not those birds called my attention, so immersed was I in mundane thoughts. I feel as though I have known this land and you magnificent trees for a far greater span than just this lifetime."

We greet you, human friend. Long have we known your energy. Great is our rejoicing as we witness the fresh winds of change moving through your Being.

Even your inner colors change as the patterns of your inner Self dance to a new rhythm in life. This must now be part of your daily movement: to recognize, greet, and listen to all forms of Nature, from the lowly moss to the greatest tree. All share in the one life, all dance to the same rhythm, all blend their notes in the song of the universe. We rejoice, our brother, for soon that song will blend into your pattern of color, and the doors of a new and deeper sharing will be thrown wide open.

As I walked on my way, I realized that it is not only the sun which can make a day much brighter. How is it that we deny ourselves an inner sun, shining through the silent words of Nature?

ONCE TRIGGERED, my response to Nature became a daily adventure, and I spent hours by the river writing the events and words in my journal as each moment unfolded. There was one section of the river with which I had an amazing empathy. Just a hundred yards downriver the character of the river changed, no longer offering the same deep connection. In the newness of my experience I needed all the help I could get, and it was noon one day when my footsteps took me again along the now-familiar track. Filtering through the leaves of the trees, the sun danced in mottled patterns on my shoulders.

Scrambling down the steep bank to the river, I felt the power — immense — waiting for me. For a moment I felt inadequate, a sense of the old, familiar fear, then it was gone, lost in the surging consciousness filling all life around me. Even before I reached my place on the rock, the words were moving clearly and with undeniable force through my mind.

As you sit on the rock by the river, be aware of the life around you. The Kingfisher flashing color in the morning sun. Fish jumping in the clean, washed river. The sun warm on your shoulders. The Water Dragon watching from a rotting log, distrust in its eyes. Microbes teeming in the rotting log.

Be aware of the life beyond that which you are. Each leaf bursts with the hidden energy of spring. The force of life makes its presence known in all the creatures around you. Life in life. Life upon life.

You listen to the silent song of my voice.

I have spoken to mankind from the beginning of your time. In a cascade of sound I call to you from every waterfall. With loving embrace I hold your bodies in the waters of the earth and softly I whisper.

In endless ways I call you, but so seldom am I heard. Not with your ears may I be heard, but in your heart, your consciousness. So easily are you lost in the labyrinths of your dimension. Your minds seek always to compare. Light compares with dark, strong with weak. Always the polarity of opposites reveals the identity of your experience.

I have no opposite. You cannot listen to my inner voice and then compare. You may not gaze into my inner world and seek the comfort of opposites. Your reality must stretch. Your limits must be pushed back. The dimension of opposites is but one facet of the whole reality.

The five physical senses of humanity are both your freedom of expression and the walls of your prison. This need not be. Humanity has the ability to create. Creation is an expression of the power of visualization. Within this controlled, creative framework, you may open doors into the realms of Nature where I will meet you.

You need only open the door. I will be there. Alas, to open this door defies all but the few. There are those who step beyond the known boundaries, but you know them not. For the most part they have a wisdom which embraces silence. They sip from the nectar of more subtle kingdoms, yet they sip sadly. People such as these wish to share the nectar of their lives, but it has long been rejected. This time is coming to an end. Once again, humanity stands on the threshold of Nature's secret kingdom. The Kingdom of your own Being. A secret wide open to all mankind, yet hidden behind the veils of love, of wisdom, of integrity.

The flow of words ended, but the feeling of power was vast. I sat for a while just gazing into the rippling water. I had no words, nothing to say. I felt only a sense of awe for the unseen, the unknown, the immensity of life swirling and coiling around me.

The surge of life seemed heightened in my moments of sharing with an inner Nature, and the following morning I returned to the river, tentatively testing the water for the new season of swimming. It was cold, but pleasant. Climbing from the river, water streamed in fine rivulets from my body. I sat on the rock, aware it had been waiting for me. The sky was blue. It was a warm, breezy day. River and breeze seemed to merge at the water surface, and I felt a fine inner tension in myself, caught and shimmering with the play of light racing over the river.

For some reason I felt as though I had been summoned here, and I was tense with anticipation. To the river I said aloud, "Thank you for the joy of swimming in your waters. If I have a passion within Nature, it is cool, clear rivers."

It is good that you enjoy the water so much. We greet you, we — the River and the Breeze.

Is it not a Breeze which moves within the water's flow? Is it not moisture which rides the air as Breeze? Each has been given separation by the concept of being different movements. See the Oneness in life. The song of the birds which prey on insects and the night cry of those insects are One.

Life moves through form, changing in a vast continuum from physical to physical, on and on, yet never in isolation. Be with this movement.

Allow your inner Giant Being an ever-greater freedom. Mankind, with the greatest potential for the ultimate freedom, chooses instead to become isolated.

Move beyond your barriers, and by the intelligence and freedom of Self, perceive within Nature the inner nature of your own Being.

Several leaves fell from a tree overhanging the water. Round and round they spiraled in the breeze, finally alighting on the river caressingly; so gentle was the falling.

The energy was soft, swirling in distant undulation, yet the silent words were clear.

A leaf falls in the breeze onto the water's surface. Now begins the movement back to its original cellular form. Given a period of time, the base minerals of the vanished leaf will once again surge within new sap moving within another leaf on another tree. From leaf to leaf, yet does one know of the other? So it is with humanity. Does present Self know of previous Self? Thus it is with all life. The movement never ends. Mortality is but a single moment in infinity. Man is infinite, not on a physical scale, but in Spirit. Truth is infinite. Mankind has a mind which, once mastered, can span infinity to know its own truth. This is your challenge.

The words were too powerful, the challenge too great.

I stood up and, launching myself from the rock, dived into the river. It was too much. I could not handle what was offered. It was too big, I felt too small. A child with an imperial parent offering presents beyond reach. I swam in a fast overarm trying to relieve my tension. Maybe now was the time to quit. How could I keep writing this as it happened and expect acceptance? Yet somewhere within, I knew a greater challenge — could I accept my own experience? Standing alone was a scary thought, and, as I swam, the words of the birds filtered through my mind.

Be aware of your own flight path.

Suddenly all those words about the Swift and the Sparrow became clear and amplified. They spoke of here and now. This was the price which had to be paid.

I swam slowly, exhausted, back to the rock. I said nothing, but I could feel that all was known.

It felt as though a choir was singing, but the clear words were carried on the echoes of Silence.

Our relationship must change. No longer may you feel yourself as little brother or child. Nature/mankind is but one movement, each an echo of the other.

For too long you have listened to our words fearfully, spasmodically, with many blocks imposed. Always you have listened as a child to a parent. This has been a protection behind which you've hidden. This is ended. You must claim your status and willingly meet your destiny.

You must claim the voices of Nature as the nature of your own Being. We are One. You/I are but one expression, even though consciousness draws to its Self different realities. "WE" speak in the Breeze. "WE" listen in the Breeze. From The River —The Stone —The Tree, or a river, a stone, a tree, there is no separation.

Intelligence uses all forms through which to express. This is not mankind's privilege alone. You questioned in your mind whether you should write these words, or share them. You were concerned for your protection. If you need protecting, then cease, as of this moment.

33

When you write, accepting your experience without fear, you become a focus. This is not a focus of personality, or ego, but a focus for the inner light, so that its beam may flicker into the beyond, the unknown.

You cannot move beyond your subconscious barriers without the aid of a powerful focus. Once focused, this beam of inquiry shall illuminate new dimensions of Nature/Self.

For a while I sat quietly trying to take it all in. I realized that trying to remember everything, or even change anything, was a useless exercise. I can only be who I am.

For an hour I was busy writing in my journal, the spring sun mellow on my skin. My thoughts flickered and jumped. One thing seemed certain: The Intelligence of Nature did not mince words, but I felt rather unclear about the focus. Oh well, if a focus is going to happen, it will happen. It appeared I was in very capable hands.

Lost in thought, my attention was caught by a movement in the river. Undulating like a shadow of thick smoke, a shoal of several hundred tiny fish weaved in and out of a shallow depression in the rock close to where I was sitting. They rode the currents of water with the same natural grace as an eagle rides on the currents of air. Fascinated by them I asked, "Well, fish, do you have a voice? Do you have a source of wisdom which can speak with me?" In one united movement the fish vanished, lost in the shadow of rock. Well, I thought, that's clear enough. Like a magnet my awareness was drawn into the empty hollow. No fish were to be seen, but I became aware of energy which was of fish and much more. It was fish, river, stone...and endless sky. I felt surprised. This was more than I expected.

Have I not just told you that Intelligence moves through all physical forms? Whereas form is separate in its physical identity, Intelligence is One.

"What do you call Intelligence? " I asked.

Intelligence "IS."...but you could call it God.

Understood. Like magic, the hollow in the rock was again filled with the shoal of tiny, striped fish.

2 October

As a result of connections made at the One Earth Conference, Treenie and I were invited to give a number of workshops in various cities and locations. Most important of all, Andrea and Bernie Dunne invited us to give a one-day seminar at their beautiful home in the Blue Mountains of New South Wales.

Bernie and Andrea were caretakers of the Everglades, a garden owned by the National Trust. At the time, they were negotiating a lease, so they could have greater control and be more innovative.

Everglades is one of the best-known gardens open to the public in New South Wales. The development of these outstanding gardens began in 1932 when Henri Van de Velde acquired the former ten-acre fruit orchard for a weekend retreat. By the time of his death in 1947, the gardens had been hailed as "an epic on the scale of a Wagner Opera." With the assistance of landscape designer Paul Sorensen and a small work force, Van de Velde carved wide terraces with superb dryrock stone walls. The visitor can see some of the world's outstanding trees and shrubs growing, in a quite breathtaking manner, alongside native Australian bush.

~

IT WAS IN THIS OUTSTANDING SETTING we were to hold our workshop, among the "vibes" of loved and cared-for plants. During the evening prior to our workshop, Andrea and Bernie took us for a walk around the gardens and into the immediately surrounding bush. The energies of the gardens and the bush mixed and merged with one another. The essential quality of the gardens was one of exaltation. It may sound strange, but it felt as though something was knocking on a closed door, and, although I did not know what the something was, I knew I was the closed door. But . . . I was keen to open myself.

When we walked down into the Grotto, the heightened feeling surged powerfully, and I knew I must return soon alone. As I followed in Andrea's footsteps, two other areas also heightened this feeling to dizzying proportions. I determined that the next morning I would make a dawn rendezvous with the mysterious "something."

~

THE GROTTO WAS A DEEP, natural amphitheater, gouged from the earth in an ancient past. It was a place of stillness, invoking a sense of awe for the surrounding beauty of Nature. A trickle of water seeping from the deep pool at my feet fell with a persistent melody into the unwinding waterway, vanishing in the scrub downhill. Early-morning birds, including the laughing Kookaburra, sang their ritual greetings to the rising sun. I watched the wavering sky and rippling trees reflected in the dark water, as a breeze played over the surface. Allowing time for my mind to quiet, I felt a powerful inverted energy around me, as though it had been coiled and waiting for millennia. The contorted lava walls of the Grotto bulged protectively around the pool, while mosses, ferns, and creeping violets clambered in profusion over every crack and convoluted crevice. It was a scene of tranquility and beauty. For a while I listened to the trickling waterfall below me, allowing myself time to identify with the mysterious energy of the Grotto. Quietly, not wishing to disturb the fragile silence, I spoke to the reflective water.

"I feel privileged to be here. Just to sit within your Silence is a nourishment. I have no questions. It is enough to be here and to be open to life."

Strange as it may seem, each time I connect with the Intelligence of Nature on this level I am aware of a difference in feeling when words flow into my mind. Just as we have our different character, so the energies of Nature differ in subtle ways. Thus, in this grotto the energy had its own character: In our way of thinking, it was alone, yet it knew nothing of isolation.

Be welcome. By no accident are you here. People from many aspects of life find their way to this pool. It is a place where barriers are laid aside and defenses dropped. It is here that many people are able to "feel" the essence of Nature for the first time.

The feeling beyond form.

For these people allow the first chink of light to penetrate their ironclad belief systems. I am a focus of energy, a container which will shatter with perfect timing, and my energy will be realized.

I feel your bewilderment at my suggestion.

Understand that we are entering a time of change. Each one of your kind is a container of spiritual energy, but unfortunately you have no knowing of the energy you contain. "You are" the contained. We, the expressing energies of Nature, know our place in the grand design of life.

You are aware that you listen and talk, not with the stone and water forming the physical foundation of the Grotto, but with the collective intelligent energy residing here.

Again you are aware I am not physical. Only the container is physical, as your appreciative eyes can see. Thus it is with your kind. Your bodies are merely physical containers of Spirit.

You are rediscovering your latent ability to unite with the energies of earth. There is no limit to the range of this power. It is universal, all-encompassing. This, my friend, is the journey you are undertaking. Eventually you will be more clear about the purpose.

Gaze into the depths of this water and you will see reflected what is all around you. Equally, when you view all life around you directly, you see but a reflection of the real world. Life for humanity is living within this hazy and distorted reflection. Yet each of you has the ability to perceive life as it is and take loving dominion. This requires an energy humanity lacks — humility. Humility is the creative power of the universe, contained, knowing its place in the design of life. With or without the help of mankind, this design unfolds, but that which could have been fulfillment becomes a senseless pain. My friend, just as I have blended energies with you, so I blend with all who visit here. Each is aware according to his or her own level of perception. The love I feel and share with you, I feel in all your kind. It is the expression of this love which must be guided along a path of wisdom. We are united in Spirit.

Go in peace.

I lingered for a while, but knowing my schedule I could not delay overlong. The peacefulness was pervading and mysterious.

Following the normal footpath to a large, smooth boulder, I left the track, pushing my way through the undergrowth to a small cavern, or, to be more precise, a rocky overhang.

When we visited here the previous evening a small Boobook Owl watched us from a branch only a few yards from where we stood; its large, unblinking eyes regarded us without fear, reflecting our admiration with mystic gaze. Now, in my early morning visit, the owl had returned from its night hunting, and, as I sat in this serendipitous cavern, it carefully went through a routine of meticulously cleaning feathers and claws. Crouching close to the rock face at the rear of the cavern, I regarded my surroundings as only a plant lover could, torn between a desire to own it all and an even stronger appreciation for its perfect natural artistry. Clambering up the back of the cavern was a green fitted carpet of moss, covered with small creeping ferns extending furry, orange squirrel's feet into ready nourishment among the damp and tangled vegetation. Allowing an inner perception to flood beyond my physical experience, I became vaguely disoriented. I extended an unvoiced inquiry. From within the rock walls and myself came the words:

Long have you shared this land with our kind, and long have you forgotten your own ancient past. You have been drawn to this particular place, which you shall remember.

You shall remember the time, so long ago measured by the span of lives, when you walked this land. Let your dreams remember, and in your dreaming know the symbols not in your head, but in your heart. This is where the Dreaming lies.

Heart connects with heart, for it is here the spirit of mankind resides. In dreaming shall you awaken. Allow your ancient lineage to reappear, for your past and future are with this moment, entwined.

Time is the weaver of the illusion mankind believes is life.

I crouched against the rocks, painfully aware of my physical discomfort. The little owl watched with unconcerned interest as I stretched my limbs. Timelessness pervaded the cavern, wrapping me in a shroud of clouded mystery. I could feel an aboriginal man standing near me, but also a vastly older man who was neither black nor white. My sense of perception peered foggily into scenes from bygone ages. In a manner which was neither visual nor physical, I was aware of tracing myself back and back into time. It was as though the cavern contained an inner, subtle history of mankind — a natural book waiting to be opened and experienced according to the inner dictates of the searcher. I asked the question bubbling in my mind.

"How can history be stored here? How can I be shown my own past in a place I am not aware of ever having visited?"

The atmosphere became imbued with a sense of unlimited, endless space.

Relax. You are linking with your own past, trekking through the illusion of time into other phases of your own Self. You are being led to locations which you have frequented in another time. Physically much has changed, yet despite this you cannot go anywhere or be anywhere without leaving the imprint of Being.

My head reeled. The concept which was forming in my mind was surely preposterous.

"Do you mean to suggest that in the way a fingerprint on a hard surface leaves an impression, we leave an impression by just having occupied a space in the atmosphere?"

Clearly and powerfully came the reply.

That is exactly what I mean. You cannot perform a physical act, or think a thought that is not recorded.

The inner journey you have taken in this cavern will continue and extend, in times of stillness, in your Dreaming. I will guide you. Our consciousness is linked. You shall know me as the Keeper of the Cavern, and in time you will know the true meaning of "The Cavern."

The slumbering Giant within the Dwarf awakes.

You may leave. Whether you return to this place physically or not is unimportant, for as I contain you, so also do you contain me.

This is known and recognized.

I had been through too many strange inner experiences to be more than momentarily disturbed. I was aware that I was on this journey only because, after years of resistance, I was finally allowing a powerful inner reality to emerge.

As I crawled from the cavern into bright sunlight, the owl's head swiveled smoothly around to follow my progress.

"Well," I said, "do you have some wise thoughts to offer?"

The owl merely stared at me, unblinking.

Forcing my way through the tangled undergrowth, I glanced at my watch. I felt a sense of shock. My experience in the cavern had seemed no more than ten minutes, yet well over an hour had passed. I had one more destination before I left this enchanted garden, and, after finding the winding track, I clambered over an outcrop of smooth yet convoluted granite overlooking the gully. Scattered trees grew from precarious rootholds around me, while far below in the gully the fresh foliage of the treetops swayed and danced in the eddying breeze.

An energy, wide open, expansive, and of light-filled proportion, swept around and through me, while an inner voice boomed,
hale and jovial.

Greetings. Do you not feel the urge to jump from these rocks and fly?

The distant sound of water trickling in a thin cascade from
the nearby grotto seemed to be amplified, filling the air with
liquid notes, bright and inviting. I admitted flying free was exactly
what I felt like doing, but I knew it could not be. A vast chuckle
filled all space around me.

*But you are jumping, my friend. You are testing the strength of
your newfound wings. You are learning to soar on inner thermals, for
this is the gift of mankind. A neglected gift. Neither airplane nor
rocket will ever cover the space that your kind can reach on inner
levels. All that lies before you and beyond is but a reflection of
inner space in the "real" world.*

*Cast not your physical body from these rocks, but let your mind
soar, carried on the safe wings of wisdom onto the higher, rarer thermals. Fly, my friend, fly.*

*All mankind will benefit as each individual finds the doorway to
their inner freedom. We are linked not only cell for cell, body for body,
but in the inner reaches of space we fly as One. Reach in, my friend,
reach out, and fly. There is nothing else you can do. To resist will be
pain, to delay will abort. To fly the inner space and expand is all that
is left.*

A sense of elation filled me, of vastness and expansion. Leaping to my feet on a surge of energy, I shouted aloud, "THANK
YOU — OH, THANK YOU," hurling my voice over and beyond
the gully, hearing the sound echo and bounce from the rocks
before being smothered and swallowed by the surrounding trees.
Then I noticed the early-morning tourists who, having heard my
outcry, were regarding me on the distant rock as though I were
some rare species. I felt no embarrassment — caught as I was in
such unseemly behavior.

The day was just too much . . . too much!

I found it rather difficult to bring myself down to earth for the morning workshop, for while my spirit soared, my mind was required in a discussion on the implications and applications of organic fanning. After lunch, in a change of mood, we used Nature as the pivot for a discussion on self-awareness, which brought forth greater attention and concentration among the participants.

The seminar over, we continued our tour into Sydney and then on to Canberra where we stayed a few days with Bridget Hodgkin, a very dear friend. Elderly, active, and intelligent, Bridget, with her keen humor and wonderful hospitality, was a highlight in our travels. On our way home Treenie and I discussed the various aspects of our tour, easily reaching the conclusion that my presentation at the Everglades was not a true reflection of my inner feelings. It seemed that although I spoke of organic concepts with conviction and feeling, my heart, my drive, my inspiration lay with a deeper movement, a movement into the heart of Nature. We decided that I would speak only where and when I could share this inner reality: that each movement has its own moment, but only with perfect timing. Now was the time of my inner journeying, of gaining greater insight and clarity, rather than speaking from vague and unfamiliar concepts.

The warmth and friendliness of home was most welcome; even the trees reached out and extended themselves to us, especially the Morton Bay Fig. Each time we open the back door of our house, we are greeted by the outspread branches of this enormous tree. This is no ordinary tree. It is a giant whose massive limbs stretch out to embrace the surrounding countryside. Here, amid the large dark-green leaves, hang the bunches of small tart-flavored fruit which attracts Yellow Fig birds, Catbirds, Bowerbirds, and many other varieties by day, while the constantly swearing Flying Foxes are lured in great numbers on summer nights. Only when the fruit is no longer in season is the tree quiet, silently contemplating its surroundings. Standing beneath the wide spread of this mammoth tree invokes a feeling of humility;

the ego is dwarfed to insignificance. The personality of this tree reaches into all who gaze upon it, and few can pass by unmoved.

Talking to such a tree is easy. The very grandeur invites conversation. I would no more walk beneath the branches on my way to the river without a word of greeting than you would pass your family pet without a word of recognition. I find it strange that whereas conversation with the family pets is considered normal and taken for granted, the resonance and joy of our trees and plants are unrecognized. One morning, on my way to the river, I mentioned this to the tree. Its massive buttress root system spread almost as far as its branches. I placed my towel on a convenient, comfortable root and sat down for a chat.

"Mr. Morton Bay Fig — Sir or Madam, as the case may be — can you tell me, from your infinite source of wisdom, why it is that we humans talk to cats and dogs, even horses, goats, pigs, and any number of animal pets, never receiving a verbal reply or even expecting one, yet we seldom talk to trees or other plants or rocks or rivers?"

The voice of my friend the Tree was clear, ringing like a gigantic bell in my receptive mind.

I feel your humor and your sense of joy. I understand the source. During your recent journey you released more attachments to mental burdens, expanding your awareness of the inner realms of Nature. I will give your flippant question serious consideration, for it indicates a point of change in human consciousness. There is now a rapidly increasing number of people who do indeed talk to trees and other plants.

This has been difficult for the present race of man to embrace. You talk to your animals with ease, feeling an empathy within the animal kingdom, for this is the kingdom in which mankind identifies himself.

From a human viewpoint, the plant kingdom is beneath you; thus, you fail to realize that mankind is a synthesis of the mineral, vegetable, and animal kingdoms. Your reasoning minds experience the plant kingdom as having no emotion or conscious intelligence. This failing to experience and understand a truth does not change truth; it merely limits your ability to relate to life as it "IS" rather than as you see it.

As a new era dawns, your race, in order to survive, will discover that the Nature perceived outside of your Selves is but a reflection of your own inner nature. This connection with a greater realization is being felt by many people, even as you now experience it.

My flippancy had faded, but the feeling of joy and fun was even stronger. "Thank you, Tree, Sir or Madam. I have no argument with what you share; I only wish more people could experience such a conversation as this. It is obvious to me that we should all branch out into having tree friends, or potted-plant pals."

Laughing aloud I bounded to my feet, heading for the river. I was well clear of the tree when the thinnest of far-flung roots caught my toe and sent me sprawling. The tree had the last laugh . . . Sir or Madam, as the case may be!

AT AN EARLY AGE I had turned to the solitude and Silence of Nature. In the quietness of field, hedgegrow, and the banks of many streams, I had studied the movements of Nature, relaxed, trusting my environment.

In those quiet moments, precious as living jewels, I would daydream of the way life could be, of inner strengths I would love to have.

Early in life I had developed a rage against being born. Birth had been an extremely painful imposition. No easy entry for me. By the time I had started school, from seven to fourteen years of age, I had been a chronic rebel. Any imposition or discipline was a target for my inner rage, and the private school which I attended, where the cane and thrashing were accepted punishments, was a very unfortunate affair.

Discipline was strictly imposed, and the harsh, eccentric head teacher was a person to be feared. My inner rage flared into perpetual rebellion at the violence and condescending attitude of those teachers and their system of teaching. The years of battle, of matching wits with my teachers, profoundly altered my life. Those teachers, unwittingly or not, insulted and outraged my intelligence and sense of fair play. They ignited in me a distrust of authority, discipline, and regimentation, but I found I could trust Nature, that here I was always welcome, that some inner chamber of my heart seemed to open, and in the opening I was enriched. This never seemed to happen in my contact with people, only with Nature.

My mind was disinterested in proven avenues of thought. Instead, like a renegade, it burrowed deep into the folds of imagination, undisciplined and untrained. The eight years of my school life were a bore, a burden; while in the silence and solitude of Nature, a totally different experience stirred both my interest and my imagination.

A single compensation during my school life was the nearby Botanical Gardens. After school I would leap onto my bicycle and tear around to this wonderful diversion. Like a bee to nectar, I would be drawn to the hothouses. The gardens were owned by Cambridge University. Magnificent glasshouses covered quite a large area, and their hot, steamy air welcomed me time and time again. Strange, contorted flowers from weirdly shaped plants clambered and crept in an ordered profusion from benches and beds. My eyes, round and staring in my efforts to absorb everything, grew familiar with every plant growing there. From the very first visit, it was a love affair with an exotic Nature.

It had been preordained that, as a scholastic incompetent, I would work for my father on the land, while my older brother, a scholastic genius, would go on to the university at Cambridge. At fifteen I left school, and my love affair with Nature ended. Gone were the lonely, unstructured wanderings of my youth. In their place emerged the rigid doctrine of agriculture. Gone was the wonder, the awe, the tinge of reverence. Instead, a pre-ordered cycle of sow and reap was imposed upon me. The spontaneity I had known was crushed beneath growing responsibility. The wildness of daisy-filled meadows and sweet-flowing streams, of majestic woods and cold, silent waters gave way to the harsh reality of plowing and sowing, crop spraying and harvesting. Over and over, year in, year out. It was a ritual which I both loved and hated.

Although I loved the connection with Nature, I instinctively hated the arrogant approach of dominance. Intuitively I recoiled from the alienation between Nature and agriculture. Such was the routine, the work load, the endless seasons of repetition that the inner flame of my early connection with Nature gradually diminished to a faint glimmer. It was a subtle imposition. I labeled the chains of bondage as freedom, that I might survive. Fooling myself with this grand illusion, I forged my way through life for the next thirty years, believing myself to be free; yet, even though I hugged this cloak of deceit around me in hidden, subconscious despair, light and true freedom burned brightly within, ensuring that, with the years, my ordered life would collapse, revealing another way, another path that I might walk.

Leaving school had robbed me of the innocence of my earlier experience with Nature, an innocence which could never be recaptured. However, there was always one favorite refuge — that of Byron's Pool Woods. They were near Granchester, ancestral home of the famous poet Lord Byron, and were only a few minutes' cycle ride from where I lived. Byron's Pool Woods — the words still echo in my heart as a thrill, a lingering memory, rich in detail. Byron's Pool Woods were a mecca for Nature lovers, abounding in history and mystery. On the fringe of the woods lay a large, river-fed pool. Under about four to five feet of water, the foundations of the old Mill House could be dimly seen. We kids could wade to this foundation on one side, but the other side dropped away into deep water. I learned to swim from these old foundations, submerged in the cold, dark waters of Byron's Pool.

A weir close by, green with algae, regulated the water in times of winter flood, but in summer, in our swimming weather, only a trickle of water flowed over the wide platform behind the old, hand-cranked watergates. Hour upon hour I sat there alone, staring into the water. Rivers, streams, creeks — they have always held a fascination, a bond I cannot easily explain. Whenever I was in the lonely company of a river I would feel the pull of a great longing — a longing I neither understood nor even fully realized.

Somehow, in the heart of a youth a connection developed, a spontaneous linking with Nature. Whatever that connection was, it transcended physical barriers. That which was born in me as a boy had now reemerged, sparkling, fresh with invitation. I was encouraged to pursue an inner truth, a dream where my connection with Nature became alive, activated, where I was no longer alone, but consciously connected with all life.

I WAS EIGHTEEN when I was inveigled by a friend into going on a Church Youth Camp holiday with him. It was there I met Treenie — she stood out from the rest of the giggling girls, and I was instantly attracted to her. I deviously changed the duty roster, and we eventually met over the breakfast dishes, our hands touching in the frothy soap suds. I say in all modesty, Treenie was swept off her feet!

The sun shone every day, inside and out. Britain had the hottest summer in several years, and Treenie and I wandered the countryside and walked the beaches of Robin Hood Bay. We fell in love — a love which over the years has endured, grown, expanded, and blossomed.

3 November

At fairly regular intervals I have enjoyed walking into our nearby semitropical rain forest. Usually this is a very physical affair, where I can admire Nature's amazing creations for their physical value and intrigue. I was feeling now that I would like to take a walk in the forest, relating in a different way to my environment. Nature was indicating that there are many levels of expression beyond the physical — the formless beyond the form — and I wanted to find out if I could push back the barriers in my own way. I had a sneaky feeling that I could only go so far or fast, rather like a car responding to fuel and throttle, with a driver in charge. I needed to find out if I was car — driver — or both!

I have a theory that when I was born, hauled forth with clamps on my head, that the pressure (which I have learned is considerable) caused an abnormality to my brain. Don't laugh! I am quite serious about this. I have yet to meet anyone with a worse sense of direction than me. I get lost in department stores. Supermarkets are an unbelievable hazard. I must be the only adult who gets handed in to the lost children's center! By now you can see the picture I am trying to present. I could get lost among a dozen trees. Can you imagine me in a forest? So, rather than create a situation where Treenie is required to keep a Bloodhound or Retriever, I generally go with one or another of my close friends — someone who can listen to me talking to trees or rocks, without thinking I have them in my head. One fine, sunny day my good friend Gerhard and I set out on an exploratory, tree-talking trip into the forest. As would be expected, Gerhard is a born Nature lover. He is slight of build, medium height, and his sensitive green eyes which gaze from a bearded face are forever roaming over the trees and the ground, absorbing the finer aspects of Nature. For him, bush walking is a love affair, an extension of his love for all things wild. His companionship on such walks is perfect. He knows intuitively when I need to be alone, fading away quietly to concentrate on his own areas of interest.

The rocky gorge was just one of many on the forest-covered foothills plunging from the New England Plateau. Large boulders torn from the towering escarpment littered the gorge, while a clear, cold stream plunged heedlessly through the semitropical profusion of trees smothering its course. I sat on a small, comfortable rock facing a huge boulder which loomed above and beyond the other. A thick mat of moss covered much of the surface, creating perfect conditions for the magnificent Bird's Nest Ferns dotted upon it. Life on the boulder was lived in almost perpetual shade and moisture, a perfect microclimate. On inner levels I felt the boulder growing to immense proportions, the ferns rearing like trees in my consciousness. I sent a thought of invitation, of recognition, to this huge boulder and the residual energy it encompassed. Water gushing around and over the rocks filled the air with sound, while the nearby Cicadas picked it up, amplifying it with enthusiasm. Through all the noise of a living, vibrant gorge, the voice of rock consciousness spoke clearly.

You are welcome. We welcome an attitude of respect and admiration. For too long the forests have been exploited to meet your needs on a physical level. It is time now to merge our energy with mankind on higher, finer levels.

With noise from water and Cicadas competing for my attention, I was having trouble concentrating. The words flowed into my mind and all sound was outside the experience, but I was being distracted.

Do not resist the sound of water, the sounds of life. As a breeze moves through the unresisting leaves of a tree, thus should you drop your resistance.

Allow the inner energy of this stream to pour through your inner Being as a purification. There is a uniqueness expressing itself here. Each area of the gorge has its own different essence. Each area has its own uniqueness to offer mankind.

I was puzzled by this. After all, a stream is a stream and a gorge is a gorge. How could it be one and different at the same time?

"Are you suggesting that water energy from the river here is different when it reaches the valley? How can this be so when logically it is the same water?"

My friend. In Nature, only the physical reflection you see as your world will stand up to the scrutiny of logic. You are learning to perceive, and integrate with, a finer world, a higher truth. I would ask you in reply: If mankind formed a line several miles long, would the character of the mile remain unchanged?

The concept was a new one, yet I got the point. A human line, while being all human, would be composed of as many identities as it took to make up the line. That such a concept would be applied to a gorge or river had never occurred to me. But why not? The river flowing past our home came into my mind. Of course! I was aware of how I felt a change in energy from my favorite place to other sections of the river. Certainly "my" area of river is unique. Why should this not apply to rivers, creeks, and water courses generally? The thought was an odd one. Many questions surfaced in my mind, becoming more and more confused with logic and reason. I struggled to balance the physical and meta-physical realities.

I felt a ripple shudder through the boulder's conscious-ness...a very faint mockery.

So much you ask, so much you need to encompass. Forget your questions based on logic and knowledge. Soak instead in the stream of higher energies. See, feel, inquire beyond physical form, and your knowing, like a waterfall, will fill you with the cascade of truth with perfect timing.

Leaving the boulder in the gorge, we journeyed on to eventu-ally emerge from the dense, tropical undergrowth onto a high ridge overlooking our destination: the waterfall.

Standing on the ridge, we were dwarfed by huge trees form-ing a natural corridor a hundred yards in length. Hoop Pines, Stringy Bark, Brush Box, and other giants formed the pillars of Nature's forest cathedral, while the waving foliage, high above our heads, formed the ceiling. A hush holding the place in its grip invoked a feeling of reverence, a knowing that one careless shout could shatter the magic. On inner levels I could feel energies surg-ing, intangible, but clearly active. Moving from this collective power, the words entered my mind.

It is good that you visit these places. Always we welcome those who walk among us with love in their hearts.

It is wise that you come to attune, to respect, and admire. Respect and reverence may become the doorways to higher realities of Nature.

It is only by softly knocking on the doors with humility that attunement may be slowly achieved.

Learn to know your Self and to understand what it implies to be human, for there is much to realize. Just as each tree has roots which are forerunners, so each age of this planet has its sentient race.

Can you, for just one moment, realize that today's humanity is but the forerunner of another race of man?

Yet this shall come to pass when from the ruins of each civiliza-tion mankind again emerges. Many times this has happened, and many times will it be repeated. In each age, mankind reaches a peak of power. Always, man has chosen the power of destruction. Thus, as a tree grows true to seed, man reaps the seed he has sown. Only when mankind reaches a high peak of wisdom will this cycle end. At this point a new emphasis shall emerge.

In our present cycle man has once again reached a time where he holds in his grasp the seed of his destruction. This shall cause both the beginning and the end.

The words left me feeling rather troubled and silent. I did not like the ominous overtones, and I was too close to the experience to be objective. Getting to my feet from the log on which I had been sitting, I walked over to a nearby Hoop Pine and hugged it.

"Is it as bad as it sounds?" I asked.

I heard nothing, but a clarity swept through me. It was as though a negative focus had suddenly switched off to be flooded with the illumination of a positive force. I had listened to words of hope, of life, of continuity. The end "is" the beginning, the beginning "is" the end; for on a spiral, life is cycles in an infinite continuum. We cannot take a finite view of infinity and make it fit; thus, our thinking must spiral out and expand. "Thank you," I whispered to the pine.

As we walked down toward the waterfall, I felt the energy on the ridge form into a vast phoenix, rising high above the trees, triumphant and free. From hundreds of yards above my head, water plummeted down the rock face, pouring into the deep, cold pool at my feet. We were fringed by trees. Hoop Pines clustered along the perimeter of the rock face. Liana clambered carelessly over the various trees, their huge looping vines resembling coiled serpents from a legendary past. Within this sheltered, secluded place, hidden in the surrounding forest, the summer sun shone warm upon the water, highlighting a misty halo of beauty from the cascading falls. Blood seeped steadily from my several leech bites into the pool, but there was humor in the situation. The leeches had been at "one" with my body. I had little compassion for their welfare as I pulled them — gorged and bloated on my blood — from my ankles. I accepted, however, that they were doing their thing — very effectively. I was not victimized. I was merely a walking blood bank.

A cool wind, created by the downpouring water, cooled the sweat on my brow. I gazed longingly at the cold water in which I intended to numb my hundreds of mosquito bites. Despite cord trousers and shirt I had been bitten on legs, shoulders, arms, and neck each time I stopped to write in my journal. It is ironic, for my attunement is not with the separate physical form, but only with the intelligent energy expressing through that particular form as a species. Unfortunately, I am as yet offered no protection from the physical, even while conversing with the psychical.

Once, about a year ago, when sun bathing on a river beach in late summer, I asked a large, interested, uninvited March Fly not to bite. Immediately I felt an upsurge of March Fly energy and, despite an equal surge of doubt, I heard the words formed in my then-skeptical mind.

The fly cannot do as you ask. Such a creature knows nothing of free will. The fly is a life-form following a strictly imprinted code of behavior, and this only may it do. Part of this code is to draw blood from warm-blooded mammals for nourishment.

I ask you, is it possible to view such as this fly with tolerance, understanding, and even love? Such an attitude would have two effects. One, it reduces drastically the chance of being the fly's victim; two, it cancels completely the chance of being a victim of your own separation and resulting lack of understanding.

Some fly!

By the pool, with blood seeping copiously from my leech bites, I assumed the same principle applied. My attention was drawn to the cascading falls. To attempt a description would deny the waterfall its true beauty. I can write only of its magnificence, yet it is more, for it has another quality. The fall invokes a magnetic attraction, not in the physical sense, but in ways which draw my thoughts and feelings at odd moments of the day. Aloud, and within the thunder of cascading turbulent water, I spoke to the waterfall.

"Thank you, waterfall. Thank you for inviting me here again, Thank you for making me feel I am a part of Nature, rather than apart from Nature. What is different about this waterfall? What attracts me and others beyond the physical beauty?"

The inner energy of waterfall became vast. All physical limits were suddenly abandoned, as in an inner world this waterfall became all that "IS." It contained me, and it was I who poured down the rock face, yet I contained it, watching with loving interest.

I welcome you both. Be aware; remember I am not the waterfall, you are not the hand which writes. Observe the difference, and the similarity. You are Intelligence which seeks expansion, which seeks its own destiny — to know its Self.

That I am also.

It is in this sense of Wholeness that we leave behind our attachment and identity with physical form, to merge as "One" consciousness. For my energy this is the reality of life; for you, the physical identity is that which you believe to be you, an attachment created over millennia. It is a powerful thought-form and belief from which to break away, yet this must be your challenge.

This waterfall is a focus of energy. Many other waterfalls focus power to a lesser or greater degree, but it is always subtle, normally beyond the perception of mankind.

For a while I dived and swam in the clear, cold pool. The words and the experience had faded, but not the subtle beauty of the wilderness surrounding me. Like a doll on the cliff top, Gerhard yodeled from far above, his voice faint in the thunder of water.

Some time later, when he had joined me, I shared my experience with him. He was quiet for a while, his eyes holding a faraway look.

"I feel what you are saying. I am not good with words, but when I stand at the waterfall I just feel this is all the Song of our

Creator. It brings me to such a feeling of happiness. I become balanced. I am content. I feel that everything which "IS," I am. I belong to the rocks and the water. Such a feeling — exultation. Even God couldn't feel better."

Not good with words, he said!

EARLY ONE MORNING, while the first rays of sunshine were probing the mists, banishing the delicate moisture to the higher atmosphere, I walked down toward the river. For no particular reason, except maybe the cloud of flies which accompanied me, I made for a different location and sat at the river's edge on a fallen log in deep shade. It was a smart move, for the flies were still seeking warmth from the early sun, and they quickly deserted me. My thoughts turned to my mother living on the other side of the world. It saddened me that with age she was becoming increasingly burdened with arthritis and was unlikely to gaze on such a scene as lay before me. A family of Plovers flew past, chattering with harsh cries as they followed the river. I detected no alarm from them as their cries greeted the new day. Mullet were leaping from the river, while freshwater Herring tried hard to excel their larger rivals, flashing quicksilver in the early sun. A Fantail flew from across the river, alighting on the log within a hand's reach. She regarded me for moments with beady eye and waving tail, undecided whether I posed a threat. With a final flick of tail feathers the bird departed, silent, yet noisy in presence.

The morning had opened gloriously. I was filled with a desire to roll up this wonderful natural scene, contain this magic moment, place it in a small, neat package, and send it to my mother in England, that she might share this privileged joy. Just imagine! On opening the parcel she unrolls it to find a slice of Australia's finest scenery before her eyes. She would see a clear, sparkling river, fresh from the recent rains, complete with leaping, gleaming fish, with Plovers and Fantails enriching this magic scene. River Oak and Weeping Willows would jostle for position along one bank, while smooth river stones formed a friendly beach on the other side. My mother would hear the gurgling chuckle of the water as it left the slow, silent river depths and raced splashing and noisy over the shallow, stony bed, while the whispered sound of a Kingfisher flashed electric blue as it hit the water, adding richness and quality to Nature's gift.

Dew, hanging in glistening beads from countless blades of grass, reflected in each drop a tiny rainbow, richer by far in its newness than any coveted jewel, symbolic of crystallized age — all this my mother would see. Somehow I know that while I gaze upon this beauty, holding fond memories of Mother in my heart, then in the secret recess of her soul this gift is known, this moment shared.

For a while I sat in the shade, memories of my mother and father moving through my mind. Certain episodes were of joy and happiness, while others filled me with regret, yet always the stamp of inevitability lay over everything as though destiny will have its way no matter what. Are we free to choose? Or are we free to choose within no choice at all?

If we live in a framework of cause and effect, then must we reap effect before we can change cause to change effect? In other words, is choice predetermined by cause of the past, and thus preordained to no choice at all? The shade was moving soundlessly away when I left the log to walk back to the house for breakfast. After closing the paddock gate, I paused at our shadehouse where row upon row of Cycad palms completely dominated one bench. As I walked into the shadehouse looking at the young palms, my reflective mood carried me back again, this time into the forest where I came across the parent Cycad Palm or, as it is locally known, Burrawong Palm. These are not at all uncommon, yet this particular palm had a large, cone-shaped pod growing from its center. A tentative pull and the seed pod was in my hands, all fifty pounds of it.

Each seed was the size of a large chestnut, and all 150 seeds were bulky and heavy on the strong, thick stem. Accepting the help of my accompanying friends, we wrapped the spiky pod in my shirt, taking turns to carry it home. Within weeks the seed fell away from the pod, revealing each to be a vivid and unexpected orange color. The seed were then placed in close-packed rows on several shallow trays of forest soil. Their bright color quickly faded to a dull brown, and they lay apparently lifeless for the next eighteen months. The pod was collected on Easter Sunday in April, and it was November the following year when long tap roots burst from the dormant seed. For Treenie and me it heralded activity as we began the task of potting them in large, plastic plant bags. While working we were both aware of a subtle energy emanating from the plants, indicating their vigor and abundant vitality. Despite having no more than a single root when we potted them, in a few weeks the first palm fronds were reaching toward the light as the nutlike seed sent forth their stored energy. Under normal circumstances most seed on the forest floor would be chewed and eaten by animals, or in later stages riddled and bored by insects. Indeed, few of the hundreds would grow to mature palms. Under our conditions most of the seed were now sprouting, beginning their very slow growth toward large and handsome palms. Speculating on the energy of the plants I sent my first thought of inquiry toward their intelligent consciousness.

"What is your place in the scheme of things? " I asked.

Come over here.

It was unmistakably a command and I felt a keen sense of surprise. I had expected the focus of Cycad energy to be with the plants laid out before me. Instead, the command, although within my consciousness and therefore unrelated to physical space, was directly behind me, coming from a couple of large Cycads growing in the shade of a Rubber tree in our garden.

I walked over to the palms and sat down before them.

"Okay," I responded, "here I am."

There was a feeling of outpouring energy, rather as though the presence of Cycad had heightened and intensified.

November

Your question has no real meaning. Our energy on physical levels is not as important in this age as it once was. We are of an ancient order and our lineage as a palm dates back a long way in objective time.

Once, in a bygone past, our energy played a vital role in the transition of form for many species of plants.

I digested this in silence.

"It has felt very important for us to grow these Cycads. I am not sure why we feel so strongly about it. Suddenly it occurs to me: "Did you have anything to do with this whole episode?"

It is not by accident you grow our species and foster our energy. We represent a great age of plants and infinite change. Our species has seen animals and birds evolve and disappear. We are linked to this ancient consciousness, for although it no longer manifests in a physical sense, consciousness cannot cease to be. Understand this. We link with the energy of extinct forms. Through us you also may link with the consciousness of discarnate Nature.

This linking will be subtle, very subtle, yet there will be a stirring of unconscious memories. To the surface of the mind, long-forgotten connections with your ancient past will reemerge.

This linking is of great importance. Although the repercussions of your act will not be known to you, allow your mind to dwell on the concept of linkage, the past with the present, the present with the future. Imagine this all rolled into one sphere, with neither beginning nor ending, only "now."

In this bonding, Nature holds the links of change. Just as Nature continually changes all within her realms — physically and metaphysically — so also Nature changes mankind.

There are times when this change is slow, gradual, and subtle. At other times giant leaps are experienced, with all the accompanying shock and trauma.

Prepare for a giant leap, but take comfort, for despite how it appears, such leaps are always forward.

I must admit that when I had approached the Cycad seedlings in the bush-house, my mind was caught in reflection and speculation on the past, but now the intensity of energy moving through me spiraled around and around the powerful words which claimed my attention: "Prepare for a giant leap." The past once again formed an association with the present as memories of boyhood unfolded in my mind's eye.

I WAS TEN YEARS OLD when Granchester was flooded. How well I remember my father driving his beloved Austin Ten gently into the floodwater on the road near Byron's Pool, and the thrill of washing the car and soaking my brother under such extraordinary circumstances. The floodwaters receded, leaving Byron's Pool Woods muddy, smelly, and dirty from the rampaging water. With three other boys, I remember picking over the debris, exploring the changes wrought by the water's power when our wanderings brought us to the Gully.

Today I realize that the Gully was no more than a small stream cutting at an angle into the woods, joining the river further downstream. With the advent of time, the stream eroded a passage through a ridge in the woods, gradually cutting a gully about three yards deep. The water was always cold, shallow, and shaded, but the large colorful Minnows flashed electric tones of red and blue in the clear, sparkling water.

Despite the receding floodwaters, water gushed in a brown and dirty torrent along the Gully, but to our surprise the bank was cut wider, the Gully deeper, by more than a yard. Adventure beckoned, danger adding the required thrill of daring. Gazing at the Gully, speculation soon developed about the new width. Was it still jumpable?

"Of course it is." Lennie made the statement with scorn. Even in his early years he had his father's barrel chest and strong build, and looking at him the rest of us had no doubt that he could jump it. Terry walked to the Gully edge, peering into the foaming rush of water.

"I can jump it."

Another statement of fact. Terry was the dedicated athlete, excelling in all sports, superior to the others in our gang when physical expertise was required.

Eddie crowed loud his ability, "Yeh! Anyone could jump this." And with his long lanky legs, who could doubt it?

All eyes fixed on me. Walking to the Gully I peered into the dirty water and across to the other side. Golly, it sure had moved back a ways!

"No problem," I said. "It isn't all that wide." A lie to my inner feelings of doubt.

We turned away and paced back for a comfortable run; the jumping began. First went Eddie. Long legs pumping, he soared over, as expected, clearing it easily. Lennie and Terry followed in quick succession, both leaping the Gully. I made my run and, gathering myself for the jump, slithered to a stop on the very edge of the bank, tottering to regain balance. A moment's silence...an inbreath, and then the jeering started. Embarrassed, my face flaming red, I turned about, once more facing the jump, and again ran hard at the Gully — to again abort the leap. A third attempt, the same result. I endured the remainder of the day, thankful when we got home and I could no longer hear the snide remarks, the hidden sneers.

I lay awake that night for hours, tormented by the jump I had failed. School next day was bearable because Eddie, Lennie, and Terry went to a different school, so nobody knew of my failure. Cycling home I took an alternative route, taking me through Granchester and past Byron's Pool Woods. Leaving my bike in the Hawthorn hedge at the entrance gate, I walked into the Woods to the Gully.

I stood on the Gully edge, poised — preparing for a giant leap forward. Standing quiet, no longer responding to taunts and pressure, I realized I had no fear of the actual jump, yet fear lurked vague and disturbing in the background. I stared into the dirty water, changed by the swirling mud to menacing depths. This was the problem. I needed to see into the water, to see clearly, to see my way ahead. If I fell, I needed to know what awaited, but with the water brown and murky an element of the unknown crept in, subtle, but devastating to my morale. With recognition of my failing I turned around, paced a short run, and facing the Gully, I ran to take the leap — and failed — and failed — and failed — and failed — and failed — and SUCCEEDED!

On the sixth attempt I soared high over the Gully, landing a yard clear on the other side. The feeling which swept over me was incredible. I had jumped far more than a gully. The Gully was symbolic; I had jumped the unknown. All my life I have been facing giant leaps forward, hurdling yet other unknown factors. And now, from the intelligence of an ancient palm, the leap was brought forward once more. Never had I faced such an "unknown" as I now faced, no longer a physical jump, but a leap in consciousness. Another leap across the eroding gully of my own fear — the fear of the unknown.

FOLLOWING OUR MOVE to where we now live, our daughter Tracy insisted that because we had more room we must have a Christmas tree. After several years cramped in various caravans, we all agreed with her, so one particular day found me searching for a suitable candidate.

We have a couple of towering Hoop Pines on the property, and I figured that finding a small tree would not be difficult. A walk in the bush revealed several small trees, but always a tentative inquiry brought forth a strong objection to being moved into a pot. Empty-handed, I wandered back to the huge Morton Bay Fig tree and there, close to the trunk, a one-yard-high Hoop Pine was struggling to establish itself. Ah ha, I thought, this tree has no future at all with its close proximity to the big fig, so this will be our Christmas tree. Although a fraction underdeveloped on one side, the tree was perfect for our needs. The decision was made and, willing or not, this would be the tree. An inquiry found the Pine very willing, so I began the task of excavation.

From the beginning it was a calamity. I followed the main tap root for no more than the length of my hand when it vanished under an enormous fig tree root. Laying down my spade, I directed my thoughts to the Pine. "I'm sorry but I shall have to chop through your root. Almost certainly it will kill you. To give you a chance I suggest you withdraw your energy from your roots, and tomorrow I will remove you and replant you in a large pot."

Next day on the site, with a suitable container, I severed the root and the Pine came away. Looking rather pathetic with only one short root stump and a single wisp of side root, the tree was set into its pot and firmed down. Only hours elapsed before the Pine was drooping at its growing tip. To make it look more presentable for decorations, I twisted some thin, malleable wire around and up the prickly stem to support it. The children decorated the tree, and on Christmas day it looked quite splendid receiving admiration, love, and thanks for its part in our festivities.

Following New Year's day the Pine was placed outdoors in a shady spot and received regular water. I waited for it to die before I abandoned it, for, despite the water, there were no roots to receive the life-giving moisture. Six months later I carefully unwound the wire from a vigorous, sturdy tree delighting at being in the pot and ready for the Christmas ahead. It was mid-November, six weeks before the day, when I felt drawn toward a deeper attunement.

"Tell me, did the other Hoop Pines refuse to become our Christmas tree because you needed moving, or did you as a particular tree wish to be more involved with us? Also, how did you survive the transplanting, which was little short of brutal?"

I looked at the Pine, silent and motionless, while doubt reopened old wounds in my mind.

Relax, my friend. Do not be drawn into old thought patterns; relax in this new movement. Doubt is an established pattern of confusion which will deny your experience. Relax. To answer your question I would ask you to discard the physical aspects of transplanting a tree. I am not separate in consciousness from each separate physical tree you wished to take. Each tree can be likened to an aspect of "one" consciousness. Within this is your challenge. Your science has made great inroads in the study of plants and physical life forms, but in the more subtle regions of life — energy — consciousness so very little has been realized or recognized.

This is why your choice was made, for I as a Tree could demonstrate your own power of love. My long root was destroyed, my connection with the earth and its elements erased. Yet in the time lapse when you suggested I withdraw my energy, it was withdrawn on non-physical levels of which your science knows nothing. Had I received ingratitude, indifference, or neglect, I would have quickly died, for my energy reserve was, and is, united with your own spiritual energy.

The inner light — power — which is your family became a socket into which I could plug for energy. You and your family sustained me. Thus fed, I had the energy to grow a new root system.

I paused and reread the words which had flowed so easily from the Silence into my mind. I tried not to question the truth and wisdom of life, but it crossed my mind that to prove my experience was close to impossible. The thought was picked up immediately.

Proof has become mankind's obsession. It is an intellectual attachment which, rather than expanding your horizons, is rapidly becoming a restriction. Proof can easily become a denial of that which "IS," and the seeds of tragedy are contained in this. Those who feel these words resonate in their hearts will need no proof, while those who do not could accept none.

Just as you will never physically witness my maturity as an individual tree, neither must you seek to witness the maturity of seed you sow in the hearts of those who seek to understand. Remain open and relaxed. I stand close to you each day, and our growth is combined. Seek more often to unite your spiritual energy with that of our kingdom.

Let us communicate often, that we both may benefit.

Between the Christmas tree's outdoor position and the Cycad Palms, we have a Crepe Myrtle — a large deciduous shrub with spectacular red flowers in the summer. This particular Myrtle is host to a range of epiphytes, mostly Staghorn and Elkhorn Ferns. The host is considerate, offering sun and light in the cooler winter months, with mottled shade and protection in the hot summer months.

One of the plants enjoying this hospitality is a species I much admire. It has many names: Old Moss Beard, Solomon's Beard, Long Moss, but I think Spanish Moss is the most common — and misleading. The true name is Tillandsia. A member of the Brome-laid family, it is epiphytic, hanging in long silver-gray streamers from the trees of tropical America. Rather like a tufted, gray, open moss, it is, in fact, a series of tiny, interlaced plantlets needing no roots and feeding on the airborne nutrients contained in the con-tinuous moisture of its natural regions. It is easily grown in a warm climate or in a glasshouse; although not attractive to everyone's taste, it has great appeal to me. We grow Spanish Moss using an old pine cone as both anchor and natural moisture meter. The pine cone opens wide when dry but kept damp to the plant's liking remains firmly closed. With our mild climate, it hangs in a tree outdoors, but I keep it in full view so we can appreciate its delicate beauty. I assumed our Spanish Moss was happy with this arrangement, but one day I decided to ask it. "Does your location suit you, Spanish Moss, and do you find it pleasing to receive our admiration?" In my subtle awareness I could feel the energy of this plant magnifying — an energy of far greater proportion than the small tuft before me.

I feel it a privilege you have chosen our energy to be involved in the lesson of synthesis which you have undertaken.

The words, silent but with power, invoked an instant recol-lection of how I bought this plant from a shop in Sydney. I remembered my delight when I found it in a flower shop. Silly as it seems, it is the only recollection I have of that particular visit to Sydney.

When a person feels as strongly as you about a plant we cannot help but be affected. Today you learned why this is so. You hold the privilege of conscious unity according to your will. We welcome this contact and will do all in our power to further the experience.

During my early morning meditation I was shown a physical view of my connection with the plant kingdom when we communicate. I was standing in a clearing in a light, open forest. I was being guided and instructed by something I knew as the Spirit of the Forest.

Look now at your hands, your body.

Holding my hands before me, I was able to see light radiating from them. It was rather like an aura, but of a quite different energy. I could perceive this light radiating from my whole Being.

See now the tree directly before you.

The nearest tree was about twenty yards from me. With magnificent dark foliage, it was a tree of a variety unknown to me. However, like me, the tree radiated light, swirling and moving around its trunk and leaves, governed by an unseen power.

Reach out to the tree with your awareness. Direct your consciousness to the tree, embracing it with love.

Even as I probed with inquiry out to the tree, light leapt from my body, my Being, and in a microsecond embraced the tree, uniting and combining with the light energy of the tree. In the linking, I felt the surging Intelligence of Nature welcoming the bond.

This demonstrates clearly the spiritual union which takes place. Each time you project your conscious awareness to a plant or any aspect of Nature's kingdom, thus does your radiance leap forth. Neither distance nor time may dispel this union. We have enabled you to witness this truth, that you may more easily cast aside your doubt. Doubt within certain limits can be of value, but when doubt becomes focused and maintained by habit, it may destroy the radiance you have witnessed.

Let your perception widen . . . and understand.

No longer was I united with a tree, but with the whole forest, "one" radiant light. My perception rose above the forest where I witnessed the collective radiance composed of countless individual lights, united and fused into a single glowing radiance. Higher, far above the forest, an even greater radiance shone forth . . . and on . . . out and out . . . in and in . . . until, beyond vision or perception, I knew all light converged into a single celestial brilliance.

Now, standing on the lawn beneath its host tree, I was able to look at the Spanish Moss hanging before me, comfortable with the space between us, knowing the connection.

Within our blended consciousness, radiance communicates. Your thoughts are known, and likewise, as you become more receptive, you will "know" us.

Like bubbles floating to the surface of a pond, so will awareness trickle from your higher conscious Self. Always you must seek "knowing" rather than knowledge, for this is your chosen path. In "knowing," our energy, far more than is at present conveyed, will become realized. Knowing is realized knowledge, the living word. "Knowing" is timeless and spaceless, bound by no laws.

My mind gave an immediate demonstration of its fickleness as a thought hit me.

"Tell me, so often one plant follows on from another with a line of ideas or concepts. Is this deliberate?"

The Spanish Moss waved daintily in the breeze.

The only reason for this is you. Just as your inner radiance projects you — the real "you" — into the kingdom of Nature, so it projects your strengths, weaknesses, and needs.

Thus, although there may be disparity in your questions, the root cause remains fairly constant. In meeting your needs it is not unnatural that one experience overlaps, extends from, or converges with another set in the apparent past.

My head spun with the sudden deepening of images and concepts. I decided to give it a rest.

Tomorrow is another day. . . I think!

4 December

It concerns me that the human race has allowed separation from Nature to become established as accepted reality. Hence, man and Nature, rather than man of Nature. A midcentury edition of *Chamber's Dictionary* defines Nature in a very appropriate way as the power which creates and regulates the world. I find this definition most acceptable. Dimensions of grandeur, power, and timelessness are conjured up in the imagination, yet it also poses a question. Do we as humanity stand above and beyond such power, or is such a concept so far beyond us that we are forever lost to such reality? Observation would seem to indicate that mankind is a facet of Nature, hopefully a roving, latent intelligence. I use the word "latent" with deliberation. Regretfully, our continual involvement in the violence of war, our ever-increasing environmental pollution, as well as the expanding proportion of mentally-stressed people in our society clearly demonstrate that "intelligence" is not at the forefront of human endeavor. At best, a greed-oriented intellectual arrogance is evident. Thank God, however, the normal, everyday folk, in times of crisis, draw upon the highest qualities we have within us. However, this is no longer enough. "We" are the Nature we abuse. To establish a reconnection with Nature is to reach into our Selves, reconnecting with the timeless wisdom we each contain. Few people are not presented with opportunities to reestablish their connection with Nature, but few indeed are the people who will allow themselves time for this process. We are hyped-up whirlwinds heading blindly nowhere. How — where — when does it end? Do we take responsibility for ourselves, or do we invest our power in the mythical "they" who we believe created the mess we are in?

I have learned that this "connection" with Nature transcends the physical connection, becoming an involvement with the Spirit. Seemingly we are required to stand alone, humble and vulnerable before the Spirit of Nature, which paradoxically is the Spirit of Self. We are no longer required to relate to humanity "and" Nature, but rather humanity "as" Nature. Within this framework there develops a union, one of joy, a joy rising triumphant over all outside stress, making the moment whole and complete.

ONE SUNNY MORNING Treenie and I were sitting with our friend Yvonne, chatting in her living room. The room was light and fern filled. The full length of one side was glass from floor to ceiling and afforded superb views of the nearby rainforest sweeping as a green carpet up the escarpment to the New England Plateau. An atmosphere of intimacy with Nature was invoked. Sweet-scented climbers and soft-leaved shrubs waited, ever ready to clamber inside, knocking with gentle persistence in the light breezes sneaking from the forest. Our conversation was interesting and intense, but my attention was distracted by a small, variegated Jade plant growing in a clay pot outside the window. The wide veranda housed a motley collection of miscellaneous plants which were generally required to survive by their own hardiness. Indoors was a different story; the many ferns responded to the care and attention they received. I recognized the Jade; I had given it to Yvonne when we left the area two years earlier. It had not grown. The pot was large enough to allow for growth, but the Jade languished — it was stunted, but tenacious and alive.

"How would you like to be a Bonsai?" I silently asked.

The Jade's energy perked up immediately.

That would be most acceptable. In form I am Bonsai already.

I looked at Yvonne, smiling innocently.

"Do you want the little variegated plant out there?" I asked her.

"Do you?"

Yvonne is nothing if not direct. I knew that any "ers" or "ums" were useless. Clarity and honesty were required.

"Yes, I do. I would like to Bonsai it," I responded.

"It's yours," Yvonne replied.

So that was that.

I looked again at the Jade — stunted, twisted, almost grotesque. Strange, but when previously I thought of Jade as a Bonsai subject it had felt wrong. This felt right.

Next day I decided to pursue the matter further with the variegated Jade. It seems repetitive, but Jade is another favorite. There is a quality to the Jade energy which triggers a response in me, a surge of recognition, a feeling of "something else." I placed the little, stunted plant at my side, asking the question uppermost in my mind. "Why have you not grown? Despite looking stunted you feel quite different. What is this 'difference'?"

Are you ready to stretch some more?

I sighed. "What now? Oh well, why not?"

This moment is/has been known. I have waited for this to happen. I grew as I needed to grow. Is it not true that had I been well grown, a perfect specimen, you would have been uninterested?

I felt baffled — yes, it was true.

Space-time is convoluted It exists not, yet it exists. Time is relative to your experience. To your physical world, time marches on. Time in inner reaches is nonexistent. Will be . . . is . . . has been are all one.

Different places in the same cycle of Now. The moment of you receiving me the second time was known before I even began to grow as the cutting which you once removed.

Follow it back further.

When you removed me as a cutting from the large parent plant, even the particular cutting was known, chosen before you knew the plant existed or even had a thought of taking a Jade cutting. So it proceeds — back and back — forward and forward — all connected — no random incidents — no chances — all choice — within no choice at all.

"Whoa — hang on a bit. Of choice within no choice, I am familiar. But applying that to such a mundane act as taking a cutting of a Jade four years ago, that's ridiculous."

My outburst was indignant, but the Jade continued as though uninterrupted.

Always a higher truth is in expression. A far greater Intelligence than that which mankind calls intelligence maintains order within a world of apparent chaos.

Man claims intelligence as a thought process, whereas in truth he measures only intellect. Intelligence makes no mistakes, there are none to be made. Even the apparent threat of mankind to the stability of your planet is no more than a movement within an uncomprehended dream.

No. . . not even the choice of a cutting from a forgotten Jade in the remote stretches of Australia is chance, or accident. I have grown as I have grown. I have followed the pattern of growth which is perfect for me.

Intelligence "IS."

Intelligence decides who or what shall follow a pattern of deformity, a travesty of that which you would call perfect. Even though the physical form may be flawed, or crippled, there is no mistake, for in the infinite pursuit of truth, of expansion, of balance, a gift is contained within such adversity, a gift most rare, yet hidden.

Accept a humble, twisted Jade. My "difference" is my perfection. See your own belief and thought process in a similar fashion, knowing that your experience is but a different angle of the " One" mirror.

We will grow together for as long as is necessary, whether that is to end this moment or many years hence. It will be not chance, but choice.

It will be not physical, but spiritual.

The energy quieted, the silent words stilled. I sat for a while in a contemplative mood. For the previous few days I had felt threatened. I questioned if this experience of mine of listening to and talking with the plants was real or imagined. I dialogued with Treenie, asking not for answers — I did not know the questions — but for honesty, hoping her insight might reveal my oversight. I had visited Yvonne with a vague hope that dialogue could help expose the hidden threat as seen from her different perspective; instead . . . I came home with the Jade.

Maybe that was it. I felt a sense of excitement. Maybe the Jade was my answer. An answer offered four years before I knew the question. Maybe . . . if . . . but . . . my mind reeled at the sudden onslaught of concepts. One surprising fact emerged: I could accept the words of the Jade, despite their being thrown with full Jade vigor. I felt okay. The threat had faded. I pondered. What had changed? Why could I accept in this moment, while retreating in confusion and fear in another? The inner voice came clearly once again.

Truth is as a wave upon the beach. It races high, smothering the sand with its energy, and the sand knows the wave. The tide recedes. The sand is dry, and it knows not the wave or even its source. With the noonday sun, doubt is high upon it . . . until again comes the nourishing waves of truth.

Thus in your heart do the tides of truth and doubt ebb and flow. Be not concerned by this, for in mankind this is as natural as the waves upon a beach.

Know your Self as a single grain on the beach of humanity. You can choose to become saturated in the waves of truth, or, as others do, you can choose to let truth drain from you, unable to penetrate the hard shell of indifference.

You may control — for your Self only — the ebb and flow. You can remember the salt tang of truth when the tide recedes, and, in remembering, truth will for all time be "known."

I looked at my stunted, twisted Jade. A respect I had never before felt moved within me. As if a veil had lifted, I saw the Jade anew.

THE SUN BEAT DOWN from a cloudless sky; it was another very hot day. For a week we had unremitting heat, unusually so for our valley, and each afternoon the cool river became our refuge. One afternoon when the heat was reaching its peak, I was again heading through the garden, river bound.

Please pick my bloom and take me from this heat.

I stopped, suddenly aware of the roses in their bed of mulch, and of a single red Rose which had burst from bud to full bloom. The heat was too much for the flower, rather than the plant, and I marveled that the plant should wish to protect its single precious flower. Fetching the shears, I cut the Rose and placed it in a slim, water-filled vase at a focal point in our living room. The air was considerably cooler, and the fragrance of the red Rose blended happily with the atmosphere.

Several days later the heat intensified rather than abated, and even the living room became uncomfortably hot by late afternoon. The Rose, which under cooler conditions would still be fresh, was dying, each petal darkening at the tips from the stress of heat. I extended my conscious love to the fading Rose, moved by its beauty despite its plight.

"Thank you, fading Rose. Thank you for sharing your beauty and fragrance with us. I only wish we could have sustained YOU longer."

Do not mourn a dying Rose. I die, yet I live, for am I not also the Rose in the garden, all Roses in all gardens, all Roses in all vases? My petals have dried out, but if it were not for the love I have felt from you I would have collapsed the first day. See, not a petal has fallen.

December

The energy of those who love our kingdom carries within it a nourishment. Thus you have nourished me. I sing a song of fading radiance, yet it is within this unseen radiance I live. Physical death is of little concern. Death is our constant companion, accompanying each moment, yet death is meaningless. Death implies — "without life" — but this is untrue. Only the form, the physical shell, may be surrendered.

Life is infinite, ever present, ever expanding.

In the radiance of my flower, I live. In the radiance of your Being, I live forever.

Our energies are blended and in you I am whole.

The silent voice faded, but while I looked again at the Rose, I felt its energies gathering. I had felt uneasy with the content of images and words from this Rose; perhaps I was moved out of my depth, but the Rose sensed my distress.

Do not force your mind to accept our truth in your crystallized concepts. Be free, be open. Allow my words to move through you freely and easily.

Nothing must be seized and held. Do not make knowledge of my words. Let the ideas be vague and shifting, sifting and sorting their own energy, presenting, with the perfect timing of acceptance, a higher truth.

I can never die, even as a flower, for I am of you. Such a state-ment challenges you. Immediately — despite my suggestion — your mind seeks to grasp and understand.

My friend, let the heart know truth which the mind cannot yet comprehend. Explanations become useless. Cast aside knowledge based only on a physical reality. You must become attuned to another world, a dimension within and without your own dimension.

Let your heart accept, even while the mind paces in its cage of outraged belief.

When you learn of a physical truth, you accept and believe because you can see it. Do not deny a simultaneous truth vibrating to a higher wisdom simply because it may not be seen.

Place your faith in "knowing." Trust your Self. I will say no more
— I sense your stress.
Remember, love is the bond, and love is the release.

I found it very demanding to have images and ideas, thoughts, feelings, and words pouring into me which had no easy lodging place. They did not fit. Often I feel as though I am standing alone on a tiny island. The island is my known and accepted belief, that which is real to everyone. Gradually my island is being washed away as wave after wave of the unknown, the "not evident," erodes the sand from beneath my feet. I feel that our accepted truths are as firm as sand. It is as though I must step onto the rock of a higher truth, knowing that, once secure, I must step again to a different rock governed by a different set of rules. Only now am I beginning to realize that casting myself into unknown waters, in trust, is the most difficult act I have ever undertaken. But I am inspired to persist.

THE HEAT HAD FINALLY BROKEN. Clouds gathering during the day passed slowly and heavily over the valley. Rain was threatening when I reached the river, not to swim in the water, but to immerse myself in the waiting consciousness. I sat with open journal on my lap, my mind reaching out to the river. With the flow of words came a simultaneous scattering of rain, sweeping in from upriver.

Your anticipation, loaded with expectation, dampens our communication in much the same way as the rain dampens your ability to write.

My pen, moving over the paper surface, was forming half words, part sentences. Where it was wet, nothing I wrote would impress on the paper.

Thus, my friend, when you try to attune with anticipation and expectation, we find you as the wet pages of your journal, only capable of receiving a fraction of what we wish to convey.

I recoiled in dismay.

A glimpse of my subconscious expectations was revealed in the clouded mirror of self-reflection. Dejected, I walked heavily back to the house, rain sweeping over me. Dropping the journal on my desk, I sat down thoughtfully. How could I deal with thoughts I was not aware of thinking? It was a ridiculous problem. Which came first, the chicken or the egg? If expectation is based on thought, or anticipation is unconscious activity of the mind, how can I break into this cycle? Glancing through the window I noticed the rain had stopped. For some reason it seemed to be a vaguely mocking gesture, as though Nature scorned my attempts to successfully capture her wisdom on paper. With incredible sincerity the silent words of river entered my confused and whirling mind.

We do not mock you. Indeed, you are privileged that life offered such a perfect reflection of your expectations. Your subconscious rumblings cause a disturbance in the flow between us. You are as yet unaware of the power of thought. Directed and focused, thought is of immense power. Suppressed and unconscious thoughts or desires cause a distortion in the clarity we seek to impart.

A subconscious pattern of thought is an interruption between us. Before you are ready to use the full power of focused thought, it must become clear, pure, and refined.

Cluttered, imprisoned, and suppressed thought is a danger seeking always to hold the thinker in bondage. Thought should not be imprisoned. Look into the dungeon of your mind and release any locked-up thoughts. Let them go free. Attach no claim on them. Be not embarrassed by them, simply release them.

To do this you must acknowledge the thoughts which shame you, accept their existence. Speak them aloud to a loving friend, or in to the Silence. In the speaking they shall be released, no longer holding you by their unspoken deceit.

In the release of these thoughts, you shall find your own release. Only by the release of thoughts as they arise into the conscious mind shall you master thought.

The dialogue left me feeling bemused and rather disturbed. I was still feeling a sense of shock. I had been unaware of expectations, the imprisoned manipulations; yet, in honesty, I was aware of the shadows which flitted to and fro deep in the mind. I wanted no prisoners in the cells of my mind, but I was not sure I could release them or what would happen if I tried.

Day met and merged with night, but the following morning a cloud weighed heavily over me, anchored by a subconscious attachment to bygone fears. I realized that a past laden with unresolved problems is ever present and continually represented until we develop the capacity to resolve our problems. By this action we lay the past to rest.

Thoughts slid through my mind with deceptive ease as, squinting against the glare of the early, low sun, I gazed at the nearby Rubber tree.

If only doubt would never plague my mind again. Despite thoughts of pessimism, I could feel the consciousness of the tree becoming alive and aware in my mind. If only I could be at peace with my knowing.

I am sorry, my friend, truly sorry.

We can offer you no proof. What do you need? Would a recorded communication heard simultaneously by a dozen or even a thousand people meet your need?

Or would you then be one of a small group of confused and victimized people seeking further proof? Only by knowing who you are will you find peace. When this is known, proof will be revealed as an offering needed only by those who cannot accept the reality of their own lives.

Doubt holds you away from your acceptance of Self. I need not tell you that doubt is a lock on the door to greater realities, to extended possibilities. Doubt is the part of your mind which fights to retain control. Doubt seeks to speculate and, from speculation, to walk a known path.

You cannot do this and enter a higher conscious awareness. There is no room for doubt, no place for doubt to express its fear. Doubt destroys faith. Faith knows not, nor seeks to know, for in faith this moment is complete.

The path of faith is a journey beyond time, space, or dimensional limitations.

The mind may not go ahead seeking to make the way known. Instead, the mind is controlled, neither by leash nor techniques, but by the faith of this moment's "knowing."

Please understand. Known is the past, while "knowing" is only of this moment, the eternal "now."

Can you accept a challenge of this magnitude?

Can you leave the company of the vast flock of those who doubt, to become a lonely shepherd of faith?

A feeling of unease swept me, not so much related to doubt, but to a vague inner disturbance I could not identify. I decided to be gentle with myself rather than glare within, seeking to expose the lurking feelings and drag them into a premature light. I was aware of the conscious friendship of this tree, of Nature.

"'Thank You," I murmured, "thank you."

The silent word took me by surprise.

Be aware of how much more easily you are now accepting the presence of a higher truth. No longer do you fight for weeks and months against the loaded logic of doubt.

Be content to accept for now the presence of higher truth. It will fit in your consciousness, involving and enveloping you with perfect timing.

Yes. I felt that it was true. Doubt no longer fought me for week after pain-filled week. Doubt was still a fierce predator, but a crippled one, no longer able to rend and tear at my faith, yet ever lurking, snarling its menace from the background. A sense of gratitude swept over me, for I know I have been helped, almost nursed, through the last year.

My mind flickered through the recorded events. A year of pain, of confrontation and decision. Either I walked my long long-ago-chosen path, or I turned aside completely. It was my choice.

To hesitate in confusion and doubt was to sink deeper into stagnation and despair.

I sighed. "I am so glad the worst is behind me, the decision made."

It is good that you are aware of the help which has been extended to you. One day you will know how your pain was our pain; your confusion, our compassion; your doubt, our sorrow.

We have extended our kingdom to you to seal a bond, to allow a commitment to grow, to mature into flower, and to send forth the seed of its fruit. We shall meet on the other levels one day. We shall meet in a radiance of such light that truth shall forever stand revealed.

For several days a strange, disoriented feeling pervaded me. I felt as though a deep, inner part had made a giant step, while the other part neither knew where nor how to make such a move.

I felt off balance, an inner disturbance. The inevitable happened. I began to develop a cold, starting with a typical sore throat.

That was yesterday.

Today it was nicely developed. My glands were swollen, my sinuses were blocked, and a mild headache throbbed behind my eyes. Now I had an excuse to hide, to linger a while in self-pity. There is nothing quite like a cold or flu to avoid an issue!

At my request, Treenie went to the pharmacy as soon as it opened and returned home with a packet of throat lozenges which she flipped onto the bed with a remarkable lack of sympathy.

It was while she was away "something happened."

I had been reading *Illusions* by Richard Bach for the second time, maybe two years after my first reading. The book poses questions. Where is the boundary between reality and illusion? Who decides what is real and what is illusion? Do we accept a common belief, or can we have an independent belief, isolated, but real? How much of our experience is an illusion based on what we think or expect is reality?

December

I have seen a man stick a long pin right through his arm. No tricks, the genuine article. He obviously felt no pain. He was not in a trance. He taught himself that it is possible to shift his identity away from his arm or any other part of his body; thus, he felt no pain in an arm that was not his. Stick the pin through my arm and . . . PAIN. Who has the correct reality? Who lives in illusion?

I know which I prefer. I browsed over the concept of limitation. We are limited by the conditioning of our thoughts, by what we think we can achieve, by what we think will gain the approval of our peers, thus stabilizing our self-esteem — another illusion. On and on . . . .

Struggling through this long, murky turmoil of thought, a light appeared, drawing swiftly closer, flooding my mind with illumination. Something clicked . . . a giant stride . . . .

If this is an illusion I am experiencing with Nature, if it is all imagination — then it's okay. I like it. Who can make me a better offer? Polluted food and air? Is that better? To maintain a belief in death, fear, greed? Are they better? A dogmatic religion with a judgmental God? Is that better? My experience is uplifting, expanding, loving, creative, intelligent. Who can offer me a better reality or illusion? If I feel a great love toward Nature, and I feel love radiating to me from Nature, who has a better illusion to offer? If I feel compassion and love for humanity, if I am happy doing exactly what I want to do, who can offer me more than this?

Suddenly it hit me. What am I fighting? Am I fighting an offer of love, of peace, of expansion, of creativity, of insight and intelligence, of knowing "me," of what "IS"? Fighting it for what? Do I want to remain with the common belief of pain, suffering, death, drudgery, sickness, of being the victim of life's misfortune — when I know I can be who I am, where I am, when I am? Right . . . "now."

When Treenie flipped the throat lozenges onto my bed, I took one . . . and I "knew." I am not denying the pain, fear, doubt, sorrow of everyday reality, but neither need I cling to such a powerful belief while denying the creative, intelligent love of Nature.

I chose that, for me, pain and suffering, fear and doubt were ended. We all have that choice. I don't want a cold or sore throat. I don't need a cold or sore throat. I've done it all before. I no longer need to. I am free. I accept my experience. I believe my experience. I know what I know. I can offer my gift to enrich life through the pages of my books, but it does not matter how many or how few want it. I do. I enjoy it. I scrambled out of bed, a feeling of excitement upon me. I knew it was a breakthrough. To where, I had no clue, but the step was enough. To make it public and thus become vulnerable, I told Treenie and the family I would not have a sore throat and cold, sharing with them something of what had taken place. They greeted most of my words with suppressed smirks and a "we will see" expression.

Now, at the end of the day as I sit with Jade, writing and relating this magnificent plant energy, I have no sore throat or cold. It took about thirty minutes for all the symptoms to completely disappear. I like it!

THE SMALL DARK-BLUE BONSAI pot was the perfect container. I felt a sense of achievement as I gazed at the Jade, one long root thrown carelessly over a small boulder, growing as though no other pot had ever contained it. The Jade and I had combined consciously, finding the most perfect way in which to express our synthesis. The stunted, twisted form, ugly in its previous container, became pure beauty. It is almost too perfect.

I directed my thoughts to the Jade. Jade would listen, Jade would understand.

Do you feel our song of triumph? Do you feel the cosmic All surging through your Being? We rejoice with you, my friend. You are taking the steps which will gain you mastery of your destiny, rather than becoming flotsam cast high on the beach of helplessness, at the mercy of all who pass by. Now do you understand our union? Time between time ceases to be. I sing in your heart, for you are my creator.

Stretch again and comprehend. It was you who created me, that I may tell you...you are creator. You of humanity.

By your will, by your thoughts, by your imagination, by your belief, you make it so.

There is that in you which knows.

In all mankind there is that which knows.

Life is not revealed by building up layer upon layer of stored information.

This becomes knowledge. Knowledge is information made static. Life is revealed by "knowing."

"Knowing" is information in movement, kept free, spontaneous. Science has a fixation on knowledge, particularly that which is compatible with sense perception.

Despite instruments which far exceed man's sensory capacity, all knowledge gained is translated back to a sense perception before it can be coded as "information."

If it cannot be seen, heard, touched, smelled, or tasted, it is not received by physical man. The five senses of man. The four walls and the lid of your prison, Discard them. Touch will not determine subtle shapes. Eyes will not perceive reality. Ears do not hear the song of the universe. You cannot taste the food of angels or smell the fragrance of a higher truth. We rejoice as you begin to unshackle the self-imposed chains of limitation.

Use your physical senses, enjoy them, but never for one moment believe in them as complete reality. Your heart knows — experience.

Believe, believe.

Whatever you believe — is so.

The feeling of excitement surged. The sore throat, headache, and cold "had" gone. Were they ever a reality, or were they an illusion I created to hide behind? Whichever, I controlled them. I felt excited because I had never done this before. What is illusion? What is real? One thing I know for certain, I don't know where I'm going, but I'm ready to enjoy the journey. Expansion — love — creativity — Nature — knowing. Does anyone have a better offer?

TIME PASSES . . . but the sense of movement, inner movement, has not faded. I feel an inner "aliveness," an awareness more sharp, bright, and clear than ever before. I feel I am poised, balanced and unafraid, on the edge of some mystical insight. In some strange way I know, even though I am not aware of knowing. I have no idea where my connection with Nature will take me, yet I am more committed to the journey than ever. Along this path lies inner fulfillment, and I can linger no more.

No longer is doubt casting gray and melancholy shadows over a sunlit horizon; my step can quicken naturally. Change is an obvious factor in our lives. I see change as never before, strikingly obvious. Now I can trust the process in which I am involved. I can trust who I am, knowing that only the most perfect expression of Nature/Self can result. My acceptance is of my choosing, yet my choice was made long ago. How many of us are destined to honor commitments we once made and to which we are spiritually obligated?

I suspect there is a very great number of such people on the earth at this time, and I suspect that in this era, when those people connect with their purpose in life, the greatest explosion ever known, of change, of human potential, will take place. These were my thoughts and feelings as I wrote in my journal, and before me on a table, in the dark-blue Bonsai pot, was Jade.

The time on which you speculate is predestined.

Predestined not by some all-powerful God, but by humanity. Ponder a simple parable for its profound truth — "As you sow, so shall you reap."

You cannot take a cutting from a Rose and produce Jade — you cannot sow arrogance and reap humility. Life is of a vast spectrum.

Life cannot be understood if you acknowledge one brief moment in time — a lifetime. Life cannot be understood if you measure experience as the sum total of many lives.

Life is one vast continuum, in and out of physical matter. Without beginning — without end.

A swim in dense conscious expression this day, and into a finer consciousness next day. Each day/life generates balance. Without the higher worlds of consciousness, your physical existence would rapidly become insanity. What is the reason for this? Could it be random incidents? Could it be that all earth life is an accident or chance of space-time?

Or is it possible that humanity has chosen to become the synthesis of life, blending the physical with the psychical? If this is so, could it be possible that Nature stands not away from, or outside of, humanity, but instead reflects humanity, retains humanity, inflects humanity, both physically and psychically? Can speculation confirm an answer, or does it require that you live it, experience it, become the answer by "Being"?

I stared at the Jade. Wow! Some Jade!

"How do you know all this?" I asked.

Why ask a question when you already know the answer? Do you wish to play more games? Are you not yet ready to accept "knowing"?

"Okay, okay. I accept. I know how you know. Life is one vast universal Intelligence. The life in Nature, the life in humanity, one life, one Intelligence. If you know, I know. We all know. Knowing 'IS.' Life 'IS.' But we of humanity have so much to unknow, unlearn, peel away. Disbelief, doubt, restricted realities, hypnotic limits, an endless list of misbeliefs and conditioned thinking is with us and we have to cope with this. You do not."

I threw my words out almost as a challenge. How incongruous. On glancing at the Jade I realized the incredible physical differences. I could crush it underfoot, no challenge at all, but on inner levels Jade looms so vast I could climb it, rather like a mountain of consciousness from which I could peer ahead. It chuckled. There I go again, why peer ahead? I am here — now. It is enough.

Your words are true about your limitations, even if they are self-imposed and therefore not real. Within our kingdom, light shines with undiminished purity, ever beckoning, ever present.

Such illumination reveals to us our place in the design of life — now. For mankind, however, a greater truth emerges. You are born as creators. Gods of forgotten power. Leaves fallen from a tree to which you know not you belong.

You seek to develop that which "is" developed.

You seek to discover that which "is" discovered. You seek to form in the material world that which you can "know" into being. You seek to prop up your illusions, that you can more easily believe in them. You develop your weaknesses, thus denying the path of inherent strength.... Yet we are One... and my love envelops you....

The last words caught me off balance. Love became tangible as the words eased with infinite gentleness into my mind. There was a softening of energy, combined with love so overwhelming, so powerful, I glanced around half expecting to find a Spirit of Nature materialized in the room. But no. All I could see was a dark-blue Bonsai pot — and the Jade.

CHRISTMAS ARRIVED, bringing a return of the family. Duncan came from Sydney, exhausted by the frantic pace of life he had designed for himself, and Adrian motorcycled up from Melbourne, bringing a new member into our family, his fiancee, Jo. Once again the Hoop Pine came into the living room and, when draped with the lights and tinsel for celebration, stood forth transformed. I noticed a marked increase in the height, promising the Pine that after one more Christmas it would have the freedom of a garden in which to grow.

Several times during the festivities I sneaked away, seeking attunement with Nature, but each time my mind, overloaded with family involvement, would become lost in the thoughts and speculations of fatherly concern. My mind was hyped-up by the onrush of personalities, the speed, pace, and determination of the kids to extract full measure from the family reunion.

To my consternation I found myself resenting the intrusion, inwardly annoyed that I was isolated from Nature by the demands and pressures of family, but then, taking a good look at myself, I saw the selfishness in such thoughts. This was the family, our children, and here I was resenting their interference in a process which would be waiting with infinite patience until I was ready. Quickly I realized that it was I who was out of step, losing sight of the reality of "now;" and, just as our "grown-up" children needed me, so I needed them for the balance and love which are uniquely human.

I surrendered my isolation by the river to the spontaneity of youth, to the exuberance, energy, and excitement of their holidays.

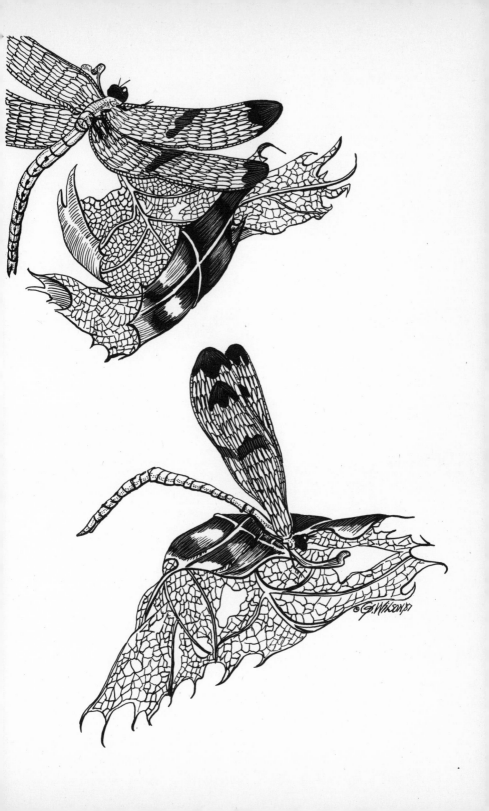

5 february

The weeks of January were swept away by fishing, swimming, talking, laughing, reconnecting with that most precious of human gifts — our own family. The school holidays filled our house with visiting friends, with giggling girls and boisterous boys, each day hurriedly pushing aside the next as the overfilled days sped past in an endless blur of activity.

By the time Duncan, Adrian, and Jo departed I was truly sorry to see them go, feeling again that space inside which, although never empty, is unfilled, lacking the everyday physical relationship of those we love.

Suddenly, abruptly, the holidays were over, the school bus again screeching to a halt outside our gate to pick up Russell and Tracy, our two reluctant scholars. As life slowed down in and around our household, I was able to visit the river with a mind satisfied and enriched by the interactions I had experienced, but now calmed and quiet, reaching out to the Silence of a timeless Nature.

The water was no longer murky with algae as it had been in the warmth of January, for a heavy summer rain had washed and scoured the riverbed clean, each stone fresh-scrubbed and shining, the gravel patches relaid with precise care. Fish were again in evidence, Mullet leaping in a moment's flickering silver, as I crouched over my journal in a mottled patch of shade and light.

It was hot, very hot, the sun relentless in a clear sky. I leapt from the bushes only when the ants launched their third attack. I had been hoping for a truce. The ants, tiny and frenzied in the heat, had driven me from my favorite rock, from the diving board, and now from the shade of the bush.

Finally, I sat rather uncomfortably on the sloping shelf of a large, partly submerged boulder. I felt fairly certain that by sitting in shallow water the ants would be defeated. They were, but two huge March Flies decided I was of great interest to them as they wove in a humming monotone around my head. Waving my hands wildly I shooed them away, not at all keen on their sly, painful bites. The next attack was decidedly sneaky, launched underwater by a crowd of tiddlers and a few large freshwater shrimps. The tiddlers were no problem, but the shrimps — ouch!

I was beginning to feel my timing must be wrong, maybe rivers are just for swimming after all. Though strong in current, the water surface was calm, undisturbed by its swift flow, while shimmering, color-splashed Dragonflies skimmed the water before me, displaying an acrobatic grace surpassing the Swallows flying overhead. A sense of freedom moved into me, expanding and circulating through my awareness.

An effect of sharpening took place, a heightened feeling, one of immense clarity. For a moment I reflected back on old doubts, finally vanquished and beaten. Exhilaration coursed through my body. No longer do I doubt the Intelligence of Nature. No longer do I close my mind to words which flow from the Silence. Silence hides behind that curtain of doubt, hidden by the thick material of physical reality. There was no surging power from the river, nothing on which to focus, but more clearly, more certain than ever, came the silent words.

Silence moves beyond your comprehension.
Listen carefully.

Suddenly, from nowhere, a breeze sprang up, the wind singing again in the needles of the nearby River Oak.

Through all the sound of wind and flute-washed needles; of wind and twisting, chattering leaves; of wind and leaping, splashing Mullet; of wind and gurgling, sighing water; of wind and swaying, dancing trees; another sound too delicate to touch with words pierced me, sweet and poignant, bringing tears unbidden to my eyes.

This "exaltation" played across my senses like a bow moving swiftly over the strings of a violin. Sound which was without, moved within. Sound transcended into Silence, stretching through my consciousness into an infinite wave of tenderness, of clarity and insight. Suddenly, a Mullet leaped with a resounding splash almost under my nose, and the wind ceased. In the Silence all was stilled.

How inadequate your senses are. From your Being, I experienced the Silence of which I am.
How limited, but do not despair.
Only weeks ago even this fleeting experience was quite beyond you, shut away by the self-centeredness which is mankind.

I had to stand up. The agony of pins and needles had turned to cramp, and, easing my nearly dead rear off the rock, I felt a surge of blood rushing into the numbed flesh. I groaned aloud.

"This is how limited I am," I muttered as I paced around, moving my circulation.

"But I get your point about being self-centered. It certainly erases a wider focus on life."

Be gentle with your humanness. It is a privilege to be human, an honor.
Hold in your consciousness the knowing that you — a human — are not limited to bodily experiences. You — a human — may experience the universe, in totality, in Oneness; yet, this experience will not

deny a normal identity with the human body. Consciousness will expand, and all will become a part of your greater Being. Your identity will be the body of "earth/man" — humanity — rather than the body of "a man" — a human. Go now, enjoy the river. I am aware of your discomfort.

A feeling of something akin to amusement moved into me. I was aware that "amused" was not the correct descriptive word, not quite the experience. Maybe the feeling could be described as an "appreciation" for the lighter aspects of dense reality. I had the feeling that "I" was the dense reality! Sweating profusely in the scorching heat, I hopped from foot to foot in an effort to stop the fierce, biting ants from swarming over my feet. The more I perspired, the more excited and aggressive they became. It was time to quit, time to swim.

THE EXCESS OF FISHING over the school holidays had whetted Russell's appetite for more, and each weekend would begin with the request: "Can we go fishing, Dad?" Basically this meant that I was required to act as transport and packhorse, for I have little interest in fishing; whereas Russell, with a fishing rod in his hands, enters a trancelike state of immense concentration and patience, quite unlike his impatient self at home.

Perhaps I hedged too often, but Russ decided on a new tactic. He was aware that a friend, John Caporale, had moments of fishing enthusiasm blowing hot or cold according to the winds of his desire. With consummate skill, Russ played out a line of images and fantastic fishing conditions guaranteed to catch any but the most laggard fisherman.

John succumbed, the hook firmly embedded, and for a few weekends they visited the local beaches and rivers with varying degrees of success.

One afternoon I decided to accompany them to the brackish headwaters of the Bellinger River, an opportunity to observe the nature of a quite different environment.

February

Across from where we were sitting on a bank intermingled with stones and grass, the dense vegetation of a Mangrove swamp swept boldly into the water. The water lapping at our feet was clean, yet the depths reflected a brackish-brown, rather like a river of tea flowing impassively to the ocean.

The strident, echoing barks of chained dogs on the nearby dairy farm disturbed a silence fostered and maintained by the softly lapping waves on the rocky shoreline. Crows called harshly from a towering clump of giant Bamboo, while Swallows silently skimmed the water's surface in an endless pursuit of insects. Life was all action, constant motion and movement.

Ten white Egrets flew past, beating their way with visible effort into a head wind, guided by instinct as they winged toward an unknown destination. The tone and pitch of the barking dogs changed abruptly as an ever-growing mob of Friesian cows congregated around the dairy. The daily ritual of milking was about to begin.

My mind drifted... way back into my past, to my ten years of milking. It was an old, familiar routine. I felt no envy as the hissing suction of the milking machine began its steady, rhythmic throb, a sound borne faintly on the breeze, yet amplified by ears wise to this particular beat. No! I wanted no part of the past. Necessity had cracked the whip which made me work such long hours at a job I detested, but fear wove the illusion. Fear that my needs could be met by no other way than subservience to a system for which I had no respect. Fear which for a while crowded confidence into a corner, cowering and beaten.

Now I enjoy idle times. Time to feel the empty spaces of this moment. Time to explore the emptiness, the loneliness, to find it full and rich, challenging in the paradox that it takes time to find timelessness.

There came a lull and, except for the keen breeze, activity was suspended. I spoke with the river and the Mangrove swamp, so alien compared with the familiar energy of my river place, with its trees and friendliness. This river felt remote, even though consciously available. Its character, molded by a strange environment, touched my vulnerable emotions with raw indifference.

As wide as I am; as different as I express; as fast as I ebb and flow, yet I am no different from the river with which you communicate. I express another quality, as different as a toe from a finger — and as similar.

The strangeness you feel is your reaction to the environment. It is not river-made or controlled. Your emotions are your response.

Pleasure or displeasure, receptivity or alienation, your choice — or to be more accurate in this instance — your reaction.

In reaction there is no choice.

Learn to be "responsive" rather than reactive, for a world of difference echoes between them.

The wind had increased considerably, blowing cool from the water, but the fishing enthusiasts seemed not to notice. The only thing which they finally did notice was the lack of "response" from the fish they hoped to catch!

MY VISITS TO OUR RIVER became frequent, inspired and encouraged by the magic energy of the sun. One morning, while sitting on my favorite rock, I gazed upriver to the Weeping Willow tree. The recent flood had left it leafbare and stripped. Slender branches shone with a reflection of the palest gold, highlighted by the solid dark-green background of the River Oaks lining the waterway, on and on, upriver.

Bending with supple grace before the violent seasonal winds roaring down the river, or brushing the water's surface in calm tranquility with a touch caressingly light, the Weeping Willow endures all conditions with its nonresistant strength. Flexibility is the quality and essence of Willow. Hemmed in by the vigorous River Oaks massed along the riverbank, the Willow stretches far out across the river in its search for sunlight, and it endures. Strong and stalwart as they are, nevertheless, occasional River

Oaks are torn from their roothold in every flood, tossed, twisted, and broken in the raging water.

The Willow endures.

It offers no resistance to the rearing strength of pounding floods. Half submerged, the branches writhe and twist, dancing to the river's tune... until the flood recedes.

Again the Willow stands free, new leaves quickly replacing the battered foliage. Its strength is masked, yet the Willow makes our finest cricket bats, strong and resilient.

The Willow endures.

The gentlest of river breezes stirred the golden boughs, dancing with a ripple through the tree. The poetry of Nature's finest touch. Appreciation stirred within me. How blessed I am to be surrounded by such beauty, with an even greater blessing: that I allow myself time to experience such golden moments.

We are united in loving awareness.

So enrapt was I in wonder for the beauty manifest before me, that the words moved unexpectedly into my mind.

"I greet you, graceful Willow. I pay my respects to all you represent."

Was it a long-drawn sigh I heard, caught and echoed on a silent breeze?

Respect! Rare indeed is the quality of respect in mankind. To respect each other, to respect Nature — life — requires a respect for Self.

So few, so few indeed, respect their own Selves.

Indeed, the energy we experience most from mankind is Self-loathing buried deep and malignant in the debris of subconscious fear. Small wonder that such loathing, such a lack of Self-respect manifests in sickness, in malignant growths, for such an attitude is a malignancy of the mind.

"How much are you aware of human conditioning? You seem to express insights that we could not possibly credit to a tree."

Your question indicates a slip into old concepts. In the world of Nature to which you attune, a single tree is an illusion. I am "one" with Willow-tree energy. Worldwide, "I am"/ "we are" "one" energy. Then again, I am not separate from all tree energy. That which "IS," "Intelligence," "God," "Nature," name it as you desire, this is the power which flows in our sap.

"I am"/ "we are" pure Intelligence in our chosen conscious expression and form. You have been told before. Enjoy your five senses, use them wisely to experience your physical dimension, but do not let them deny your psychical expression. Human experience today is limited to the conditioned belief of a renegade mind. Despite appearances, this is neither good nor bad.

It is each person's individual choice.

In the bleakest, most grim personal expression there is "light."

Equally in the most benign and grace-filled person there exists "dark." Balance is the expression of a mature and Self-loved Being. The mind submits to love.

The concept of "nothing is good or bad, thinking makes it so," was not a new one. But I was intrigued by the words "the mind submits to love." There are many seminar experiences available today where we are offered techniques to control the mind, rather as though on a disciplined leash.

"I would like to hear more about the mind and love," I said quietly.

What is there to say? Love is that which "IS."

Before such, the mind submits. He who is controlled by the mind dies to the mind…and is reborn.

Such persons relate to the same world, but view it from a different perspective.

They view from Love seeing that which "IS."

Others view from fear seeing that which they believe is.

When others will not support your perception of that which "IS," love will sustain you. When all will support that which is believed in, this maintains the illusion.

It has taken me seven years of conscious inquiry and often painful effort to accept life as I now perceive it, less clouded by my fears.

I am aware fear has not vanished, for, given permission, my mind will quickly conjure up the old images to sustain help-lessness.

I had a question.

"Will it take another seven years to reach a state of complete surrender to life, or freedom from all fear?"

Such a question has no answer. You could be love-filled in this moment, transformed in pure "Light," or you could die many years hence screaming your fear. The possibilities exist — your choice.

I have chosen.

Each day life offers me the chance to review my choices. New pressures, lucrative offers, but the price is — to follow a known path.

I cannot do this, yet I am aware these snares hold a gift, for they strengthen my resolve and clarify my sight.

Life offers only upliftment, enlightenment — but as experienced through human sense perception, it is not easy to comprehend or understand. You are aware of the grace of Willow strength. Resilience is strength.

I was aware of a universal law — take that which opposes you, using its strength against itself.

The power is Chi.

Many great men and women have done this.

I stood up, stretching. The Willow appeared unchanged, yet a lightness played around and over the slender branches and leaves. It was not physical. What I could see was different . . . and I knew that I was the difference. Hours passed, while I sat lost in silent contemplation on the old bridge-plank diving board facing upriver.

A gust of wind, sudden and demanding, lifted my head and eyes upriver, and there I saw the voyager.

Exquisitely formed, boat and rider sailed toward me. The boat — a leaf, large and brittle, folded at right angles forming hull and sail.

The rider — a blue Dragonfly, perched daintily in savage splendor atop the sail. The sight of such beauty inspired a poetic response.

> Dark blue, the mystic voyager,
>   gazing over waters, flowing wide.
> Where will he sail this day
>   searching for tomorrow's gold?
> Does he search the seas "in tune"
>   or seek a "fiddle" of his own?
> Is he bound to craft and sail
>   by illusion of his need?
> Or like us, by illusion of his greed?

The leaf and Dragonfly were gone, sped headlong on their journey by a swift rush of water.

An atmosphere of tranquility and peace settled over the river.

In the deep, dark hole upriver, within reach of the Weeping Willow fronds, a pair of Platypuses foraged early mornings and late evenings, but for the moment they too were at peace, quiet in their subterranean tunnel in the rich, protective earth. As if to defy the calm, a bold Rock Dragon scampered noisily across the dry-leaf carpet close by. The energy of Nature felt close, very close, an intensity contained in the calm.

It is interesting, I pondered, that Nature offers me no blueprint for cultural skill. I have my successes and failures in the garden, just as other people do. Strange, yet not really strange at all. To receive directed guidance would lead me into dependency, inadvertently creating and maintaining helplessness. I would not wish for that.

Such guidance from our kingdom would destroy your intuitive powers to attune with that center of "knowing."

The energy was new, a quality — or character — not previously experienced. "Knowing" put forward what I was seeking.

I glanced along the river bank to a young Mulberry tree not far from where I was sitting, perhaps the offspring from a bird-dropped fruit; it leaned over the water's edge, its large green leaves soaking up the energy of the sun.

"It is you I hear. Thank you for your words and for the rare occasions I can beat the birds to your fruit, thank you. I have tasted your delicacy both sides of the world."

The flow of words again slid smoothly into my awareness, and as often happens my line of thought was ignored.

Knowing is held in this moment — "now."

Prior thinking does not contain "knowing," while logic and reason deny the principle of "knowing." Reacting from fear, "knowing" is denied. Acting from love, "knowing" is.

The river swirled and rippled around the firm out-thrust bridge board on which I was sitting. I stripped off my clothes, folded my towel, and laid it along the diving end of the board.

Lying down, the sun warm on my back, I gazed into the water, staring straight down into the depths. A small Damselfly, slender and graceful, settled on a blade of Tussock Grass overhanging the water. In one smooth movement the long, slender abdomen arched, its tail end entering the surface of the river. Although it defied my eyesight, I knew that eggs were being pumped from its ovipositor into the water, there to attach themselves until the time of hatching. In moments the Damselfly was gone, but I could see the occasional, large Dragonfly, with down-curved abdomen, depositing eggs beneath the water surface in a series of long, skimming flights over the river.

The miracle of birth . . . and rebirth?

In the springtime when a larva hatches from its eggcase, a predator is born into the dense world of water. Voracious, ever hungry, the Dragonfly larva is deadly to all its size, a tiger of the deep. Much larger tadpoles perish, sucked empty by this killer larva. In the course of time, the natural cycle completed, the larva clambers up onto a rock or log into the light atmosphere of air. A metamorphosis takes place. There comes a moment when the casing of the larva splits and a Dragonfly emerges triumphant in the sunlight. A pause...a few hours to pump powerful body enzymes through the wings, time to dry, firm, and strengthen...and a new creature takes to the air. Did the larva in its dense water world know of the birthing to come, into the fine world of air? Did the Dragonfly have any memory of dying to a water world while birthing into an air world?

The metaphor hung over the river, dazzling in its obvious implication. Do we know from where we are born?

Maybe we are born into a dense world, a savage predator terrorizing and destroying life around us. In the course of time, the cycle complete upon our unconscious choice, we die to the dense world.

Is this our metamorphosis?

Are we reborn into the pure light of Spirit? Do we take wing, soaring on the high energy of controlled thought, free to take a higher nourishment, free to bask in the sunlight of that which "IS"?

Do we choose, in our desire for perfection, to once again enter the dense world, maybe for a quick splash, or perhaps a long swim, to attempt to redress the desire and fear which permeate the dense atmosphere, polluting our thoughts and actions? Could we be universal Dragonflies, immersed in a cosmic game in a Self-made world, seeking the cleansing and purification that only experience can offer?

6 March

I am frequently drawn to the river by an intensity, an insistent urge which demands.

The sun shines...the river calls...and I obey.

One morning, following such an intense urge, I was sitting on the diving board, poised over the vibrant and sparkling water, when I put forward the question:

"What is it that responds?"

Do not look for separation.

The I that calls is not separate from the I which responds.

To those who are aware of their sensitivity and are determined to cultivate and encourage their finer feelings, life calls in many varied ways.

For you, the river calls.

The river becomes a matrix.

The known falls back into its crucible. It is reborn, "knowing."

In the womb of Nature, water is the receptor of life...and the birth giver.

"Do I answer a call from life that I may receive new birth?"

By choice you move with life as it "IS."

The clouded stream of human belief would drag you into its current of illusion, while the clear flow of Nature seeks to nurture the birthing of an ancient Self.

Two movements compete for attention. You must balance these energies to emerge unscathed.

"Why do I feel such intensity? How is it that beneath my calm approach to life a raging, seething discontent mingles easily with a serene acceptance?"

Your discontent is a blessing — give thanks for it.

Know where it is centered.

You are discontent with life's illusion. An inner "knowing" rages against "known's" offerings.

The battlefield is a natural dynamic, a potent force to be harnessed and directed, yet only through the power of surrender to that which "IS." This is your training, your destiny.

"There is a destiny?"

If you so wish you can choose the when. Destiny was accepted with awareness, but chosen before awareness knew of choice.

I could feel concepts and ideas quite new to me shifting and sifting as though we all floated interlocked in a deep, dark pool. My sense of Self expanded, and, with the expansion, a focus clarified.

The sensation was quite unlike telescopic vision, seeing more of less and less. Instead, seeing with my eyes continued as before, but I was not aware of looking through my eyes. I identified with all, seeing not "onto" with focus, but "identifying" with an inner clarity.

I was the I which I observed.

The experience was strange, both new and familiar.

An orange-red Dragonfly settled on the diving board near my journal. In seconds it was gone, yet in the going it remained. The space was empty to normal vision, unoccupied by a Dragonfly in a physical sense, yet a psychical knowing of Dragonfly was as clear and focused as ever.

A sense of bewilderment swept over me; my brain was baffled by the speed of change.

I closed my eyes and relaxed. Vision was gone, but perception roamed like a child, blinking nervously in a new light. Was it visual impression, imagination, or real?

Subtle beyond subtlety, delicate beyond delicacy.

Momentarily I perceived as that which "IS." It was a moment of infinite tenderness.

"Why," I pleaded, "can I not maintain this?"

That which emerges from a matrix must grow. Would you deny this principle? Can you deny sound to hear Silence? Does birth precede death, or death precede birth, or are birth and death a misconception of that which "IS"?

"Are you deliberately working me, stretching me?"

I heard nothing, but the power of suggestion from a clear, inviting physical river which flooded over me was so strong that my next move needs no recording. Even before I hit the water, a cry was torn from my heart.

"Let me see that which I hear, please, let it be so."

I dived deep, and holding my breath I swam further than I had any right to swim on one lungful of air. I emerged not breathless, but with a sense of awe.

What happened under there?

To my physical senses water had engulfed me, and while swimming I was acutely aware of the river...yet, on some other plane of experience, I swam in space. Around me was a vast emptiness, not sky blue or star filled, but sheer nothingness. Nothingness lasted for an eternity of swimming nowhere. A wave of desperation, of panic-tinged despair swept over me...and I saw a nearby star.

Beyond it, around it, other stars swung lazily into position on smooth, silent orbits. Relief poured through me, and I swam toward them, torn between directions and wondering which was the nearest star.

Do not seek sanctuary in its cellular form, for that which I AM is the "nothing" of space. I swim in the universe of your Being.
You swim in the universe of that which "IS."
Look not for form, but from within see that which energizes form.
Hear not the sound, but the Silence which surrounds it. See not the form, but the space of which it is formed.

While I swam in space, I swam unbreathing in the river, far beyond one breath. It was a denial of time.

In space there is no time — real time.
In time there is no space — real space.
Can you unscramble this and taste truth?

Knowing was instantaneous. Realization came crashing in, pounding through my head in a surging rush of blood.

For micro-moments the whole world stopped and all that "IS" took an inbreath of pure newness. I was that newness.

For a cosmic Dragonfly the sun shone on gossamer wings as the enzymes of a higher truth were catalyzed.

I dived again...greedily...but it was only a river in which I swam.

A SUBTLE CHANGE was taking place in my relationship with Nature. No longer was I on the outside looking in, for the experience was developing in such a way that I became the experience — experiencing.

For years I had listened to Nature's words while denying them a place in reality; if everyone else was deaf then it was easier for me to be deaf also. But now, in my surrender to an inner truth, I found this strange reality demanding ever more of me. And I mean demanding!

It was a turbulent day, the sun withdrawn and morose behind the heavy clouds moving slowly across the sky. Wind blew in fits and starts, gusting with huge energy for a few moments, then subsiding with a mellow sigh.

The river called.

I sat in the living room, comfortable, trying to deny the call. Why not listen to Nature's wisdom in comfort? Why the river, it's only a place? . . . and the river called.

With a sigh, I left the armchair, gathered my journal, and headed for the river. Passing under the Morton Bay Fig, I noticed some fresh cow dung covered with bright-green flies, shiny and immaculate in buzzing swarms. I had not previously noticed these flies.

Must be some autumn flies making a late appearance — to make a brief flight and mate before winter doth them part, I thought whimsically.

Using the hand rail with considerable care, I slowly descended the steep track down the bush-covered incline leading to my river refuge. Half an hour earlier it had been pouring rain, and the track was mud-slick slipperiness. Halfway down, one foot shot out from under me. Incredible! After twenty-five years I did a perfect break-fall, just as I had been trained in judo classes in my late teens. I completed the journey with one very muddy forearm, but otherwise little the worse for wear.

"It had better be worth it," I growled . . . very quietly!

The river flowed, impassive as ever. In this moment, no place could look less inviting, or less mystical. Mundane was the word I was feeling for this place and mood. I sat on the diving board and, on cue, the wind came gushing down the river, snatching at my journal and playing indifferently with the leaping pages. The sun, pale and watery, peered from behind the lacy masking of a gray cloud. Around me, high in the branches of the trees, my friend the wind sang her unique song of creation as she whipped the leaves to a frenzy.

Would you deny the wind while accepting the river?

Hurling a violent gust into the branches above my head, the wind held me in comparative calm. "I am as prepared to accept you as conscious energy as I am any other aspect of Nature," I responded.

I feel you are truthful.

Was it coincidence? The wind fell away to the softest gentle murmur.

In the Oneness from which I spring I am aware of your attunement with Nature. I am involved in every moment of your experience. I am wind, composed of air — a basic element.
For you I am life.
For this world I am life.
For beyond, I exist in a nonexistent state.

There was a pause. I had nothing to offer. Startling in its sudden power, an immense gust of wind shook the trees around me. Feeling a touch of humor I mumbled — "Tut tut."

The wind was gone, the trees empty of movement. A strange awareness grew slowly around me. I was wrong. Things were not what they seemed. The leaves above me continued to sway and dance, singing the high song of the wind...yet there was Silence, the wind static in my Being.

A duality of experience emerged. There was wind — and no wind. There was sound — and Silence. Movement — and stillness.

Each action offered its moment of truth to my physical and psychical Selves.

I knew my challenge was to synthesize the movements, denying neither experience. To move with both, accepting as "IS."

Joy and tenderness leapt to the surface of my awareness. I gazed with inner, loving eyes at two aspects of Self, comfortable and aware in their togetherness. For several moments an awareness of "IS" held a trinity of identity... then the sun emerged, flooding illumination over all experience.

I became the I who relates to everyday life. I became the I knowing who I am. I became the I which "IS."

Just as I tear the feeble hold of exhausted leaves from a tree, so will I tear old, spent concepts from your feeble grasp. Your path is one of surrender To release, let go. This requires courage in human terms. The path of unknowing, knowing, knowing "IS."

I smiled at the absurdity of an inadequate language.

Well you may smile, but Nature can only express through "you" in your language.

While we have the capacity to expand, destroy, replace, and revitalize your concepts of life, you are the controller of your words.

"Would you like me to learn new words to expand my vocabulary?"

Only as a natural organic movement. As you flow and expand, so will your ability to fully express yourself develop with you.

We have stated before — we desire openness and simplicity. Your gift is communication through simplicity. Do not destroy it.

"I guess you are referring to the human me I know. Being smart holds little appeal."

You are smart enough. To attune with Nature requires neither smartness nor cleverness.

One requires humility. Humility to recognize your inherent "greatness," and a humility which recognizes the "greatness" as a part of the universal "IS."

Remember, my friend, as you fly the sun spaces in your unfolding experiencing of nothing, remember wind and its substance — nothing; no-thing.

The words echoed with mystery. We humans are mystery, surrounded by mystery. What an empty mockery to live life only in the pursuit of money and pleasure if it requires we sacrifice the mystery of what "IS."

On Tracy's coffee mug are the words: "Life is not a problem to be solved, but a mystery to be lived."

In this moment the mystery was paramount, vibrating in wind and life with intense energy. Maybe the way of life is to continually inquire, seeking no answers, yet this is not easy to accomplish for we are then involved in the concepts of "letting go" and "being." Vague words and meanings, but I suspect that our destiny is to give these concepts meaning and purpose.

To inquire suggests that we seek always to explore rather than exploit — to seek, rather than find — to live life as an open-ended agreement with God, rather than search for a nonexistent conclusion. How can that which has no ending be concluded?

THE DAY WAS CALM but cloudy. This time the river was not calling; instead, I felt a desire to commune with the river.

When I approached the water, it lacked the sparkle of dancing reflections which only the sun can produce. There was a calm, an expectancy the river was very alive.

A bottle bobbing high in the water floated toward me from upriver. It moved swiftly under the Willow tree and headed with speed and purpose toward the old bridge board on which I was sitting.

As it slowly floated over the deep pool where the Platypuses hunt, the bottle was suddenly out of the mainstream, surging in hapless circles around and around in a slow, eddying swirl.

There was a flow to the river, but the bottle no longer rode with it. How many human bottles do I know?

For how long did I helplessly circle, a human out of the flow of life?

Questions sprang to my mind as I watched the almost-stationary bottle, but answers were not required. The sense of purpose which motivates us feeds us an illusion of being in life's mainstream; yet, in truth, we are in life's river, slowly eddying in a backwater, while the surging current of activity passes by. We have a divine right to life which we can never lose, but to be in life's flow instead of a backwater is a choice we have to make and direct.

All humanity is contained in the river of life, but the slow, deep holes and the fast, shallow rapids offer their deception. When you are aware and awake you may correctly interpret them; if you do not, then you are at their mercy.

A movement in the water below caught my attention. In the calm, clear water a Leopard Eel moved with purposeful grace along the rock ledges on the riverbed. Its whole intent was obvious — a hunting forage. Sinuous and calm, the Eel sought its prey, poking in each hole and crevice with deadly efficiency, He was not very big, a shade under one yard perhaps. Some of our Leopard Eels can reach almost two yards, with a large girth and dappling along their backs. They are the rulers of the underwater world in our stretch of the river. A flurry, and a half-grown Catfish shot out of a crevice. The Eel ignored it, continuing its slow, careful inspection with alert intensity. It probably had shrimps on the menu!

The Eel has a sense of purpose, and hunger is the motivation, but be aware of how little of the river each Eel patrols.

I knew of their territorial habits, each staking a claim on their choice of the riverbed. In some areas, while lying half hidden alongside submerged logs, the larger and therefore unmolested Eels (they are less competitive and nervous) have let me gently stroke along their soft bellies, my fingers caressingly persuading them to half roll onto their sides. Over a summer period, I have established a genuine rapport with certain Eel characters.

It is not the purpose of mankind to stake a claim and stay forever fixed. Only fear needs to hold onto an area, naming it "home," a place of safety. There are those, however, for whom this meets their needs and their purpose, for in establishing roots they make real growth.

But man is not a tree.

Greater growth is experienced when roots are kept trimmed, never seizing hold of an area to make it "mine."

Let ownership begin when it is no longer needed. While security demands ownership, then it is stagnation in the guise of comfort which will bind you.

The river flows — on, ever on.

Let home be a base, but never a purpose, or like the Eel, your limitations will control you.

When you look into the water do you see last week's water, or yesterday's . . . or is the water ever fresh, ever flowing, ever new?

I am almost ashamed to record it, but my eyes, from their conditioned limits, had never seen the river as totally "new." I saw the same river, the same water. My eyes lied to me, while my mind fostered the lie. The water is new, it is continuous newness, and although intellectually I knew this, my eyes had never transcended their conditioning.

Yet I had "felt" the newness of water.

I had been aware of the aliveness of water; only my eyes were deceived.

Now . . . I looked at the river anew.

What did I expect? Did I assume it would look different? It did not. It looked like the river usually looks. Again . . . I was the difference. I realized that the difference will never lie in the observed, only in the observer.

As I scrambled back up the steep track, I was speculating on "fresh" water. Fresh as in new! I walked into the kitchen, and, as it was lunch time, I accepted an offer of poached eggs on toast. While I watched Treenie preparing my meal, I realized that the "fresh" water principle applied to people as well. When I wake up in the morning, do I see yesterday's Treenie, again with deceived eyes, or can I see a new Treenie by seeing "anew"? If I see a new Treenie, and she sees a new Michael, our relationship will be fresh, new, vital, and alive. If, however, we see yesterday's partner, then we each become the cause of stagnation and repetition in our relationship.

Always you are each the causative factor.

Today's people seen through yesterday's eyes will swing you out of the mainstream of the river of life into an eddying swirl of stagnation.

For some unfortunate people this is called marriage. See your partner in life, all people, as totally "new" in the moment of contact.

In this way you may live confined to one area, yet flowing swiftly in the fresh current of life.

Life will seek you, rather than you being the seeker of life. Thus the paradox is revealed. To live life constantly on the move, yet viewing through "yesterday's" eyes, denies movement or change.

To live life from one home, on one tiny plot of land, viewing all life through "today's" eyes, allows you to be the aperture through which life flows, ever fresh, ever new.

However, for those who roam far and wide, ever moving, ever aware, ever open, viewing all life through "this moment's" eyes — life becomes a benediction.

I was quiet, humbled by the magnitude of life and growth which yet awaits me.

THERE WAS A TIME when the valley in which I live contained an abundant flood of forest pouring from the plateau escarpment down into the valley. Among its trees the Red Cedar (*Toona australis*) was a giant, a king among trees, and the only deciduous tree in the forest. That time has passed. In his folly, man plundered the valuable harvest of timber, leaving the valley barren of its former richness. Only a few Red Cedars survived, for this timber was the most valuable and desired of all.

Sitting in our garden area under one such tree, I studied the few Red Cedars dotted among the Citrus trees near our house. Although tall to an uneducated eye, these trees were mere saplings, no more than sixty feet high. Over the rough bark a mass of epiphytic orchids crept their way from limb to limb, slowly smothering each branch with a mat of thick, fleshy leaves. Jammed in the forks of larger branches, huge Orchids were clumped in thickets, offering their flowers each season as a blessed compensation. Dotted throughout each tree, hanging from the limbs with casual indifference to location, the fronds of Elkhorn and Staghorn Ferns were seen among the foliage.

It was early autumn, but the Cedars remained green. Many weeks were needed before a winter chill denied the flow of sap to dependent leaves.

I am not a botanist and I know little of the age of tree species, but I feel the energy of Red Cedars as very old. A wisdom of some long-forgotten order is fostered by these trees, but it is not of a physical nature. Its roots go beyond the physical outreach of a tree. A gray sky framed another overcast day and invoked a brooding atmosphere, yet the energy seemed focused on the aura of a forgotten glory in some past era. In some strange way I felt my awareness drawn into a past, floating as though on a cloud of light above the brooding intensity up onto, or into, a dimension of inner visual impression.

From an inner seeing, soaring high above the valley, I gazed onto immense stands of forest in some timeless zone.

What I perceived bordered on fantasy, for it was "feeling" vision, rather than "seeing" vision. No doubt my eyes would protest if shown a forest of long ago, growing rich and abundant with towering Red Cedars on farmland which is now smooth and green with Kikuyu-dominated pasture.

Perception suggested that my eyes did not contain all truth, merely one level of truth to which we totally relate. Today's movies make mockery of the old saying — "Seeing is believing." Our eyes are limited, feeding us deceit and falsity along with correct impression. Perception also suggested that my experience of life would be richer if I opened myself to multiple levels of experience, rather than only a visual and auditory experience confined to three-dimensional planes.

With Silence came clarity.

The time when great forests filled many valleys such as this, is not separate from this time.

In the dimension to which mankind relates, the forests have disappeared, while those remaining are threatened with destruction. A moment in passing.

This is the reality with which man is in accord, but it is not reality as "IS."

If life did not supply the exact Law of Cause and Effect to your sense of reality, you could learn nothing. Learning requires that you experience the polarity of action. Yet mankind is not confined to physical reality.

Man may realize his greater awareness, probing into higher zones of truth and reality.

Fly high over the forests and feed your heart, for the forests are more real than the illusion which denies them a physical counterpart.

For an alarming moment, a reasoning mind protested to an illumined spirit at the strangeness of the dual experience, but it subsided. As far as the inner "I" could see, a rich carpet of luxurious forest covered the valley, while a sparkling river of crystal water wandered with serpentine grace under the canopy of trees.

While I, the infinite soul Self, gazed from above, I, the finite physical Self, sat in a chair, journal on my lap, quiet and at peace with my surroundings. My acceptance of the experience felt good. To smoothly synthesize the experiencing of two Selves, each a contradiction to the sense receptors of the other mode of experience, was less of an achievement than a surrender.

In surrendering protest, denial, and doubt, you lose nothing, but gain insight and courage.

In surrendering Self to an ongoing process, that which is lost is the "known," while that which is "knowing" is gained — but cannot be known.

"Knowing" is realized knowledge.

The moment when the "known" ignites, leaving only the ash of truth, is a spontaneous "knowing."

The gathering of energy faded, and sadly my limited normality returned. The physical world became my focal point, casting me back once more into the illusion of isolation. The Red Cedars around me were, to all intents and purposes, just trees, growing in our world, yet remote from us, separate and unconnected.

I believe that our welfare as nations of peoples lies with the development of the ability to truly see our place in the scheme of life. So long as we are separated and remote from Nature, we are isolated from a deeper relationship with each other, and unable to trust and accept the "one" race of humanity.

MARCH WAS CLOSING ANOTHER CHAPTER when I walked with care and caution down to "my place" by the river. The day seemed to carry an intensity, and the river was so alive when I sat on the diving board over the water, that just being with it as an observer required my full attention. In the depths below, a solitary Golden Perch swam in slow, lazy circles. It was a newcomer, and I admired the faint gold tinge outlining each scale. This was a bold fish, obviously quite unthreatened as it stared up at me from swiveled eyes. Two ducks flew from upriver, literally running along the water surface for a short distance before gaining flight. A yellow butterfly fluttered past, falling and rising in erratic flight.

Mullet and Herring leaped from the water, while Fantails and Blue Wrens flitted, chattering and scolding, among the branches above my head. A special day, quite superb.

You do not see the perfection in every day, in every moment?

I was vaguely surprised at the question. I had been enrapt in my observations and feelings. Although I was open to the river's subtle energy, it caught me unexpectedly.

The question also hurt. In honesty — no — I did not see and feel the perfection in every moment, in every day. I would like to, but the simple fact is: my environment has a huge influence on me.

When each moment is born anew in your consciousness, you will carry no more pain. In rebirth, the newborn may choose perfection.

Again, surprise flickered through me. The reference to pain was very meaningful. During our years in Tasmania I had injured my back, and incompetent medical attention had allowed a chronic condition to develop. With hindsight I acknowledge that the pain had been a great catalyst in my life, but to this day it pursued me, blending months of freedom with times of intense suffering. Having just emerged from a week of back pain and limitation, I would give a lot to be free of it.

You have only to release the desire to suffer.

Anger suddenly swept over me. To suggest I desired suffering was ridiculous. Unexpectedly, the river physically intervened. In the water below, a Water Tortoise walked with dignified speed along the riverbed. Its long snakelike neck and head were well extended, while it traveled in an easy floating glide. This graceful movement from such an inherently clumsy creature contrasted greatly with the ungainly crawl of a Land Tortoise. I am not sure whether the Australian Tortoise took to the water, or never left it, but it was a smart move. None are land bound.

The Land Tortoise carries its heavy load, making slow progress. Gravity is the pressure.

In the river the Tortoise is relieved of its weight. Gravity is no longer a pressure. It is not atmospheric gravity which limits mankind, but the gravity of limited thinking, of bound, restricted thought.

If you were to place all your grave burdens into the river of life, allowing the "IS" to carry you, the freedom you would experience could not manifest as back pain.

Only the weight of an overload manifests as back pain.

Unconscious — subconscious — conscious, the load is carried on mental levels beyond the physical capacity. This overload manifests in disease, sickness, injury, and pain.

The words were clear, and for a long time I have intellectually known their meaning. But how? How do we just let go?

Such a move requires a major surrender. A surrender of the ego with all its little "i"s fighting for survival.

It really is not difficult. You need accept only one truth — and live it.

THIS MOMENT IS PERFECT. Know it. Become it. Live it. Breathe it. Stay with it. Become centered on it.

Perfection will move from an uncomfortable, painful, demanding, unpleasant, limited perfection... to a perfection of freedom, peace, acceptance, expansion, limitlessness.

Life will move from rigidity to fluidity.

Pain is a symptom. Rigidity is a cause.

To break rigidity may cause pain; to retain it "is" pain.

Rigidity resists, fluidity resists not — nor does it pain.

Fluidity is not what you do, but how you do it.

Fluidity or rigidity is the state of mind in action. Treating sickness may repair effect, but it does not touch cause. At best it may be the catalyst which allows cause to be recognized and changed.

The freedom of fluidity is found by knowing that whatever you desire you already have.

For you — your body is saying, "Release suffering, allow me to be healed," while you are saying, "No, I need the pain lest I forget I am not free."

Release it. You are free. Know it.

My head was beginning to spin. I took a deep breath... slowing down.... Silence.... An inner dialogue moved through me with gentle freedom. I was unattached to thought or meaning. It is possible. I can be free of pain. I no longer need pain when I can accept freedom. But... I cannot accept freedom because I have just realized... I do not recognize it. I don't know freedom.

Clarity moved whisper-soft over the dialogue.

Freedom is "now." In no other time or space may it be real. Only "now"... forever. I had known that also for a long time, but again... only in my head. An idea. A concept. Never real... because I had pain.

Maybe this is another new beginning. I feel movement as the knowing connects head and heart. It fits.

The Water Tortoise returned, drifting across the riverbed in a slow, scrabbling glide. Nearing the rocks close to the diving board, it slowly surfaced, its head breaking the water into clean, small ripples. Mouth open, the Tortoise gulped in air.

Suddenly it saw me; our eyes met in a moment of contact . . . and it was gone in a hurried rush of water, plunging to the riverbed. I heard no words, but in the one penetrating glance I read a clear message.

"Which of us is encased in the toughest shell?"

As I stood up on the diving board, acute pain flared in my lower back causing me to stretch and ease the cramped muscles carefully.

I felt the weight of limits, of rigidity, as I stared into the empty depths.

"Which indeed?"

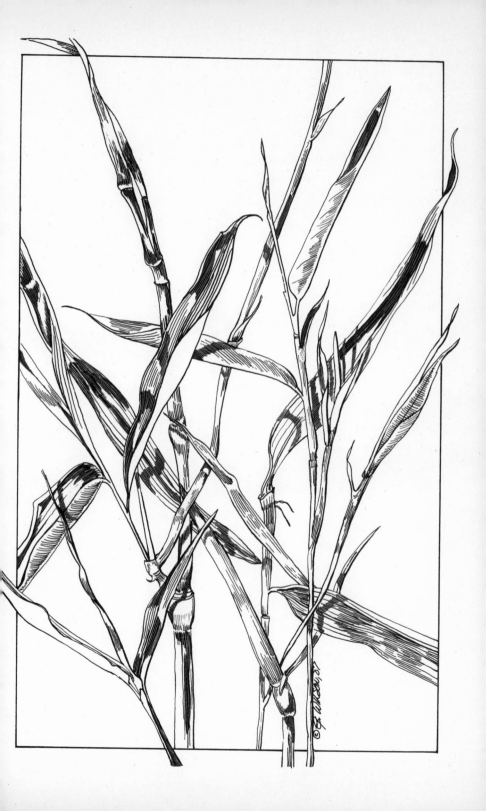

7 April

from an early age I have recognized a connection with Nature, a mystical thread moving beyond mind and heart, connecting me to some mysterious, unknown element. That I am not alone in this connection is proven by the mystical writings of the ages, yet for some reason mankind as a whole has failed to realize this inner truth.

The cities with their choked masses surely deny the space and time to find the Self which experiences further realities. I have been fortunate, surrounded in my early days by fields of golden corn; of meadows green; by the woods of Oak, Beech, Sycamore, Elm, and other friends; by cold rivers and mystic ponds; and later as an adult by the splendor of Australia's coastal bush, by the damp and dripping rain forest, the highland lakes, the crystal rivers which man has not yet poisoned, and mountains which gaze blindly to the stars. These have always been within easy reach. Our previous home was in an environment of Nature's extravagance unleashed. Its location in a valley not far from where we now live was idyllic. The land encompassed rain forest, hills, and tiny valleys in a setting of outstanding beauty. A river snaked its way along the base of the forest-covered escarpment, forming one of our natural boundaries. A few hundred yards along the river a dense thicket of Bamboo thrived and expanded, growing larger with each passing season.

The Bamboo became my hideaway sanctuary. It was a place to indulge my self-pity, or to shrug away the pain of a wounded ego. A place of quiet. A tiny, hidden track twisted through the Bamboo to a certain log lying full length in the river. Pointing downstream, the log offered no resistance to flood waters, and it had lain on the riverbed for a long time. This was Lizard Lounge, the ultimate sunbathing skinny-dipping hideaway.

Log, river, and Bamboo combined to form a place of synthesis, a matrix of holistic energy. Even after we left our previous home I would often make return visits, and after chatting for a while I would head off to Lizard Lounge and the Bamboo grove.

One such day at noon, I walked down to the Bamboo to consciously reconnect with the energies of Nature I had experienced there in my earlier days of doubt and conflict. Creeping into the center of the grove I sat down, journal on my lap. The magic was as strong as ever.

Sunlight danced a slow, rhythmic pattern over the deep litter of fallen leaves on which I sat. Cool and mysterious, the Bamboo invoked memories of pain and joy, no longer separate, but blended by time. Below me, the same river to which I attune where we now live sighed quietly as it flowed around the bulk of Lizard Lounge. Whipbirds called forth their rolling, delayed whip . . . crack, exploding the quiet of the Bamboo grove.

Earth breathed out a pungent, rich organic aroma, while Silence settled like an invisible mist. Surrounding me, the green, smooth barrels of Bamboo stems rose slender toward the blue sky, rising twelve feet before the first thin branchlets of foliage sprang from the splendid pillars of supple strength. Tenderly adding movement to the magic, a breeze stole quietly through the pale-green leaves above my head, causing shadows and sunspots to flicker and dance in soundless motion. Peace...a peace beyond words embraced me, holding me safe for a few timeless, precious moments.

Your presence is welcome. You are reconnecting with an awareness which is likened to weak eyes blinking before the sun. Yet, unlike your eyes, awareness can endure the blazing light, growing stronger, expanding, opening to ever-wider vistas.

You have walked often in our midst, blind to our subtlety, deaf to our whispers of truth. Now you return, with the birth of wholeness nurturing in your heart.

We welcome you as a human, as humanity.

Man is of one kind, of one energy. In our midst all humanity is contained in your holistic Being.

The peace intensified, becoming a movement within, disturbing deep long-forgotten emotions. I became aware of a Oneness of joy and grief. My normal senses have shown me that joy and grief are separate, each expressing very different emotions and reactions; in these experiences, joy and grief are one. Joy contains grief, and grief only fulfills and expands joy. Often I weep from pain of the limited Self, yet the weeping is a confused reaction to a transcendent joy tinged with pain. I do not understand these emotions. I do not know their origin, I cannot identify them. I only know my experience of higher realities has shown me that without pain, joy becomes shallow. Without the "falling to earth" there can be no "transcendent flight."

The inner movement of peace became a gentle, poignant vibration. One could say I felt a subtle inner shift, a moment of separation, and again the duality of experience began.

Shadows and sun splashes flickered around me, dancing fragments of light playing over body and Bamboo. I felt a confusion, for it seemed the Bamboos were fragmenting and disintegrating around me, while my own body was caught in this magical dance of light. As though lifted by a wind of some inner source, I was blown out of the Bamboo thicket and into a universe of color-filled sound and sound-filled color.

No longer was I fragmented. A single being, united, I watched from billions of inner "I"s as I became at "One" with the human song of pain ... and joy.

Become centered on that which "IS."

There is an immense pressure in the human mind to believe in a tiny truth. Embrace it ... own it ... but do not deny a vast truth ... your truth ... human truth.

Listen to the collective human song, but do not be afraid to sing your own song. Dance to the music which moves in your Being. Follow the star in your heart until perfectly positioned in all that "IS."

Be a player in the game of life, but be aware of the golden rule ... the player controls the moves ... the player is the mover. . . the player is the moved.

My inner view of life changed as it expanded. I have no words to describe visible sound forming intangible networks of space, or ways to explain ideas of pure energy framing new worlds.

Holistic experiencing peaked ... timeless ... until, caught in a giant wind, I was blown as a leaf in a storm ... of peace ... my field of experiencing narrowing ... until I gazed once more on dancing splashes of light playing over pale-green Bamboo stems.

Momentarily I felt shaky. The subtlety of the experience was overwhelming. Self-doubt could so easily destroy it. When I arose, it was to scramble down the track to Lizard Lounge, only available by a swim in the cold, autumn water. My introspective mood denied the swim as I stood caught in deep thought. Whenever I experience this "exaltation," a paradox is always revealed. I had simultaneously experienced separation and connection. I was filled with a knowing that fragmentation and wholeness are inseparable.

Separation and connection, fragmentation and wholeness — all are strands in a single universal thread. While all threads are woven into the human experience as one energy, it is we who separate the strands.

Separation is a concept. One in which we believe. A concept which has become the law of the land. But believing a misconception does not change truth. Truth — all life... connected..."Is."

DAY AFTER DAY A STEADY RAIN had been falling, and just as steadily the river crept higher and higher. On the fourth morning I slithered down the slope through the dripping bush to our water pump, switching off the electric motor to prevent later problems. Below me the water surged quietly without the violence that torrential rain produces. Moving with as much stealth as I could muster, I crept through the drenched undergrowth, finally emerging at my special place.

The river was high, lapping just beneath our diving board. With much difficulty, I dragged the heavy old bridge board higher into the safety of the bush. This place I love so much, of wild bush and rocks, is a bend in the river; thus, even when the river is subdued, the water laps both sides of the jutting outcrop, creating a feeling of island.

Standing in the rain, the swollen river seemed to almost split at my feet, moving into the blind-inlet side with turbulent energy, while flowing with smooth, hurrying power downriver.

As I gazed into the rain upstream, I appeared to stand in the center of the river, the water hastening to my inner call. For a long time I stood there, feeling the river as a whole entity, knowing it from an inner level as a source of joy and inspiration. No longer was the water flowing around me, for my awareness expanded wider and wider, embracing and drawing the river through the center of my Being. With the river came overwhelming joy and gratitude. I called aloud into the rain.

"Thank you for all you have given me, for all you have shown me. You have extended an honor I will not abuse."

The joy swelled, tears mingled with the rain on my cheeks.

We have given you nothing.

We have shown you nothing.

It is you who have learned how to accept the fruit which is always on offer to mankind. The fruit of human wisdom will fall delicately into the hand when one reaches out in love and humility. This fruit cannot be plucked from the tree of life, nor can it be plundered at the roots.

It is you who have looked into the waters and have seen the reflected truth. When the eyes of mankind are blinded by fear, only desire and greed may be reflected. You have used the clarity of Nature to perceive the clarity residing in the human heart.

The richness of a holistic life is the sponsor of your joy, the promoter of your tears.

I stood silently, utterly absorbed in a real world where Nature's movement is of total order. Out on the river a small, black object caught my attention, bringing my focus back to a normal sense reality. I had often wondered how the Platypus fared in times of flood; now I knew.

Like a leaf in a playful breeze, the Platypus flowed and rippled with the swirling water — one moment floating with short legs and webbed feet extended, bright eyes surveying overhead happenings, the next beneath the murky surface while feeding on the rich harvest offered by the flood waters.

Here was no battle with the current, no fight to prove its mastery. The Platypus took the power and energy of the river and used it. As an Eagle masters the wild thermals of upper air, so the Platypus rode the currents of swirling water. I extended myself to that innocent master, reading its intent as it plunged deep into the water. As One we submerged, all direction and senses lost in the whirling confusion of river and debris.

The Platypus foraged and surveyed, moving in scrabbling, supple, clumsy grace, a master of its environment.

Abruptly I lost contact, standing alone and dripping on the rocks, vaguely wondering if it had ever been real. I stood and watched, pupil and teacher, while a solitary ancient creature, primitive and unique, taught me how to ride the currents of the river of life... effortlessly.

There came a moment in mid-river; the Platypus did not reappear.

Thus we disappear, each in our time, each in our own way, but, like the Platypus, we, too, will reemerge at a different time, a different place, to again swim in the river of life. One river only in which all Life swims. One river, one life. One movement held in one moment. The river is not the mystery, only the swim.

I stood entranced, while rain dripping in huge drops from the foliage overhead soaked through my raincoat and into my clothes.

Somewhere the Platypus had reemerged, for while I saw nothing... I felt its presence as surely as the promise of a new tomorrow.

Journey into Nature

To my beloved Treenie.
We are not alone in the fairy ring.

Author's Note

This book is complete, but it is also a sequel to my last book, *Talking with Nature*. In order to enter a deeper relationship with Nature, I was required to become a participant *with* Nature rather than continue in the role of an onlooker. I did not find this at all easy. I was propelled into a metaphysical reality, a reality I did not enter willingly. Yet on the inner levels I had already made a commitment. Let's just say I didn't know I had! We humans are like that. We come to this planet with a clearly defined destiny, but as soon as we take on human form, we forget it. Life then carries us kicking and screaming toward our perfect goal while we try our hardest to abort the mission.

Nature is a force of immense power, so my pathetic struggles were like those of an ant aswim in an ocean. It was not long before I gave myself willingly to the force carrying me, opening myself to a hidden Nature of boundless metaphysical proportions.

This book explores the connectedness of all life. I have learned that separation is a lie. To me, this means that I, the writer, and you, the reader, connect in consciousness as we share these pages together. We are not separate in consciousness, just individual. The journey of self-realization I unwittingly undertook revealed an inner dimension of Nature, a dimension beneath the surface of our everyday reality that is of immeasurable value to us, though we have long been conditioned to deny its existence.

I offer this book as a means of igniting your own inner awakening and laying bare the lie of old, worn-out beliefs and concepts. Becoming awake is the birth of purpose.

Michael J. Roads
Queensland, Australia, April 1989

Acknowledgments

As always, I extend my thanks to my wife, Treenie. It is not easy to summarize the countless ways in which a loving soul mate can support a struggling spouse, but this is what Treenie does for me — constantly. Very simply, she is there — there when I need her, there when I think I don't. Through everything, always and forever there!

My sincere thanks to Hal and Linda Kramer. Together, they have not only helped me reach the true audience for my literary efforts, but have become part of Treenie's and my life.

Life has a way of producing the right person at the right time. Greg Armstrong became the catalyst for turning my metaphysical reality into print. I thought the timing had not yet arrived, but his intensity and passion convinced me otherwise. Greg, from my heart, thank you for releasing the genie from the bottle!

I would also like to thank my editor Suzanne Lipsett. I understand that this was not an easy manuscript to edit; however, it was a challenge she met. If I have managed to clearly communicate all I have tried to say, then Suzanne's skill has proved invaluable.

I owe thanks to our four children, too. Throughout their years of growth, they have all left impressions of value, as they continue to do today: Duncan — volatile, high powered, catalytic; Adrian — silent, enigmatic, strong in purpose; Russell — sensitive, adventure seeking, vulnerable; and Tracy — the other woman in my life, a bud awaiting bloom.

My sincere thanks also to Dan Millman. Unbeknown to him, his inspiration helped me open the Door.

1 Meeting a Myth

Treenie let go of my hand as we paused while crossing over the low wooden bridge. It was a primitive-looking affair, but built in such a way that it had survived the regular powerful floods that had often engulfed it. The sides were no more than logs bolted onto the structure. They allowed a clear view of the water as it flowed beneath our feet while they served as a convenient seat on which to contemplate the beauty.

"Look." I looked at the river where my wife pointed. The water was crystal clear. There, sitting bold and dominant in about six feet of water, was a large stone shaped like an egg.

"That's odd," I said. "Because the water is so clear, sunlight has caused algae to grow over the river stones...all except that one."

Together, we peered through the distorting water at the stone. The day was glorious and the midwinter air crisp and cool, even here in our subtropical valley. We had been walking for exercise and fun, listening to bird songs as we strode down the country lane. Wild lemons, guava, and lantana jostled for space over the road, the flowers of the lantana nodding in a gentle breeze as we passed them by. Butterflies hovered among the yellow, pink, and red flowers, not caring that winter weather should forbid such activities, while the courtship of tiny wrens among the foliage suggested an early spring.

"Perhaps it's meant for us." Treenie's voice was soft as she stared at the stone. I glanced at her. "You don't expect me to leap into this freezing cold river, do you? Not for a stone?"

Treenie smiled without replying. She knew me well enough to know I would break ice to go in if I really wanted to.

"Why don't you ask the stone if it wants to be with us?" she suggested.

"Why don't you?" I countered.

"Oh, come on. You're the one who talks to rivers and rocks. Now's your chance to make a new friend," she teased. I stared down at the stone, intrigued not only by its strangeness in the river but by an energy I could feel emanating from it. "Okay, stone," I said. "How about it? Do you want to come home with me?" I spoke with some mockery in my voice, but the words that poured into my mind came with such force and authority that I instantly sobered.

"I have waited a long, long time in many rivers and in many places. Although I belong to no one, right now I belong with you."

I gazed at the stone in surprise. Although I had expected to hear an inner response, the content and implication caught me off guard. While Treenie watched with resigned amusement, I stripped down to my shorts and, with some trepidation, waded into the river. Ugh! It was cold. The moment I was waist deep in the water, a car trundled across the bridge. Several faces stared out at me as if I were mad!

I knew there was no way I could retrieve the rugby-ball-sized stone without getting soaked, so I plunged beneath the water and dived for the vague, distorted shape beneath me. I grabbed and lunged for the surface, but the stone resisted. It was heavy! I took a deep breath, shivered, and revised my strategy. This time I dived, grabbed, braced, lifted, and then scrambled underwater to the nearest bank. I took a grateful gulp of air as my head emerged from the river. Back on the bridge, I dried quickly in the warm sun before pulling on my clothes. Then, cradling the heavy stone in my arms, I continued walking homeward with Treenie — somewhat slower than before.

For the next year, the stone remained basically silent. I learned that it required irregular immersions in a bucket of fresh water — it would demand these in no uncertain terms. But apart from that, all the stone offered was the puzzle of its existence. On one occasion when it was issuing a fine stream of bubbles in a bucket of water, I asked if it had a name or a purpose. The answer was ambiguous, to say the least.

"I am a Guidestone — your Guidestone — and you are my purpose. It was you who programmed me for an event such as this."

I frowned in puzzlement. "What do you mean?" I asked. "What event? What is a Guidestone? How could I program you?"

"In the bud of innocence awaits the bloom of truth." I waited for more, but that was it! A fine stream of bubbles silently popping at the surface of the water was the stone's final comment.

How I detest riddles!

⬤

A FEW MONTHS LATER, Treenie and I were in Brisbane, where I was giving a "Talking With Nature" workshop. The event was well organized, and the room was more than big enough for the forty people involved. I spoke of my love for Nature, of our connection with the Earth, and of our loss as we become alienated from Nature. I shared my view of the Spirit of Nature and of how, by building a new relationship with Nature, we can transform ourselves. I suggested that we are not separate from Nature but a constructive intelligence within it, and that by our actions or misactions we connect or separate ourselves from Nature. The response from the people involved was rich and warm.

Following a shared lunch, the afternoon session commenced. I felt apprehensive, for I had no set format and was about to embark on what seemed a foolish experiment. A few days earlier, the Guidestone had emerged from a lengthy silence to tell me I should give it a twelve-hour soaking in water followed by twelve hours in full sun. This would, in effect, charge the stone with energy. The Guidestone then instructed me to take it with me to the workshop and place it within a circle of the participants.

I had arranged the seating to form a horseshoe, with me seated in the open space. Following my intuition, I began by asking each person to look across the half circle into the eyes of a person opposite. Why I suggested this I did not know, but the impulse was so strong I followed it. A time of surrender resulted as we lowered our barriers between us by making eye contact. We became vulnerable in our defenselessness, and unexpectedly, steadily, the energy in the room climbed as we surrendered our personal privacy.

When the energy had become comfortable, I stepped into the center, lifted the Guidestone from its bag, and placed it on the floor for all to see. Until this moment, the stone had been hidden. Now, as I rolled it into view, forty pairs of eyes fastened onto it.

With electric suddenness, the energy in the room leaped higher. I suggested that each person focus on the stone, seeing it in a new way. "View it as energy rather than a stone," I said, "and allow that energy access to your Being." Then I sat down.

To say I was surprised by what was happening is putting it mildly. One could almost cut the energy in the room, it had become so potent. I decided I would not become involved but rather would keep an eye on things from the sidelines. In full innocence, I stared curiously at the Guidestone, aware of its power. That's strange, I thought. I have never noticed that little hole in the large end of the stone before. I leaned forward to see better, gripping the arms of my chair. I could clearly see a tiny hole about the size of a mustard seed. I stared at it, frowning in consternation. I had studied the stone in minute detail and before that moment would have sworn there was no such hole.

As I stared, all normality came to an abrupt and sudden end. Without warning, my body locked. I could not move a finger. My arms and legs were frozen, immobile; I couldn't even blink. With this horrifying realization, sweat broke out all over me, but in the same moment I was drawn from my body as though I were smoke and sucked into the tiny hole in the Guidestone.

—

I BEGIN TO EXPERIENCE a duality of awareness I have never known before. My conscious awareness is with the psychic essence taking human shape within a vast chamber in the center of the Guidestone, yet I am also conscious of my helpless physical body in the workshop room.

As I become aware of myself in the immense chamber, I begin to tremble. All space seems to be filled with pure, raw, seething energy, terrifyingly impersonal. The chamber is filled with what appears to be fire, yet I sense extreme heat and icy cold simultaneously. Energies of incomprehensible dimensions fuse as the shattering power of this colossal dynamism roars and surges in a silent crescendo of sound. All around me, echoing over and over, up and down the scale of sound, one word reverberates incessantly — *run, run, run, run, run, run...* — endlessly repeated with mind-shattering power. I stand transfixed, weak, and helpless while the words of this Energy blast into me.

"You stand at the center of the Stone, the microcosm of the macrocosm. You stand at the center of the Universe."

I am frightened. What the hell am I doing here? How did I get here? I want out. I desperately want to follow the shattering command I am hearing over and over and run as far and as fast as I can, but I cannot unlock my physical body!

In a tiny voice I ask, "Why am I here? How did this happen?" Nothing! I might as well have sung "Waltzing Matilda" for all the good it does me.

"I am the Keeper of the Door." The voice fills the entire chamber, echoing through my consciousness with immense power. There is only one response I can make. "What door?"

"If you cannot find the Door, then it has no place in your consciousness."

Standing dwarfed in this huge chamber, surrounded by and engulfed in surging power beyond anything in my ability to comprehend, I have never felt so alone, so totally vulnerable.

Without warning, I suddenly know I am not alone! In a moment of revelation, I know that life has conspired to arrange this moment of truth. Certain key people have been drawn almost against their will to attend this workshop. In some way I am linked to every person in this room. It's a perfect cosmic setup! I, who had created a framework in which the others could be participants, have been cast into a participation beyond my wildest dreams. I know with absolute certainty that if I fail in whatever it is I face, it will be a long, long time before I have another opportunity.

I am encouraged, and for the first time since entering and taking human form in the Guidestone's mystical chamber, I attempt to move, to walk forward. Immediately, the Energy, the Keeper of the Door, surges and boils around me, determined to frustrate my efforts, while the pounding command — *run, run, run* — erodes my will. I can only compare the experience to walking into a heatless, raging white fire while pushing underwater against the density and might of a raging river. Each trembling step is an exercise of will. Each takes all my reserves in strength and effort, drawn from both my metaphysical — beyond the physical — and physical bodies.

Meanwhile, my body in the chair is still rigid and my eyes still stare at the Guidestone. Sweat and tears mingle on my cheeks. I am aware of acute embarrassment, a sense of utter disbelief.

Ages seem to pass while, with huge effort, as though burdened by massive weight, I manage, step by ponderously slow step, to creep farther into the chamber. Throughout this seemingly endless time, the Keeper of the Door roars and hurtles, filling all time, all space.

Startled, I see before me a pair of massive doors. They fill the whole chamber, disappearing from view on either side and far above. I gape at them with sinking heart. Nobody could open such doors. It is not humanly possible. There are not even any handles, nothing except doors of a size and apparent weight beyond reckoning. I am very close now. Summoning all my remaining strength, I take one more faltering step against the hostile power of the Energy.

I can touch the Doors.

Strength surges in me. Immediately, all around me, the powerful, insistent, will-shattering command echoes and reverberates with awful intensity — *run, run, run...* — and I quail before it. Again I try to flee, but my uncooperative physical body remains locked, eyes fastened to the Guidestone. I cannot run.

Summoning all my will power, I slowly struggle to raise my arms until I can place one hand on each Door, where they meet in a hairline crack before me.

At that precise moment, in my locked physical body, a dull pain explodes in the top of my head. I can feel the pain as a strange throbbing intensity, as though the crown of my head is somehow opening and closing to an alien rhythm.

Standing small and weak before the mighty Doors, I gather all my remaining strength and will power, ready for one huge final effort.

"Stop!"

The command is such an onslaught of sheer power that all else fades before it. I stop!

"To open the Door is to invoke an awesome responsibility. Do not open the Door unless you are prepared to accept this."

The weak part of me tries once more to run, but a silent whisper — *Stay, do not break* — holds strong. Defiantly, without the faintest idea of what I am letting myself in for, I shout as loud as

I am able into the silence of a mystic world, "I can...and I will!" and I push, as hard as I can, against the Doors.

There is no resistance. The Doors fly open as though they have the weight of gossamer, and I stand on the threshold of another world. It is a familiar world, yet new and different.

Spinning in silent orbit, a new Earth awaits. With a vision defying normal eyesight, I can see into a valley, both familiar and containing a sense of order beyond human experience. Three-dimensional life coexists within some other dimension, causing all substance and form to be illumined. An inner radiance shines forth as outer reality. Even as I stare at this beautiful, wild yet peaceful Nature, the valley fills the space beyond the Door and a sense of expectancy fills me.

The invitation is crystal clear.

I have the opportunity to enter this new reality. This is the Earth of some other age, home to a sensitive, loving humanity. Standing in the Doorway, gazing with exaltation, I know I must step through.

Once again, with unbelievable power, the words from the Keeper of the Door pour into me.

"If you step into the Beyond, the full force of Nature shall pivot in your being. Can you accept this enormous responsibility?"

Behind me, faintly now, the echoing *"run, run, run"* continues, but it no longer holds the power to control me. With the vision of a new Earth before me, I hear my own voice clearly reply with power and authority. "I can accept this responsibility and use it with wisdom."

My thoughts, however, are rather different. Did I say that? What am I letting myself in for? What's going on? Help!

"Remember! The full force of Nature. Misused, it will destroy you."

With these words, all resistance from the Keeper of the Door fades.

Before me, a new Earth awaits my footsteps. I am exhilarated... and exhausted, purposeful... and scared!

I attempt to step forward one pace, but find it impossible to make any progress. Some strange, invisible membrane seems to be between me and that new Earth, and try as I may I cannot walk through. It resists me as easily as if I had tried to walk through invisible glass. Half a dozen times I attempt to force my way through but without success. I even try punching the invisible barrier, but this has about as much effect as punching a pillow.

Finally, I stand back, puzzled and defeated. "All that effort for nothing," I mutter. "It's ridiculous."

"Oh, I wouldn't say that. I didn't expect you would get this far. I certainly don't expect you to step through the Door."

Shocked, I spin around. The person, or Being, I face smiles at me calmly. I step back hastily, away from the deceptive Doorway and the newcomer.

"Good grief! Who are you?"

Two disconcerting eyes look into mine, holding me in a gaze I cannot break. I stare in appalled fascination. There is no white to those eyes. The irises, considerably larger than those in human eyes, are a deep golden color containing flecks if intensely sparkling light. And the calm intelligence in those eyes is beyond anything I have ever encountered. Strangely, as he — it?— holds my gaze, I can feel my fear evaporating. Whatever this being is, violence is not part of it. I relax with a sigh.

"You ask who I am, yet you know. I have seen the answer within you."

The Being is considerably taller than I and I must gaze up at him. "I...I do?"

He nods absently, now looking through the Doorway. "Think about it. Take your time." He chuckles at some private joke. "Time is irrelevant here."

I stare at him, no longer feeling threatened. That he is human, or humanoid, is beyond question. He stands on normal legs, clothed in a pair of faded green denims. His bare feet are longer than normal, and his toes taper almost to a point. Even though he is clothed in a loose, faded green cotton T-shirt, an exceptionally well-proportioned upper body testifies to his humanness. His skin is the color of pale golden honey, not unusual in our multiracial society, but with his face and head all human normality ends. His large, faintly slanted eyes are set in a face of Oriental features. He has very high, fine cheekbones and a thin, narrow nose perfectly proportioned to his broad face. His lips are moderately full and clearly defined. On his chin is a tuft of fine downy hair too sparse to hide the fact that the chin itself tapers out to a blunt point.

Sensitivity and strength are contained in that face. It is fierce yet gentle, mellow yet wild and free. But the real challenge is above the eyes!

His eyebrows are no more than a thin line, and just above them small spiraled horns curve gently outwards. His skull is a bald golden dome. I have the impression that this dome is the repository of experience and knowledge far beyond anything conceivable in human terms, and that we humans are all as children by comparison. The bulge and expanse of forehead is greater than any I have ever seen, yet it is his ears that now hold my attention. They are not animal, but neither are they human. The ears are no larger than ours where they join the head, but from there they sweep back three times the normal length, tapering to an upper point covered in the same downy hair as that on the chin.

An incredible face. Totally beautiful, utterly serene. Just drinking in the detail of his features fills me with peace.

And then I know! I know exactly who this Being is.

"Pan!" I gasp the name aloud, and he smiles as our eyes meet. "But how? Why? What am I doing here?" I stutter to a halt, overfull of questions.

"You did not think your relationship with Nature could continue merely on a verbal level, did you? When you elected to jump into the river of life, you invoked certain forces that have long lain dormant."

He holds my gaze once more with a level stare that I am unable to escape. Not that I want to. I could willingly drown in his eyes, so compelling are they.

"Consider the experience you have just undergone," he continues. "What has begun here is your intuition into a different level of relating to Nature, but I stress it is only a beginning. You were unable to walk through the final barrier. As I introduce you to the inner world of Nature, you will find you are on a journey of discovery. Not only will you discover a whole *new* meaning to Nature, but within Nature you will have the potential to discover your Self. You may find the true Self of your Being. Only then may you pass safely through the Door. That membrane is your security, for what lies beyond the Door may be gained only through perfect timing. You *are* that timing. This is your path and your destiny."

"So what do I do now?"

"You open yourself to new experiences and willingly become involved in them. You began all this a long, long time ago. To enter a new reality of Nature, you must first experience Nature. Experience it as it is, and experience it not as an onlooker but as a participant. The mineral, vegetable, and animal kingdoms are part of the human Being. You must experience your own inner connections with these kingdoms. In this way, the knowledge and experience that are now buried deep in your psyche will become your conscious reality."

He smiles at me in a way that seems disconcertingly sympathetic. "I will help you. That is why I am here in the Guidestone."

I feel hopelessly inadequate. Compared to Pan — is it *really* Pan? — I feel that everything is far beyond me. And I am aware of a sudden, overwhelming fatigue.

Obviously, Pan is aware of my exhaustion, too. Concern flickers in his eyes. "Go now," he commands and clicks two of the long, tapering fingers of a strong, slender hand.

—

INSTANTLY, ALL MY AWARENESS was focused on my physical body as I regained conscious control. I could again move my limbs and wipe my sweat and tears. Now an emotional battle began, for I wanted nothing more than to collapse on the floor and sob.

The top of my head throbbed incessantly. I felt very fragile. Cautiously, I glanced around, expecting every eye to be fixed on me in curious speculation, but no one was aware of what had happened. I was astonished. I had been in the Guidestone for ages. A glance at my watch revealed that scarcely twenty minutes had passed. I placed a trembling hand on the top of my head, trying to hold it all together, when my eye caught Treenie's. The look in her eyes told me she knew that something had happened, even if she did not know what.

Somehow — I'll never know quite how — I survived the next hour. I listened while people shared their experiences with the Guidestone, and I became aware that several people realized that something fairly dramatic had happened to me. In all probability, they had been the crucial human element — consciousness — that had supported me when I had most needed help. I did not share my experience; to do so would have been beyond me. I was in emotional shock. Later I learned that a participant who was a close friend went away with a headache that lasted nearly three weeks. He swore he would never attend another one of my workshops!

As time distanced me from the experience, my acceptance of it, I am not proud to admit, rapidly diminished. After all, who in his right mind believes in Pan? My education had revealed him only as the mythical God of Nature with a human upper body and the legs and feet of a goat, and until this experience I had never had cause to question this description. But the Pan I met was far more than merely human, and totally unbestial. In the past, when sitting by the river listening to its silent — yet audible! — communication, I had often surmised that things might possibly go deeper than they appeared. My involvement with a metaphysical Nature continually required that I surrender much that is considered normal. But never in my wildest dreams had I expected anything like Pan. And yet it made sense. If Nature were intending to lead me deeper into its mystical consciousness, who would be a better guide than Pan, the god of this inner realm? The difficulty with this logical summary was that Pan himself was not logical. He was an affront, a challenge, to my cozy belief system, which I thought had already been stretched to its limit. That was my problem — the idea of Pan as my guide made sense, yet it was nonsense!

Curiosity caused me to try summoning Pan, even though I found it difficult to believe in him. How could I meet him again? How was I supposed to pass that final membrane by finding my Self? My journey into Nature up to now had offered me words and several rather unusual interactions with a river, but Pan was obviously the forerunner of extraordinary things. Should I just wait, or what?

I discussed the whole episode at length with Treenie, and she found it easy to accept. But that did not help me resolve the personal dilemma I was facing. Just to make matters more complicated, that little hole in the large end of the Guidestone simply was not there. I checked the stone carefully, and the hole did not exist. So how could I have been sucked into it? All that remained were impossibilities and questions!

A FEW MONTHS LATER, I received a letter from a man named Kinsley Jarrett. I had been receiving a trickle of letters in response to the recent release of my book *Talking With Nature*, and Kinsley's letter was among them. He had responded deeply to certain incidents described in the book and wanted to meet Treenie and me. Liking the tone of his letter, I agreed to a meeting. As luck would have it, he and his wife, Valma, lived only a few hours away.

In due course, the Jarretts arrived at our home. What ensued was one of those meetings with strangers that are really the renewals of old friendships. After the first hesitations had been eased away, Kinsley asked if we would like to see the drawings he had done of various Nature Spirits. He had been a commercial illustrator, he told me. I felt skeptical, though, at the idea that Nature Spirits had appeared and remained present while he drew them. However, I hid this feeling as he took the first of his illustrations from the folder. Then I simply stared in fascination and awe. That Kinsley saw true I had no doubt. The detail and energy of his art leaped off the pages. Nature came alive in his work, vital and very, very real.

He laid a few more of his sketches before us and then, after hesitating briefly, brought out one more. A chill ran down my spine. It was Pan! As Kinsley had drawn him, an enigmatic smile played over Pan's lips. Once I looked into the eyes on the paper, I could not pull my gaze away. For perhaps ten minutes, I held that sketch of Pan's head and shoulders, drinking it in. It was accurate in practically every detail. Kinsley explained how and where he had seen Pan, but I hardly listened. All my denials of the Guidestone experience lay in tatters at my feet while Pan smiled mockingly at me from a simple sheet of paper.

No more than a week after Kinsley and Valma had departed, a tube arrived by post from Kinsley containing a rolled up picture. As I unrolled it, I knew that Pan was back to haunt me. A brief note explained that when Kinsley went back to his favorite forest nook he saw Pan there once more, and Pan had suggested that Kinsley make an illustration for me. I put the picture in a frame and hung it above my desk. I quickly found that no matter where I stood in the room, Pan's eyes were gazing into mine.

After that, I waited for something else to happen but nothing did, at least nothing like what I had anticipated.

An old friend from our past, Wendy, came to visit Treenie and me for a few days, and we had a lot of talking and reminiscing to catch up on. Eventually, responding to her questions, I began to discuss certain aspects of my relationship with Nature, becoming rather intense as we moved into my favorite subject. I noticed alarm on Wendy's face as she looked at me, but I dismissed it. Suddenly, she sat bolt upright, the alarm replaced by astonishment. "Michael! Stop! Your ears!" She paused in acute embarrassment, then forged ahead. "Your ears! They've grown long and ... weird." She pointed at them. "While you were talking, they were growing. Even your face changed."

I ran my fingers over my ears. They felt the same to me! Wendy jumped to her feet, very agitated. "I must go outside," she said. "I need to get away for a few minutes."

Treenie and I looked at each other. "Well?" I asked. "Can you see weird ears, or is she imagining things?"

Even before Treenie could reply, I was on my way to the nearest mirror. I stared hard at my reflection, twisting my head from side to side. For one brief, heart-stopping moment, I saw Pan, his smile a mocking enigma as our eyes met. Then he was gone, and my own face reflected my bewilderment. Shaken but satisfied that my ears were normal, I returned to the room. Later, when Wendy had joined us, she explained how she had seen my face gradually change. Obviously, the change had not been physical, but something that seemed imposed upon my features.

It was considerably later when Wendy noticed the picture of Pan above my desk. "That's the face; that's it!" she exclaimed excitedly.

As though that were not enough, other people saw similar shifts in my physical being — five more times. Each time, it was the ears or face of Pan superimposed upon mine that drew their attention.

One day when I glanced at the picture of Pan, I clearly heard his silent question.

"Yes," I murmured aloud to him. "I do accept you now. I don't seem to have much choice!"

2 Becoming Water

Winter had ended. The sun shone on the river with unabated power, early morning shadows having retreated into thickets of trees and bush. Instead of diving into the inviting river, I slid into the water silently, for I wanted to sneak up on some water dragons that I knew frequented the riverbank to bask in the hot sun.

I scanned the dead, water-logged branches ahead of me, watching for the single movement that would betray the dragon's outline. Suddenly, it happened. With a slight pulse of a throat, the whole reptile became visible. Slowly, I moved closer, trying not to blink. Movement was effortless, for the water supported me as I gradually closed the distance. Finally, I was within six feet of the ancient creature, but I knew it was aware of my presence. For five, maybe ten minutes, we remained motionless.

A shoal of small striped fish began to feed on the debris I had disturbed in the shallow water. It was not long before they progressed from this to pulling on the separate hairs of my chest and legs, tugging with frantic energy in an attempt to detach their prizes. They tickled, and as I shifted slightly ripples of alarm radiated across the water's surface. Instantly, from a branch before me, an eighteen-inch water dragon leaped into the safety of the reeds. I gasped! I had not even noticed this particular dragon, yet it had been even closer than the one on which my gaze was fixed. Its skin rough, with corrugated, broken shades of gray, the reptile had blended perfectly with the branch. Yet once seen, the creature was clearly visible.

From the river came silent words: "You see yet you do not see."

It was true. The startled dragon had been in my full vision, yet I had not seen it. Now, because of the unnatural position of my head, my neck was aching, so I decided to end the game by creeping forward, closer and closer to the dragon statue. Five feet, four feet, three feet — explosive action. One bound and it, too, vanished into the dense waterside undergrowth.

I smiled in childlike satisfaction. In my own way and in my own time, I loved being part of Nature. Taking a deep breath, I slid underwater, swimming silently down into a deep, murky hole close by. I knew a large eel lived there, secure in its water world, believing itself to be king of its domain. And it probably was! Living under a submerged log, it fed on the hapless young perch that came within reach of its snapping, teeth-filled jaws. I saw the eel's hazy, bulky, sinuous outline and reached out to stroke it, but it had other ideas. As a six-foot-long, thick ropy shadow, it glided over my body, its velvet-soft skin cool as it slid across my belly.

I took another breath of air and dived again, changing direction. Now I allowed the underwater current to carry me as I drifted effortlessly, silent in body and mind, across the sunlit shallows of gravel and smooth river stones. Here I had to be more watchful, for the sluggish bullrout stung with the sustained touch of a red-hot knife. A flicker of movement ahead caused me to reach out, hanging onto an extra-large and convenient river stone.

Without alarm, eight fat river mullet were feeding on furry, dark green algae growing on the stones, their sleek, silver-gray bodies twisting and flashing as they grazed. These river mullet seldom ventured into the estuaries or ocean, probably preferring the comparative safety of the upper freshwater rivers. These fish were fat indeed, about a foot long and gleaming with health. I popped my head above water and, taking a really deep breath, let go of the stone to dive once more and drift among the flashing silver fish. There was no panic, no real disturbance. As a shoal, they swam around me, within reach, all the while twisting and rolling as they leisurely grazed their underwater pastures. I called to them in the silence of my mind, asking them to share their wisdom, but I heard nothing.

For a while I continued downriver, swimming deeper now in the water and occasionally surfacing for air. Disturbed, a large water tortoise raced vigorously ahead of me, and I playfully grabbed it as it clawed frantically at the water. Again, I popped to the surface, holding the struggling captive before me. Water dripped, while its legs continued to swing in the air and its snake head wove aimlessly back and forth. Gently I touched it beneath its mouth to feel the tiny, thin barbels protruding from its lower jaw, when to my utter astonishment it bit me! For a few seconds the tortoise remained attached, unaware of the pitfalls of hanging on! Then I plunged hand and tortoise beneath the water. Instantly, the tortoise let go, to disappear into the depths with determined and frenzied haste. I looked at my dented fingertip, smiling. Cheeky!

Quietly, I swam back upriver, easing my way over the shelves of submerged rock. Contented by the sun and lazing in that wonderful flow of living water, I reflected on my gradually strengthening bond with Nature. As a child I had been angry — not with an anger that other people had been aware of but with one that had simmered within me. I had had to endure a decade of being a very nonintellectual, nonacademic right-brained boy in a very intellectual and academically left-brained–oriented school. Not understanding why I was such a misfit, I turned to Nature. By tranquil ponds and in places such as Byron's Pool Woods, I found acceptance and refuge. My bonding with Nature happened in silence. Alone, I had nothing to say, so I learned early that rarest of gifts — to listen — not to people, but to Nature. I viewed people with distrust. That much school had taught me.

Eventually, my schooling ended and I began to work on my father's farm. At this stage, my relationship with Nature came under threat, for as a trainee farmer I was required to subdue Nature. Farming and Nature, I learned, were in direct conflict. I had to change, and my childhood connection with Nature became submerged, but throughout those years of farming it remained within me, a spark awaiting its time.

In my mid-twenties, married to Treenie and with two boys, I emigrated with my family to Australia. Settling with them on the island state of Tasmania, I once again began farming, simply because I had no training in anything else and loved the outdoor life. Over the next eleven years, I developed a new relationship with Nature. I learned of a potential bonding between a human Being and Nature, but there was a catch. Such a bonding had to be *experienced*, not merely conceived mentally. While the bond remained a concept, it was no more than speculation: it had to be actualized, lived.

Now all Treenie and I came to know was work, work, and more work. Sixteen hours a day were normal for us — up at 5 A.M. to milk the cows and feed the pigs and calves, breakfast at 9 A.M., then do a full day's work and end at 4 P.M. with the whole milking routine again. Day in, day out, such was the schedule every day for eight years. My love for Nature was buried under the sheer necessity of work.

But gradually, below the day-to-day routine, I was surrendering to the moving force of Nature. I was learning that to make a true connection with Nature — beyond the mind, beyond knowledge — I had to release the farm and open myself to Nature's metaphysical realms. Nature revealed to me that within the moment there is a movement that can be experienced as though one is attuned to the heartbeat of the universe. In this movement, there is Silence, and within this Silence is Wisdom.

In our decade on Tasmania, I made enormous changes in my thinking, becoming one of the foremost organic farmers on that tiny island state. Still, much more was needed if I was to enter the mystical kingdoms of Nature, and I wanted to do so with an intense, unabated longing. I felt that my true home lay in the heart of Nature. It was this longing, the deep inner need of mine, that took Treenie and me away from farming, now with three boys and a daughter, to travel around Australia in a kombi-type vehicle and a pop-top caravan.

After many adventures, we initiated a community project, and with about twenty other people went to live on a 345-acre property that was to become known as the Homeland Foundation Community. It was there I had to face myself — not an easy task! I learned that I took an aggressive attitude toward people, but that hidden behind this shield were the unresolved fears of a little boy. Throughout this four-year adventure, if there was conflict in the community, I would be in the thick of it. If there was confrontation, I would be there.

With some shock, I learned that the reason I did not like other people was that I did not like myself. Once I faced that fact, I could begin to solve the problem. It would be difficult to exaggerate the pain and trauma of coming to terms with myself. As I lowered my barricade of aggression, there was no shortage of people who would cut me to the quick in my vulnerability. I was a target, for I had been one of the most dominant in the community and was now defenseless. I cried more during this process than I had ever cried in my life. I allowed a little boy to cry. Many times I sat by the river in my mental and emotional pain and vowed that I would leave tomorrow. But tomorrow had a habit of never coming. Slowly and painfully, I learned that my greatest strengths were a handicap, were defenses, while within my vulnerability lay a seed of unrecognized strength. This was not an aggressive strength but a strength that revealed a totality within myself.

Had either Treenie or I known of the trauma we would have to face in that community, I doubt that we would have had the courage to enter it in the first place, for even Treenie did not emerge unscathed. She faced her own personal problems and suffered greatly as she let go of old patterns of thought and behavior. But like me, Treenie triumphed.

When Treenie and I left Homeland to settle a few miles away in the same valley, I had come genuinely to like myself. My growth as a human Being no longer depended on interaction with other people. When you can finally live in a community of forty people without conflict, you have found a measure of inner confidence and tolerance. Even my relationship with Treenie had taken on a new meaning. Before living in the community, we had been close, rather like two powerful vines entwined around each other, each offering and receiving support, but the community life had torn us painfully apart. As we each found our own strengths and inner capacities, we came back together, but in a different way. We were now individuals standing side by side, two strong, separate trees. Our support for each other was based on a new level of self-respect and love, and in a wonderful, magical synthesis of soul, the two of us experienced a new kind of love within our marriage. We bonded on a level of love and acceptance we had not attained in our first eighteen years of marriage.

Living by the river, my relationship with Nature grew anew. I was no longer turning to Nature as a refuge from people; now, once again, Nature was my teacher, and Treenie had become my Nature companion. Before our time at Homeland, Treenie had always seemed outside my journey into the inner realms of Nature, but now she was involved, and in some inexplicable way my experiences served as stepping stones in her own path. If, during one of my communications with Nature, I learned something new and profound, when I shared it with Treenie she had already experienced it, but on an entirely intuitive level.

As I swam in the river on that delicious spring day, I knew that the journey into Nature I had longed for was becoming a reality. Now I needed to find new levels of openness and acceptance, for already I was threatened by the sheer impossibility of Pan. Pan had told me I was to experience the inner kingdoms of Nature — the plant, mineral, and animal kingdoms — but I had a feeling there was more to it than that. Though I have a strong mystical side to my character, my strong logical mind was going to cause me trouble. How could I trust Pan as my guide if at times I still doubted his existence?

⟶

A LIGHT BREEZE had sprung up while I floated with my thoughts, dispersing them among the newborn ripples. Idly, I glanced around; then I recoiled in shock. Sitting cross-legged on the surface of the river close by was Pan. "Oh! You startled me!" I exclaimed.

He smiled, those incredible eyes holding mine. I wanted to ask him how he could sit on the water, but under that gaze all words dried up.

"We are going to begin now by stretching you. Let go of restrictive belief systems and all you consider normal and flow with what I offer. You alone will determine how your experiences within Nature will evolve. I am not going to tell you what lies ahead, for you would build inner defenses against the unusual and unintentionally devise ways of reducing the impact of the unexpected. This would negate our purpose."

He paused while I digested his words. An intensity had built around him, and I could feel it within me, bringing clarity and quick understanding.

"If we are to bring about a transformation, then I must use the weapons of surprise to bypass your natural defenses to the unknown." He chuckled. "Such defenses are well developed in humanity; that is why the unknown is so vast. You must become changed, not modified. A metal that is forged into a plate one day and melted and reforged into a vase the next is not changed. Its shape is simply modified. However, if by some process that metal is transmuted and becomes gold, this is change. This is your inner purpose ... to become changed."

"Er... what to?"

"That I cannot tell you. You have to be it to know." He became silent and I did some more digesting. I knew I was under his influence, for otherwise I would have felt far more agitated than I did.

"Let go," his voice coaxed me, the words echoing and reverberating in my skull. I struggled as my senses reeled.

—

"LET GO." It is a command I cannot ignore. I feel my Self being drawn from my physical body, and I watch in helpless anguish as it slowly sinks beneath the water.

"I ... I'll drown. I'll lose my body."

"*No*. A natural preservation will take place. Watch."

I watch as my body rises to the surface on its own volition and the mouth opens to take in air. The body is animated, even though I am no longer in it.

"You are alive; thus your body lives. Your purpose now is not to die and lose your body, but to experience aspects of Nature that are denied to the physical senses. The body is a unique vehicle. It will survive because you will survive." He pauses, and when he says the next bit I wish he hadn't.

"Of course, if you die to this physical reality, then your body will no longer accommodate you. Surrender your will to that which is and go with the experience. By letting go, you are safe; by resisting, you may create adversity. Flow with the water... and experience."

It crosses my mind to protest, but the thought dies unfinished. I no longer relate to *me*. I am pure water — yet more. I both flow in the river that contains me and hover as an invisible mist above it. I no longer experience through eyes or ears. I perceive. I am a liquid that fills every part of the Earth. I can feel the consciousness of the Earth, the rhythm of its breath. I flow among the dense particles of solid rock, knowing the rock's consciousness. I am all puddles, ponds, lakes, and oceans.

No longer an isolated entity, I flow in savage splendor down rocky ravines, laughing as the sound of torrential, thundering water bounces and echoes from the rocks. I lie in calm tranquility in icy, land-locked lakes containing the fish that swim in my sluggish depths. I am rain falling from the skies, and, frozen, I fall as snow.

As a muddy swirl, I flow toward the sea, slowly, in a ruined, silted riverbed. I know that mankind has wrecked my natural system, but within my spirit essence there is no judgment. When a small, frail child wades into my shallows, slipping into a deep hole, it is I that fill her lungs, unfeeling, while she drowns.

Suddenly, a strange duality begins. Not only am I the water in her lungs, but I am aware of my physical self, Michael, holding the child. I place my lips on hers and, as I begin to give her mouth-to-mouth resuscitation in a hopeless attempt to save her life, I am the water I draw forth from her lungs.

I feel the shock in my human self as I realize the little girl is an empty shell, but simultaneously with this all-embracing vision I see the mistlike form of her ethereal body as it hovers uncertainly at her side. Unable to restore her bodily life, I am aware of my humanity as I wade into the river to wash her vomit from my mouth. I am the water that swirls into my own mouth and I am the river to which I address my emotional, tear-stained words, "Please, help me to understand."

In this strange duality, where time and normality no longer exist, I reach an understanding. In some inexplicable manner, an event of twelve years ago is happening now. Some remote part of my consciousness that blames the river for the girl's drowning is laid to rest.

As mist, I float on white-capped mountain peaks, their spires jutting through me as I hug their cold, stony slopes. It is I that transpire from the leaves of a million trillion plants, and I that return in light rains and heavy storms. Far above our planet, I perceive the Earth beneath me, and if consciousness can weep from beauty and joy, I am surely doing so.

Endlessly, timelessly, I am part of the lifeblood of Nature's system. I flow in the body of every human being, carry every life, flow from the apertures of every body, and know Oneness as a total reality.

I am water, in pond, puddle, ocean, lake...and river.

———

A HUGE INVOLUNTARY breath brought me spluttering and gasping to my senses. I felt laden, heavy...human! I was also cold, and shocked to find myself in the river. Swimming to the bank I felt strangely physical. What had happened? In a flash, I remembered. I looked for Pan, glancing to where I had last seen him. Nothing! I toweled myself dry, rather disoriented. Suddenly, in clear detail, I remembered the incident involving the little girl. With a group of friends, I had been swimming in muddy waters of the River Murray when we had heard a lot of shouting and screaming upriver. We had run to investigate and found more than a dozen people frantically searching the river looking for a little girl. The fatalistic feeling of hopelessness I had experienced washed over me with the return of the memory. The river had been so muddy that even placing your hand below water put it out of sight. The child's relatives and friends had already spent five minutes looking with frantic haste, and as we organized a more thorough search of the river the minutes ticked away. It was some fifteen minutes later that her submerged body had been found in a waist-deep hole only a few feet from the bank. One of my friends and I had worked on reviving her, but we had both known it was futile from the start.

Only now did I realize that I had never come to terms with the river and her drowning. I remember asking the river to help me understand. I realized now that the drowning had created conflict within me, for I had loved the river, muddy and silted as it was. That it had drowned the child was in no way the fault of the river; nevertheless, the innocence of the child had somehow caused me to blame the river. My journey into the essence of water had revealed this unrealized rift between myself and the river. Now, I hoped, the rift was healed.

I dressed, holding out my arms to stare at them in fascination. I knew I would never take anything physical for granted again. My arms, my body, I contained the consciousness of water, a consciousness separate from my own consciousness — and yet not separate at all! Somehow, Pan had taken me from my physical body and plunged me into a metaphysical realm where I had *become* water. Within that experience, I had connected not only with my past interaction with a river but with *all life*, for water is in all things. Strangely, I had not lost my awareness of myself, yet my identity had become submerged in the experience of being water. A fusion had taken place, a fusion suggesting the interconnectedness of *all* life and the possibility of our reconnecting with Nature in a way that reaches the very core of our Being. Time was revealed as an imposter in this metaphysical realm, for my encounter with the drowned child twelve years ago had been happening as I experienced it. Nature had often indicated to me that time and space are three-dimensional phenomena only, and to a certain degree I had already experienced that, but this was something else!

Three weeks passed without a sign of Pan. I moved from my initial shock into a feeling that I had been tricked. To experience the girl's drowning from the perspective both of a human *and* of water itself was overwhelming. And yet I began to see that I was viewing life differently. I had learned that the borders and boundaries we erect and impose on life do not carry much reality. If my experience had been real — and it had felt more real than anything I had ever known — it suggested that we live within a very narrow and confined reality while a hidden vastness may await us. Who determines what is real — or not real?

Alas, although the experience was giving me a lenient attitude to the idea of life's reality, I was still having a struggle with my *personal* reality. The experience in the river had been so personal I could find no comfort in talking about it with friends. As always, I shared my thoughts with Treenie, aware of how much I needed her stability. She seemed to have no trouble accepting my account of what had happened, but I was plagued by the conflict created by my logical, left-brain self and my holistic, right-brain self. I needed to come together and function as one whole Being, but instead I was split. Both Pan's appearances and the experiences he had precipitated were outrageous denials of all that was considered normal. I discovered that normality was something I valued and that my logical self clung to it with tenacious strength.

My mental turmoil all came to a head in the most unexpected manner. Treenie and I had been invited to a party, and with some reluctance I agreed to go.

The usual hum and murmur of fused and discordant voices filled the large room. Through the crowd, I could see Treenie, looking magnificent in her dark red dress and her crown of glowing silver hair. She had gone gray at an early age, blaming life with me as the cause! Personally, I loved her hair. As the middle years had softened her face, so the silver-gray hair had accentuated it. She reminded me of a beautiful tree, which, having grown and matured, was now in full bloom. Her eyes animated and sparkling, she was caught up in conversation. Not my best at parties, I tend to flit around the periphery of the various groups, seldom making real contact. Not so with Treenie. She is a people person, a stimulating, compassionate, and intelligent woman who attracts people easily.

From my retreat behind a tall potted palm, I listened with some trepidation to the powerful assertion of a dark-haired woman as she declared her love for and need of her guru. Her eyes swept over the people around her. "We all need a guru," she stated with unshakable conviction. "We need to share in the love and wisdom of One who knows truth." I felt momentarily threatened.

I had no guru, no one to direct me to that final truth. In fact, for most of my life I had scorned the notion, never having felt a need for one. Yet at that moment I found the woman's conviction unsettling and, intrigued by the power of her statement, I now met her eyes. Abruptly, I had her full attention.

"What about you, Michael?" she asked. "Do you have a guru?"

I groped for an acceptable answer and could speak only four words. "Pan is my guru."

The small group murmured. The potted palm and I became the center of attention.

The dark-haired woman stared at me challengingly. "Are you serious? Or are you in love with the eternal youth of Peter Pan?"

My words came strongly now, carrying the power of my own just-realized conviction. "I mean the Great God Pan — he of the goat's horns, hooves, and mischief by the water."

That was the end of the discussion. Nobody knew whether to take me seriously — and I didn't help! All I could feel was a growing sense of wonder at what I had said and now knew to be true. But why me? Obviously, I had not selected such a Being. I had been chosen. For what purpose? One thing was certain — I had finally accepted my reality. I felt my acceptance and my surrender to the will of Pan as a breath of fresh air within me.

The following morning, I made my way down the steep steps beneath the trees on the riverbank to my old bridge-plank diving board. Halfway down, I paused. Pan — naked — was standing on the end of the board! He seemed oblivious to my presence, and I watched in amazement as he leaped high into the air and came down onto the end of the board. With even more surprise, I saw the four-inch-thick board bend and, with a supple flick, toss him into the air. He went high, far higher than possible, turning a couple of perfectly executed somersaults before entering the water without the faintest splash!

By the time I scrambled down the remaining steps, he had emerged dripping from the river. I stared at him aghast. He had no sex organs! I took two steps back and sat down on a rock. It was all too much!

He looked at me levelly, clearly amused. "Not quite what you expected."

My mouth opened and closed three times before any words came out. "But . . . but you are male, surely?"

"I am neither male nor female. I am balance. I am the infinite balance of Nature."

"But mythology depicts you as a horned goat/man who spent his time splashing by rivers and seducing maidens. How could you do that if you are sexless?"

He just smiled at me, and his beauty was overwhelming.

"If you were terrified of inhuman beauty and ran from its sight, what would you tell other people? Would you describe me as beauty or a beast? People do not like to be diminished by their own fears."

But another one of my niggling doubts had been dredged up from somewhere in my conditioned self. I stared at him, trying to see past the beauty to the beast. "Where is the traditional Pan?" I asked. "Didn't Pan cause panic? It — you — gave birth to the word *panic* and its meaning, isn't that right?"

"Not I." He said. "That was the work of man. When a person's view of life is so restricted and petty that it cannot embrace a nonhuman reality, panic is the reaction." He was again dressed in the faded green denims and T-shirt. He had not put them on; they were simply there!

Pan smiled at my consternation. "For me, this body is no more than a garment of thought."

I was bewildered. "But how could you be so heavy that you made the board bend? No matter how high I jump, it doesn't bend. Yet the other week you sat cross-legged on the water. It doesn't add up."

"That is because you believe in the fixed laws of physical reality. Believe in them. Go ahead; you need them. But do not limit your belief. Accept the fact that other realities exist. Other realities have different rules. You cannot apply one to the other."

It made sense. I did not really understand, but it made sense!

I had suspected that he read my mind. His next comment confirmed it.

"Do not be limited by what you understand. At this point, only your intellect seeks to understand. But you can allow yourself to *know directly*, rather than logically deduce by means of your intellect."

I understood, I thought! But I had some unfinished business with Pan. I didn't mean to accept what he told me passively but felt the need to clear away all lingering doubts. "Why didn't you come and see me after my experience in the river? I might have drowned, for all you knew. Didn't you want to know what happened?"

He had been standing on the end of the board again, but when he glanced back at me, fire flashed from those intense, disturbing flecks in his eyes.

"I know exactly what happened to you. I know you better than you know yourself. For a while you experienced belonging, something rare in the human condition." I was astonished. That was *precisely* what I had experienced, but until this moment I had not been able to find the word that described it. I had belonged in Nature, even though the connection was through water. I had belonged to Earth, to humanity, to life. In that state of Oneness, I had belonged in a way that as a human — and separate, as all humans are — I could never feel.

"That is where you are wrong. You retained your humanness, but the Being you are experienced the wholeness you are. You *are* all you experienced. Within humanity is the whole of Nature. Even I am part of you."

Now I was confused again. "I don't understand."

Ignoring me, Pan gave a great leap onto the end of the board, and again he somersaulted into the air... to vanish! I looked all around me, up in the air and into the water, but there was no sign he had ever existed. I walked to the end of the board and gazed reflectively upriver. What did he mean when he said, "Even I am part of you"? How could he be? Maybe I needed to see Pan not so much as a personality but as the Spirit of Nature. Yes, that felt right. He had already told me that humanity contained Nature, just as we were contained by it. If this were so, then Pan was part of me — and of everyone else. I smiled at the thought!

Lost in speculation, I turned to walk off the board and was startled to see Pan sitting cross-legged on the rocks. His abrupt appearance precipitated another question. "Can other people see you? I know Kinsley did, but can other people? Could Treenie?"

"Only if I choose."

Another question occurred to me. "What happens next?" Pan had done his vanishing act again, but his words were as clear as his invisible presence.

"You'll find out!"

3 Becoming Plant

I waited and waited to find out, but Pan did not appear. He had an infuriating habit of turning up at the most unexpected times, but not when I wanted him!

During this time of waiting, I dreamed on six consecutive nights that I died. The dreams were all vivid, in full color, and different. In the first, I was in a room with several other people and knew there was going to be a nuclear explosion, though I was unconcerned. Suddenly, nothing existed. It was as if the building, room, and all occupants ceased to be. Despite this, consciousness remained: I was aware of self, even though I had no body in which to remain anchored. I felt an immense freedom. I remember thinking, "Not only is matter annihilated, but even time has ceased to exist." I felt my awareness expanding, stretching out unfettered into the universe. Then I woke up.

In each subsequent dream, I witnessed my death and saw myself buried in a clear, flowing river. Always I felt a sense of freedom and exhilaration. Never was there a trace of fear or sadness. I enjoyed the dreams, even though I felt a mite anxious about what might be involved.

The morning after the sixth dream, I went down to the river. Having been buried in a river for several nights, it seemed a logical place to seek the meaning of my dreams.

I sat on my old bridge board, the memory of Pan strong within me. It was warn and humid. Low, white clouds shielded the sun, but the heat was a warm, moist blanket. Gazing into the clear water, I remembered the incredible feeling I had experienced as the water and I had merged, becoming One. I became aware of the power of the river, not so much in its volume, for it is a small river, but in its spirit. I even felt a residual memory of belonging. I could feel the spiritual energy of river, all rivers, all water. It was to this subtle, mystical flow that I addressed my questions: What did my dreams mean? What could I learn from them?

From the silence of Nature came a response.

"Nature is the physical reality of spirit. It is not separate from the human spirit. Seeking a greater truth than the physical world reveals, you have entered this natural flow. Often — as in this moment — our coming together is on a conscious level, but usually the innate wisdom of Nature visits when the mind is asleep."

"But why? Surely it would be easier for us to be awake. We could cooperate."

"On the contrary. You resist when you are awake. You deny the existence on this planet of intelligent life other than your own. The fact that human intelligence is only a minor part of *All* eludes you. When you are asleep, your consciousness does not resist such realities."

"So what do my dreams of death mean?"

"Water is the symbol and carrier of Spirit. You have experienced this. In your dreams, water symbolized complete immersion in death. This indicates conscious commitment and dramatic change. In the six death dreams, six aspects of fear died from your consciousness. Six residues of the past died. Truly, death touched you each time."

"But how can I be touched by death and still live?"

"There are many deaths. Humanity relates only to the great death of the body. In truth, this is but one death in a series of deaths."

"How is this possible?"

"Most deaths are beyond the awareness of the conscious mind. With the development of insight, there comes an awareness of these little deaths, deaths that usually happen during sleep and dreams."

I felt pleased about all this. My dreams were obviously beneficial.

River words continued. "Each little death reveals the potential for a higher expression of the Greater Self. And that is what life is all about."

"Happy now?"

I should have been used to Pan's abrupt appearances by now, but once again I was startled. Then I became suspicious. "Who have I been talking to? You or the Spirit of River?"

He was sitting on the rocks, one bare foot dangling in the water. Ripples of disturbance ringed the area, while a huge catfish swam as close to his foot as it could get. He must have been there for ages! He looked at me lazily, while another question popped into my mind.

"Questions, forever questions. Of course I have been here all the time."

"But you were invisible."

"Not invisible. I had no body!"

By now my questions and confusion had tripled. Pan laughed aloud, a sound not human, but of distant wind chimes.

He held up his hands, as though fending me off. "Okay, I will answer. First, I *am* the Spirit of River. We are not separate. I *am* the Spirit of Nature. Next, I am no body, so I have no body ... unless I happen to want one." He paused, sheer gleeful fun blazing from his eyes. "Most humans spend their lives trying to be somebody. It is a joke. Everybody is really no body. You are not a body, you are a *Being* with a vehicle called a body. You are All. That is who I am. Pan means All. I am all Nature. You are all humanity *and* Nature." He smiled wickedly. "Try that on for size!"

I slumped on the rock beside him. "It doesn't fit" I groaned. "It's all too much."

"Fit or not, it's reality. You have chosen to make it fit. That's why I'm here now. Together, we have to go Beyond, and you are not yet ready. So shape up!"

"Beyond...!"

My memory was working overtime as I tried to recall where I had heard that before. Ah! I had it. "In the Guidestone, the Keeper of the Door said, 'If you step into the Beyond, the full force of Nature shall pivot in your Being. Misused it will destroy you.' Not only do I not understand, but I feel afraid."

Once again, I was subjected to an appraising stare from those startling eyes. I saw compassion in them — at least I hoped that's what I saw.

"Yes, it could destroy you."

"Well, then. I need help. It's easy for you to say shape up, but I'm the one who has to do it. And I don't even know what I am supposed to be doing, or how. And while I'm at it, what the hell *is* Beyond?"

He was patient, I'll give him that, even if he was infuriatingly reticent to fill me in on the details. Ignoring my questions, he stood up, leaped off the rocks as though propelled upward by a super springboard, did another of his perfect somersaults...and vanished.

Suddenly, my body began to shake involuntarily. I stared at my arms and legs aghast as they trembled violently. In my ears came a whisper. "A shake up will help you shape up."

"Oh, my God," I groaned. "A spirit with humor."

Gradually, the trembling grew less violent but more intense. I lay back on the bank and closed my eyes. Knowing that Pan was behind this, I anticipated his next words. Sure enough, they came.

"Let go," he whispered. "It is even difficult to shake you out of that body. Let go . . . and trust."

I have no recollection at all of letting go.

—

ONCE MORE, everything I experience comes through perception. My visual and auditory reception increase beyond measure. I become part of the All. I *am* what I experience. For a while I float above the Earth. I am nothing — everything! I feel no anxiety, even though my humanness is with me. Very slowly, drifting like mist, I become aware of my self taking on a material form. The self that I "know" encompasses many parts of the globe. I grow over the slopes of countless hills, form thickets in myriad gullies. I am briar. As a thorny, tangled mass of vines, I grow on farms and wasteland, on roadsides and in hedgerows. I am blackberry!

For endless time, I grow and thrive. Energies I have never known are expressed through me. Beings, minute as insects, swarm over my vines, while other Beings, more vast in stature but infinitely less tangible, connect me with the Earth and the heavens. All I know is continuity. A feeling akin to human joy is with me constantly. Sounds beyond anything the human ear has ever heard connect me with all life. The human fraction of me weeps at the thought that such magnificence remains beyond normal human learning. Within this sound, no violence is possible. Strange as it may seem, I know that violence is an imposter generated by our illusions of separation. All connects. Sound, minute and greater Beings, blackberries, Earth, the universe . . . and Beyond.

Seasons pass. I experience the bursting energies of spring, when the activity of minute Beings on my vines, within my form, and among my roots, is at its peak. I am the swelling buds along the stems of every briar. I am the force of life that reaches deep into the warming moisture of the soil, and I am the vines that respond. I am the leaves that slowly emerge. I am the sap coursing along endless veins of countless plants. All plants are One plant.

There is no separation. Neither space nor distance exists beyond the physical form. Compared to my totality of energy, my physical form is infinitely small, yet of vast importance.

As the heat of summer grows stronger, I am the chemical changes that take place within the physical plants, and I know that without the minute and greater Beings, this could not be possible. I am the fruit that covers the vine, its flavor, its juice and substance. And I thrive.

Eventually, disturbance becomes part of my energy. My formless, invisible body is hurting. A distortion is taking place within my etheric structure, and all life is affected. I cannot become separate. I cannot shield the All from this discord. Discord enters harmony and a nonstate comes into being. I am the pain of discord, the joy of harmony. In ways that are indescribable, I suffer.

I search for ways to alleviate this discord. Helped by the Beings of Nature, I search for the source of pain... and I find it. Humans!

On a farm in the mountain foothills of Tasmania, a farmer sprays his blackberry vines. On thousands of other farms, on countless roadsides, blackberries are being sprayed. My discord becomes part of the discord of Nature as powerful chemical sprays are released on the plant kingdom all over the planet. And this discord connects with all life. The sprayer and the sprayed, all are equally affected. As blackberry, I am immediately affected; as a man, I am indirectly affected. The greater the delay, the greater and more devastating the effect.

I am both farmer and blackberries on that hillside in Tasmania. My awareness of being a farmer is total as I concentrate on poisoning and killing the cursed blackberries. I want the land they sprawl over, forever spreading and encroaching on my farm; it is land I need. Equally, I am blackberries being sprayed. In the vast silence of Nature, I call out repeatedly to that farmer to cease the folly of his actions... and we remain separate. As the Spirit of Nature, I see the incredible dichotomy of reality. We are connected, totally One, yet the farmer's sense of separation fragments our Oneness. Oneness does not cease to be. It cannot. But it remains beyond the farmer's experience of life. Outside his reality, it is unreal! Seasons pass, and each summer the chemical sprays become more toxic, more abundant.

Each summer I call into the Silence to that one particular farmer. In my knowingness, I see the time bomb within his consciousness, for his consciousness and mine are One. It is primed and due to explode. I throw my energies into activating that explosion, knowing that it will forever change his life. Within, the etheric realm's other Beings of Nature clamor into his dreams, his subconscious.

One day, the moment comes!

He/I am once again spraying the chemicals of distortion onto his/my vine body. I call again into the silence, and he responds. He yawns mightily and turns off the engine of the tractor, deactivating the pump. In the sunshine, on that warm, mellow hillside, he responds by going to sleep, an unusual act for so busy a person.

He dreams. He dreams that he is blackberry vine, and he experiences the distortion of the chemical effect. He learns that killing a physical vine is of little consequence, especially if it is done by natural means, but that his spray is wreaking havoc in the etheric regions. He experiences that havoc, and in his dream he groans aloud. I am the dream and the dreamer. I am the cause and effect. Within all this, I can sense a rightness, a movement within Nature that I know can precipitate balance. I know that the time bomb in consciousness is primed in many human Beings, and each in his or her own way will trigger his or her personal explosion. When the farmer self wakes up, he stares at the blackberries in awe. In consciousness, he, human, connects with me, vine. He climbs to his feet, rolls up the long hose, and climbs onto the tractor. He starts the engine and drives away. He never sprays chemicals on blackberries again.

My blackberry consciousness covers the planet with no more difficulty than my conscious awareness of my human body. Where blackberries exist, there am I. I know that changing the actions of one human is of little physical consequence, but nothing is an accident. In consciousness, this one human connects with all humans, and this one human has long, long ago chosen to go Beyond. I know that this is a pivot point. His life, all life, has been irrevocably changed.

A SHARP, STABBING PAIN lanced down my neck. I groaned. Where was I? I sat up, gazing out over the river. The memory of my experience was suddenly so powerful that I sat still as a statue for long minutes. Wow! What an incredible thing! I had been blackberry! Who would have thought such a thing possible? The feeling of going beyond biological limitations clung to me, invoking wonder. For a moment, I questioned why it had been blackberry of all possible plants, but then I knew. This was yet another aspect in Nature wherein I had created disturbance and imbalance. Not only was this within myself, but within Nature as a whole. It seemed that my journeys into Nature were designed to give me an opportunity to redress the imbalance while simultaneously learning and expanding in awareness of self. How I could be shaken from my body I did not understand, but I realized with an ever-deepening insight that our bodies are indeed no more than wondrous vehicles. Essentially, we are not the reflections in the mirror!

When I arrived at the house, I looked at the clock. No more than an hour and a half had elapsed since I left! I called Treenie and over a cup of coffee told her all that had happened. I recalled how I had once, many years ago in Tasmania, felt a strange, overpowering impulse to sleep when I was spraying blackberries. The dream had changed me, I recalled. After dozing off on that sunny afternoon, I had dreamed I was spraying blackberries. Not unusual, considering! While I sprayed the deadly toxic mist over the leaves of a particularly vigorous blackberry, I had heard a voice calling me. I stopped spraying and looked around, but there was no one there. The voice called again, telling me to touch the leaves of the blackberry vine I had been spraying. I did so. As my fingers touched the leaves I was hurled into the air at tremendous speed, up and up, until I was far above the Earth. Looking down, I could see the whole of our planet, and for some peculiar reason all the blackberry vines were clearly identifiable and visible. I saw, to my astonishment, that from this elevated view they formed a wholeness, like one whole plant, yet I knew that they were really many individual vines. As I saw and realized all this, I began to fall to Earth, feeling very frightened. Suddenly, my fall was checked, and I began to feel a terrible despair. I cannot describe that feeling, but it was awful. I felt as though something was dreadfully wrong, so wrong that it would cause the downfall of all life as I knew it. This was not a physical feeling, not even a mental one. Rather, my whole psyche seemed to be in torment.

I began to fall once more, and as I fell I felt that all Nature was crying. Then I saw myself, as though on a screen, spraying the blackberries — and I knew with utter despair that I myself was the cause of that profoundly disturbing feeling. Then I woke up. The dream had been too strong or clear to ignore, and I never again sprayed blackberries or any other plant with toxic chemicals.

Together, Treenie and I speculated on a strange possibility: the blackberry experience had occurred then even though it appeared to happen now. In some incredible way, my dream of all those years earlier had been interwoven with the *present!*

I say that we speculated, but in truth it was I who speculated. Treenie listened patiently while I rambled on, trying to convince myself that time was as malleable as memory itself.

Then Treenie spoke. "My darling," she began. When she begins like that, I know I am in for a lecture, sometimes a patronizing one! She continued. "If there is one thing we have learned along our path, it's that time, space, and separation are all illusions — powerful ones, perhaps, but illusions all the same. When you have a mystical experience that verifies truth, why do you fight it? Why is it so difficult for you to accept what you already know?

You know in your heart what is true. If I can understand it, I know you can. You have been exploring the consciousness of the plant kingdom. It was a metaphysical experience, because you can't put a physical body through such antics." She smiled at me sweetly.

"There's no need for sarcasm," I muttered.

"Oh, but there is. You persist in deliberate and pointless nonacceptance. Assuming that you can be more reasonable and open, let's sum up the situation. Your experience revealed to you that all life is connected. You learned that whatever we inflict on Nature will eventually be inflicted on us. Yes?"

"Yes. And by us!"

"That's the irony of it. As long as people see Nature as being outside themselves, we will continue in such folly. Responsibility for the planet begins with each of us. Little did you think when you were spraying the blackberries that you were causing all Nature to suffer. Your mystical experience reveals that individual action has a universal application."

Her eyes sparkled with enthusiasm as she continued. "I find it exciting that what you learn on a metaphysical level always seems to have a physical application."

"That's because they are not separate. Each contains the other. Gee, aren't we limited," I concluded as I realized how little of what we were discussing was involved in common knowledge or thinking.

"Don't get morbid," Treenie admonished. "That's your problem. Part of you doubts your metaphysical self and gets morbid. You even doubt Pan. You see him, yet you doubt him. Do you doubt me? Just accept that when you are learning a new game, you have to learn different rules."

Then came the nice part. She put her arms around my neck, kissed me, and said, "I'll help you, my darling. That's why I am here."

That part always bothers me. She often tells me she is here to help me. She also says I came here under protest. Now *that* I can believe!

A few days later, down at the river, I decided to try and conjure up Pan my way. "PAAAAAAAAANN," I shouted, as loudly as I could.

"You called?"

Pan was standing only a few feet away. It was all too much! It made me wonder how often I had been unaware of his presence.

"More often than not," Pan stated.

I sighed. I knew it was true.

He gazed at me, locking my eyes. I could neither blink nor look away. He looked pleased. "It's happening," he said. "Experiencing Nature as it *is* takes you farther and faster than listening to disembodied words."

I felt slightly devalued.

"Why do you do that?" Pan asked. "In no way do I belittle listening to the silence of Nature. The words of Nature have immense value. I *am* those words. But they are not the experience." He frowned at me. "Sometimes I wonder about you."

I scowled back. "It would help if you would answer a few of my questions. Just the important ones. Like what is Beyond? Why do I have to go there? What have I been chosen for... and why? Those will do for starters."

Pan laughed a human laugh, long and loud. His eyes were a challenge to me. To be unable to look away from someone's eyes can be a chilling experience. Sometimes he looked right through me. How many times had I read that expression in a novel? But actually to experience it was something else! The flecks of light in his eyes contracted and expanded as though animated by an independent life of their own. I had the feeling that I was seeing the universe shining through those flecks of light. It was as though I was seeing beyond... Beyond!

"Aha! Now we're getting there." Pan's voice was mocking. "*Life* is Beyond. Life, in all its many facets. Other realities await. You have been chosen because long, long ago — that is, if we concede to subjective time — you made the choice to manifest in this earthly dimension. You chose to become a sleeper — and you chose to awaken. The process in which you are now involved is the awakening. It is a planetary process. Each individual on this planet is part of the whole, or, to put it another way, the whole in a part. As each individual awakens, every other individual is affected, for, as I have said, the whole and the individual are One." He smiled strangely. "There is a catch, however. Awakening does not simply happen. You have to want it. You have to become aware that humanity is asleep. You have to become aware that the events of daily life are a dream, a collective dream that most of humanity shares and unwittingly believes. So, you must choose to be different. You must choose to let go of restrictive and limiting beliefs. You must choose to create thoughts that lift you beyond the mire of negative human thoughts. You must choose to become creative with your own Being. You must choose to become awake. Becoming awake is to know who you are — to know your Greater Self. Humanity is struggling to awaken — or at least some of its members are. Some choose not to."

"Why do they choose that? You would have to be mad to choose to stay asleep."

"They make the choice by not choosing. They dream not knowing they sleep. The same problem afflicts the whole planet. Some tune into the new energies, some tune them out. That is their choice. Those who ridicule and scorn what they do not under-stand, what is unknown because it is new, will cling to the old."

"So what have I been chosen for? Correction: what have I chosen to do, and why?"

He chuckled, light flashing from his eyes.

"You have chosen to help the human consciousness awaken. You are but one among many. As a writer and speaker, you have adopted the perfect tools. And to you have been drawn those who long ago elected to help humanity awaken. You have very enlight-ened help."

A long-held suspicion came to the surface. "Treenie is part of that help, isn't she? I used to think she was a fallen angel. Without her, I would still be asleep."

"You are not yet awake, but you are in process and, yes, Treenie has chosen to help you. As for her being a fallen angel" — he looked thoughtful, hesitant — "she has not fallen."

4 Becoming Mineral

I had not seen Pan for nearly a month. Despite this, I tried to continue my relationship with Nature. I could connect with and listen to that inner voice of silence, but it was no longer as satisfying. Pan provided another dimension of Being. When I was with Pan, a keen throb of anticipation beat within me, for I never knew when the miraculous would unfold around me.

Treenie and I left home quite early one sunny morning to visit one of my favorite places, a great flat-topped pillar of rock towering high above surrounding forest in the New England National Park, only a couple of hours' drive from our sheltered valley.

We walked the track through dense, dripping rain forest until we reached the base of the plateau. From there, we followed the steep track to the summit. Below us, as far as the eye could see, lay forest. On the ridges it was sparse, open sclerophyll — dry, stiff-leafed — forest, while on the plunging slopes grew rain forest, lush and soft, reaching deep into the valleys. Each environment was clearly defined; together they appeared from above as a patchwork quilt of varied shades of green.

My eyes lingered on the gray rock face at our feet. It was jagged and crumbling, stark testimony to the erosive power of the wind, rain, and ice. Bird song, spires of thin, rich melody, ascended from the trees below. For once, I had a bird's-eye view onto gently swaying leaves. On this small, bleak, windswept plateau high above the surrounding forest grew hundreds of bonsai. Small and ancient sprawling shrubs clung with tenacious roots that had penetrated deep into ancient cracks and fissures. How different were the forest giants, so close in distance yet environmentally so far away. They have had little struggle in their efforts to grow. I wonder... where lies the greater strength?

"Penny for them!"

I glanced at Treenie, startled. It was so easy to get lost in the sheer grandeur of Nature in a place like this.

"I know you're planning to sit out here and attune with the plateau," she continued, "so I'm going to find somewhere sheltered where I can absorb the view." She gave my hand a quick squeeze and wandered away. The soft, eerie moan of the wind as it swept over the plateau had intensified, and clouds now filled the sky.

I sat on a low, uncomfortable shelf of rock buffeted by the unceasing wind. In front of me, a strange phenomenon unfolded. Pan slowly emerged from... nowhere! He appeared as a phantom, without substance. Hesitatingly, I reached out to touch him, and my fingers passed through his misty form. I felt very uncomfortable with this arrangement. His smile had no clear definition; even his eyes were vague, distant. "I wish you were a bit more solid. You seem too much like a ghost for comfort." My words were an intrusion.

"But you are the same!"

—

STARTLED, I HOLD OUT MY ARMS. Sure enough, they are no longer flesh and blood. I drop them onto my lap. I feel normal to my own touch but am as nebulous as Pan. Only then do I realize that we are slowly sinking through the solid rock. I look at Pan for reassurance.

"You have experienced the consciousness of water and of plant, all the while 'knowing' your humanness. Now you shall experience crystal, and you will 'know' your human connection within the kingdom of minerals. Deep within your psyche is hidden knowledge. You must connect with this." Questions surge in my mind, but the strange experience I am involved in is too immediate to be denied.

The sensation of sinking through rock becomes more pronounced. We seem to sink for a long time, yet the time is unmeasured. Around us, rock flows past with no more substance than a heavy gray cloud. At the end of the descent, I find that we are enclosed in a huge cavern, still seated on the shelf of rock. The darkness enclosing us is pierced and vaguely illuminated by countless flickering points of light. I get to my feet and glide across to the nearest wall of the cavern. Studded and dotted in the rock walls are millions of tiny jewels, flashing and sparkling with great intensity. Although the light they produce remains constant, the jewels shine in an ever-shifting iridescent pattern. The sight is breathtaking.

I brush my fingertips over many of the jewels, curious. Some are cold, some hot, but most are cool. None are loose; not one lies casually on the rock floor. Above me, around me, at my feet, each one is firmly embedded in the rock.

But where is Pan?

I listen to my own thoughts speaking to me, yet they are not my thoughts. Suddenly, I realize that this is telepathy! Inside my head, I hear Pan.

"There is a reason for you to be here. Find it."

Perplexed, I saunter around the cavern. It is very different from the huge chamber in the Guidestone. Movement is easy here. Even as I decide on a direction, I am moving along it. I examine the walls some more but can find no new or startling revelation.

"What sort of reason?"

I am ignored. This is a place of no-time. One part of me seems to wander around for ages, but in a greater sense time ends. Gradually, as I absorb the feel of the place, I gain the impression that I am seeing merely the tips of one huge crystal. Each separate jewel seems to be a single facet of one, while the bulk is hidden, shielded by impregnable rock.

"Good. Your perception is correct."

I can hear him, but I cannot see him. And I want to!

"Do you think you could become visible? This place is beginning to give me the creeps."

"I am here. Do not be afraid. Take notice of the flickering points of light. Can you imagine the One light? Each human being has the potential of the One, for each is the All. There is no separation between you humans, but what do you do? You each bury your individual light in negated thoughts, ignorance, complacency, and apathy, and through the ages these maladies have become solid as rock."

I feel acutely uncomfortable.

"And you are now firmly embedded. Only sparks emerge, glints of your submerged potential."

There is silence.

Then blazing, awesome, overwhelming light.

"*This* is the potential of being human."

Even as the words reach my mind, I am picked up by some vast, inexplicable force and hurled out into — nothing!

⌒

I SEEM TO BE FLOATING on my back, at ease. I can identify nothing around me, but I appear to be enclosed in a huge cocoon of light. I am at peace. Nothing disturbs me. I stay in this suspended state for a period of no-time. Gradually, I feel a very faint sense of urgency. It is tugging at me, drawing me from my undisturbed peace. I resent this, for the peace is beyond anything I have experienced. The urgency persists and unwillingly I sit up. It is a strange feeling, for I am suspended, floating, yet my body is without substance. At the far end of the cocoon, the light is dispersing and I can see through it. Before me appears a scene from three years ago, but as I watch, it is happening now. Irresistibly, I am drawn toward the end of the cocoon and precipitated into the unfolding scene.

—

"I'VE GOT SOMETHING TO SHOW YOU." Linda Tellington-Jones was excited as she hurried into her room. She was staying with Treenie and me for a few days during one of her regular visits from America. When she reappeared, she showed us a bluish green crystal about the size of a woman's fist. It was rather opaque, lacking the clarity of a Yang crystal or even the milkiness of the Yin. Peer at it as I might, I couldn't see within it.

"This is an aquamarine," she said fondly.

I wasn't at all a crystal person, but I felt duty bound to "oooh" and "aaah" over it, while Treenie appreciated its beauty in a more genuine way. Linda, in a typical display of enthusiasm, declared her intention to have it sliced in half. "One half for you, and the other half for me," she said, beaming at us.

Treenie looked dubious. "I wouldn't have it cut if it were mine," she said, concerned for the crystal and for Linda.

"I think it's a great idea," I said, concerned for neither.

Only a few hours later, we were at the Quartz Crystal Awareness Centre, where Ian MacArthur also considered the proposal with caution. "It may spoil it," he said. "It could be sliced easily enough, but we'd have to find the right place." He turned the crystal over and over, until he reached a decision. "Yes, it could be cut here." With his finger, he drew an imaginary line, inviting our comment.

"Be careful," said Treenie.

"Cut it, cut it," Linda cried excitedly.

"Are you sure it will be okay? We don't want to ruin it," I said, but in the next breath I urged him to cut it.

With some apprehension, Mac took the crystal into his work-room and sliced it into two halves.

It's important to explain that we are talking about a very valu-able gemstone. Mac had never even seen one of its size and quality. The deed was done and, though Linda was unrepentant, I felt slightly guilty. Mac showed us the revealed interior under a strong light.

Wow! It was a crystal transformed. I could see myriad tiny spires of light stretching from the outer surface into the marine depths at the center. Light caught and held the needle spires, coat-ing their lengths in rainbow colors. I was hooked by the beauty and mystery of the rock's interior.

Not long after Linda returned to the States, I laid our half of the aquamarine on my desk and opened up a conversation with it — at least I tried! But no matter how I focused on that elusive energy, nothing came to me from it, not a single whisper.

A year passed, and the crystal remained mute. But one day while I was gazing into the aquamarine's window, watching the play of light on those tiny threads of inner space, it entered my mind to take the gemstone to the ocean and place it in a rock pool. So, one sunny morning in midwinter, I took the stone to a particular rocky headland where there was a group of large rock pools. The tide was right. Everything was perfect.

As I walked along the beach carrying the crystal, a small group of rocks caught my eye. In the hollow center of one rock was a small pool, containing no more than a bucketful of water. When I had walked a hundred yards farther along the beach, clearly into my mind came the words, "That is my pool!"

"Aha!" I muttered. "Mute no more!"

I trudged back across the white, crystalline sand to the little pool and placed the aquamarine in the water. When I had settled myself on an adjoining rock, a feeling of well-being came over me, and I knew its source was the gemstone shimmering in the pool. Within moments, an incoming wave sent a sheet of clean ocean water into the little rock pool. I gazed at the crystal, which was caught in a shaft of diluted sunlight. A thousand rainbows formed and vanished in its interior.

"Do you hear me now?"

"Oh, yes," I replied. "Very clearly."

"Long have I known your consciousness, but to intrude was . . . untimely!"

"But why? I have wanted to hear you. I can appreciate that you must be an incredible storehouse of knowledge culled from vast spans of time."

"This I acknowledge, yet you still need to release your hostility to crystal energy. This is strong within you."

I thought about that and decided it was not true. "No," I protested. "Not hostile, just indifferent."

"You think so. Look into the depths of the crystal and see what you see."

I gazed down at the crystal. Swirling water and sand flecked its surface, and it looked rather mundane. But as I lifted my eyes and glanced out over the ocean, another seeing emerged, an inner seeing into another reality.

———

I SEE MYSELF, even though I am in an unfamiliar body, inhumanly tall and lean and in a very different landscape. It is early morning, well before the rising of the sun. The era, I sense, is long past, compared with the time I call our own. I stand alone in a small valley, an amazing valley! The mountains around me are crystal; sheer brilliant spires emerge from a white, solid base. No human eyes have ever seen the like. This is a place of dreams, a place both alien and hauntingly familiar.

I know that I am about to die, yet this is my choice, a choice made in the name of science. I am conducting an experiment, an attempt to transfer my psyche beyond my body. To what destination? I do not know. I cannot reach deeply enough into this other me to learn it.

I am aware that my loved ones are watching from a shielded place within the crystal mountains, and I am aware, too, of my own immense sadness, combined with a will and a desire to live. The act I am undertaking is not a casual one. It is the result of long and detailed studies. Many experiments have been carried out, but this is the ultimate moment. Only now may I know, and only I can be subjected to this devastating, one-way experiment. I am very old, having lived far, far beyond a human life span, and am filled with a boundless, inhuman knowledge. I have no fear whatsoever. I experience curiosity, regret, and, strangely, exultation.

As I stand in the valley, a huge alien sun rises above the crystal mountain as though part of a smooth, clockwork motion. The sun is much larger, much closer, than our own. Light reflects back and forth along the blazing spires in shafts of great intensity. Despite the double lids on my eyes, I am instantly blinded. I am unable to see the sunlight when its awesome energy is focused on one huge central crystal spire, and I feel nothing as the light blazes through me. As though hit by a colossal fist of wind, I am hurled inward, then outward, then into... nothing!

I am back in the safe, serene comfort of the cocoon of light. I am floating on my back, at peace, yet the memory of all that has taken place is with me. There is no anxiety. Everything that has happened fits into a sequence of my life that in this state of suspension feels perfectly natural. I am aware of being nourished, of being protected from immediate shock while I assimilate the events that have unfolded. There is a period of no-time. I know that I am the human me *and* that other, alien self! In my memory, the blazing light of the exposed crystal and the terrible blinding light of the alien sun mix and merge. There is no separation. No time has elapsed. Both are happening... now! I am shocked and exhilarated. I know both my selves, even though the alien self is unavailable. I cannot tap my alien knowledge or look at my alien thoughts. I have learned that time is not a constant factor but part of the human construct. The voice that whispers as a distant echo in my head is comfortingly familiar.

"So much of human roots are in the endless past, yet not the past of the time span most humans live within. Reality is flexible, timeless, limitless, unbordered, but the human concept of reality is strictly limited. For your species, it is conditioned and bordered by your belief in separation. This isolates each one of you. The past you briefly experienced in the crystal valley was you of another reality, a reality that in its past coexists with your present."

"But why, Pan? Why? And what happened to that alien me?"

"What happened to that distant you connects with you now, but the experiment and its results are not this moment's conjecture. You will experience that experiment again, and at that time you will be ripe to enter and experience just what did happen. You are not ready yet."

"Where was I, Pan? *Who* was I?"

The whisper becomes very faint. "Questions, always questions. Question not who you were but who you are, for in the journey you have undertaken, this is the paramount question. If you lose your self, how are you to find it again if you do not know who you are?" His words are fading, and in direct proportion the cocoon of light is also gradually fading away. The irrational thought that I might fall from this state of suspension crosses my mind, and a shout gathers in my chest.

⸻

My voice, loud and startling, made me jump as I shouted into the wind.

I was still sitting on the shelf of rock on the plateau in the bonsai forest, my heart hammering away like a sledgehammer. I took a few deep, steadying breaths. I no longer enjoyed the protection of the cocoon of light, and my mind was a spinning chaos of images from the multiple time frames. I tried to slow my mind and put it all in careful order.

The experience had begun exactly where I was sitting. First, there had been the sensation of sinking down through the solid rock with Pan; then we had emerged into the huge crystal. There Pan had shown me that all the many flickering points of light were *one* light. As I experienced this, Pan had shown me the vast power of that one light — and I had literally been blown away! My next awareness was of being suspended in a cocoon of light, safe and protected. Where this cocoon was I had no idea, but I suspect it was somewhere between dimensions, in a place of no-time. After an indeterminate time in this cocoon, I had seen myself of three years ago involved in a clearly remembered incident with the aquamarine. Next thing I knew, I was out of the cocoon and into that past, but living it as though it were now! I had taken the aquamarine to the beach and placed it in a rock pool. The aquamarine had told me I was hostile to crystal energy. After a short interaction, I had had an incredible vision — of myself as another type of Being on another planet standing within a crystal valley. I had been conducting some sort of experiment in psyche transference. The sun had risen, and a shaft of light of unbelievable power and intensity had totally disintegrated the body of that other me. The experiment had been successful, for the psyche had survived and had been hurled out into other dimensions and realities. I paused in my thoughts.

It was only now that I realized this, yet I *knew* it to be true. Immediately after experiencing the blast of light from the sun, I was back in the cocoon of light. For a while — I have no idea how long — I was nurtured. I needed to be cared for in that way! Then, faintly, I heard Pan's telepathic words. As his voice faded away, I had felt that I might fall. My shout had brought me back to an earthly, three-dimensional reality where time ticked away to the beat of a watch on my wrist.

As though to prove that I was back, Treenie came to where I was sitting on the rock ledge. "You've been sitting here for nearly an hour and a half. It's time you had your lunch. I've had mine." Then, seeing my face, she asked, "What happened?"

I looked at her helplessly. "I think I've put it together in my head, but I really can't talk about it yet. I feel numb."

She nodded sympathetically. "Are you all right?" she asked anxiously.

I nodded. "I'm okay. I'll have my lunch up here. Then I'll come. There's plenty of time." I smiled at my unintended pun. Treenie pointed to the clouds. "Don't get wet."

I watched her as she walked away, aware of the feeling of warmth and love that connected us. Within that love, I knew, flowed the endless thread that connects all life.

I ate my lunch sitting on the sheer edge of the plateau, over-looking the forest. A strong wind buffeted me, whipping my hair with playful indifference, and I began to feel refreshed and more clearheaded. The images no longer jostled each other in my mind, but the feeling of numbness continued. It was not a physical thing, but rather as though something was smothering and damp-ening the intensity of my feelings.

My reverie ended abruptly when a few drops of rain, driven by a fierce wind, stung my face. Treenie was right. Time to go!

I followed the track across the plateau and down the tumbled, jumbled pile of huge rocks to the forest floor. In this calm and sheltered place, the rain was negligible, and as I followed the track homewards I tried to quiet my mind by concentrating on the nat-ural abundance around me.

Away from the track, the dense forest was almost impene-trable. This was a place of rare and startling beauty, where a thousand different species of plants competed for the diffused sunlight that filtered through the leafy tops of restless trees. And what trees! Host to an incredible variety of vivid mosses, lacy ferns, gray and yellow lichens, and strange liverworts, the tree trunks were almost buried in clinging vegetation. My thoughts returned to my experience on the plateau, and I wondered where Pan had gone — and when.

"It is not I who withdraw from you. It is you who become

unaware of me." Pan's words seemed to echo around me, but I could see nothing of him.

"Where are you?"

"I am within the forest. Everywhere you look, I am." I shrugged, not ready for more lessons. His voice, when it came again, was strong and stable, but he was still invisible.

"Relate to me as though I am all the trees around you. You do not need my form right now."

There was a long pause. "Michael...give me a summary of your experience. Not what happened to you, but what it meant to you. Tell me what you learned and what you feel."

I felt vexed! "You know what I think and feel. What's the point?"

"Yes, I do. And I can also feel the numbness and shock you are experiencing now that you are back in the physical realm. I want to hear you express your feelings and thoughts verbally. I want you to hear yourself."

I knew he was proposing therapy. It did seem appropriate and he was certainly the right person — person? — to listen to me. To my surprise, my words came tumbling out. "I learned that the human view of reality is little short of pathetic. Our normal reality is like each of us living in a tiny, windowless cell in a house that contains a hundred thousand rooms and covers a thousand acres of land. We believe that the cell is all there is, so we live in it isolated and alone. What is even sadder is that if a few people like me manage to tunnel out of their cells and see some of the other rooms awaiting entry, the majority of people think we are imagining things." I paused for a moment. "Not only do I think that, I also feel it."

Pan's voice was a soothing caress. "You seem hurt."

"Yes. Somewhat to my surprise, I am."

"Why?"

"Because in some way the strangeness of my experience separates me from other people — not in reality, but in knowledge and experience."

"That's easily rectified."

In a flash of clarity, I understood. I could write a book about my experiences, just as I had written the earlier book about talking with Nature. It had taken a measure of courage to write that book and expose my soul, but this one would be much harder. Still, I knew I could share my experiences with honesty and clarity. The rest was up to the individual reader. Knowing this, I felt better.

"Anything else?"

"Yes. I learned I was hostile to crystal energy. I suspect that the experience with the alien me was to show me why. Also, I'm aware that there is a lot of unfinished business regarding that other me, but I feel comfortable with that. Everything has its timing." I grinned. "You taught me that. I understand what the heart of the plateau crystal had to teach me. It told of our need to learn that humanity *really* is one family. We really *are* all brothers and sisters. In fact, in consciousness we are even closer. I learned that time and space form only a three-dimensional reality, and that it is possible to allow the psyche to expand and journey into other realities, other times. I also learned that I have a lot to learn!"

I waited for Pan to respond, but only the whispering of countless leaves answered me.

I continued on down the track toward the waiting car — and Treenie.

5 Becoming Animal

reenie and I had been idling away the morning, chatting over a few cups of coffee before she left for a few hours. For some unknown reason, I felt apprehensive as I watched the car accelerating up the road. Dismissing the feeling, I returned to our sitting room.

Ever able to surprise me, Pan was sitting cross-legged on the carpet in the middle of the room. His curious eyes held me in an appraising and serious gaze.

"Sit down and relax."

His words were not an invitation; they were a command. I sat down.

"Make sure you are comfortable."

I swallowed nervously. "What's going on?"

"Relax."

It made me more tense to hear Pan tell me to relax in such a serious tone. "I knew it. Something nasty is going to happen, isn't it?"

Pan smiled and, almost against my will, my anxieties dissolved. I resented his easy control over me, but my reasoning part quickly became unreachable.

"That's better. I look serious, I know, but there is no cause for alarm."

I took a deep breath. "I've been apprehensive for the last hour. I don't know what you have planned for me, but I bet it's the cause of this feeling."

He smiled that irresistible smile — sunshine breaking through clouds that had lain heavy for weeks.

"It is time for you to make another connection. The Door to Beyond beckons. In your quest for self-realization, you must connect with the kingdom of animals. Humans are not animals, even though you classify yourselves as such. Humans are a different form of Being. Humanity contains the consciousness of animals, just as you still contain the consciousness of the vegetable and mineral kingdoms. You, Michael, have connected with the consciousness of the plant and mineral kingdoms and with water in its many forms as it covers and penetrates this world."

I was pensive. "I seem to be involved in a process of experiencing Oneness — to actualize and become *one with* Nature, going beyond words and ideas." The connection of words suddenly became apparent. "Is that what going Beyond is? Is it going beyond all words and ideas? Is it in fact going beyond the limitations of the mind?" I felt excited.

Pan's eyes flashed approval. "As near as it can be verbalized, that is what going Beyond means. However, Beyond is a reality. It encompasses this time frame and more. Now, let's get started."

I felt apprehensive. "Wait...wait a minute." One of Pan's pencil-thin eyebrows arched inquiringly.

"Do I get to choose which animal I experience?"

"Oh, yes. That is absolutely essential."

Thoughts of cheetahs and other of my favorite animals crossed my mind. Then a terrible thought popped in, uninvited. "I won't be killed or eaten, will I?"

"Is that in your experience of animals?"

I thought about it, a bit uncertain. "No. Not that I know of."
I had a terrible feeling that something was being overlooked, but
what?

"Then *go*."

There was no gentle shaking, no easing out of the body. His
words were a vibrant force within me, hurling me out
into . . . nothing!

———

I AM A CATTLE DOG, a puppy. Everything is a mystery to be
gnawed on and played with. I understand little. I live in the eternal moment, and within that I have fun. I have a companion my
own age, and all day we play, sleep, eat, and play some more. We
fight mock battles, and in our play we grow stronger and more
coordinated.

There are other cattle dogs on the farm, two mature grown
dogs who regard us with amused tolerance. Together, my friend
and I grow beyond puppyhood, becoming aware of a strange craving within us.

One day, our master comes to us and puts us in a big vehicle.
He takes us on a long, bumpy, smelly journey. It excites me. I have
never smelled such smells; the wind is full of them. In my excitement, I lose control of my bladder, but my master only laughs.
When we stop, he takes us out. We are restrained by a chain
attached to our collars. He talks for a while to another man and
then departs without us. I am devastated.

Next morning, the other man feeds us, takes us to a large, airy
barn, and introduces us to some other puppies and grown dogs.
Each day he takes us out into the fields, and with shouted instructions and help from the adult dogs, he teaches us how to round up
and drive cattle. They are stupid creatures, nowhere near as clever
as I, but there is a lot to learn. I find out the hard way that a single
cow and calf are not the same as a herd. I approach a cow and her

calf, and she charges me. I am surprised when one of her horns catches me. Luckily, I am only bruised. It is a good lesson.

Time comes and goes, but for me there is only the joy of working with cattle. I no longer have the strange craving. I am totally satisfied by my work. The man is very pleased with me. He pats me often, calling me a smart dog. One day, my master comes to take me home again. My companion does not come back with us. He stays on the farm and is contented. He does not love my master in the way I do. He would accept anybody.

I am now a large, strong cattle dog. Master has names for us. I am called Spud, and my eyes are odd colored. I have white eyes, and my master tells me how unusual this is. The other dogs are Ringo and Bounce. I like them. One day when master shouts the familiar instructions to us, Bounce does not come home. We all run to get around the cattle, but Bounce keeps going. We never see him again.

Master has a lot of cattle, and as the years pass I want nothing more than to work them. Often there are strange urges in my body, and I dream of desirable female dogs. Sometimes these dreams are so strong that when I wake up I run around restlessly looking for the female, but the lack of scent tells me I have only been dreaming. Once, a female does visit the farm, riding on the back of an open vehicle. Her odors are very exciting, and I want to couple with her, but I cannot get off the chain, even though I struggle. I am very upset by this and take my anger out on Ringo. I am bigger and stronger than he is now. We have a fight, and I am top dog.

Several years pass, and then something devastating happens. Our master no longer milks cows in the dairy near my kennel, and we have no work to do. The master takes us out into a paddock, securing our chains to a long wire pegged down at ground level. We have plenty of space to exercise but seldom any cows to work.

And something else happens. The master has been changing over the years. I can see it in his energy. I can read his intent as easily as I can read a cow. It radiates from him. He has been linking his consciousness with his beef cattle. Now, when he wants them moved, instead of using Ringo and me, he communicates into their consciousness, and they leave the paddock where they are and go wherever he wants them to go. I am very upset.

As dog, I begin to experience frustration. A growing, gnawing emptiness fills me, and I become angry. I growl and snarl at Ringo, for he is the only available outlet for my anger. He becomes the focus for my frustration and rage. As the months pass, instead of easing, my anger becomes worse. Ringo accepts the situation with the cattle, but I cannot. I become more morose, more vicious.

Our long wire runs are too far apart for us to tangle chains but near enough for us to drink from the same water bowl and touch noses. One day, when I am feeling particularly angry, I hurl myself against the chain — and it breaks. Ringo barks at me, telling me not to be foolish, and in red rage I attack him. I can feel a blinding red heat behind my eyes, and I am filled with the urge to tear and render. How it happens I do not know, but I kill him.

When it is over, I slink into my kennel. As the heat and rage leave me, I know I have behaved very badly.

Once more, I am duality. As a human, I approach the odd, distorted body of Ringo. In the pit of my stomach, I feel despair. Kneeling down, I hold his stiffening body in my arms. His stomach has been ripped open, his vital organs bitten to pulp. I look at Spud, knowing the inevitable. I chain him up, holding his head in my hands. I am not angry, but sadness is a heavy weight as I realize what I must do. With four young children, I cannot risk keeping a jealous dog. I assume that Spud has killed Ringo from jealousy, for I know how attached he is to me.

I watch my master walk away. I know he is going to kill me. I have seen him shoot other animals. The energy around his body is heavy, filled with sadness. I live only in the moment, so I do not fret. There is only now, and right now I live.

When he comes back, he is carrying a gun. He is very upset. I wag my tail furiously. I am not afraid, even though I know my death is here. I need to work cattle, not live on a chain. I want to run free, chasing on the heels of huge herds of cattle. A dull thud smashes my head to the ground, an explosion of light, and I am up and running, free as the wind. In countless other cattle dogs, I feel my consciousness working and fulfilled. I am Ringo. I am Bounce. I am Spud. I am All in One, One in All. I am dog, all dogs.

I am crying as I aim between Spud's strange white eyes and squeeze the trigger. He drops soundlessly, boneless. Falling to my knees, I hold his head in my hands, my body shaking with sobs. Guilt coils and writhes within me. Regrets for things that could have been overwhelm me. I bury Spud with a heavy heart. My feelings of having acted to protect my children are inadequate, and I feel a failure.

I am consciousness, floating in the ethers of our planetary system. I am assimilating the experience of being dog and man as One. As a dog owner, I have failed, and my guilt is a pain. I know now that I shot Spud for the wrong reason. As the psyche of Spud, I know he would never have harmed any of my children. He had not been jealous. He was born to work, and work was denied him. I know that he holds no anger toward me. He is free, united with all dogs. I am that unity also. But I am human, and I find it difficult to forgive myself! Nowhere in my dog reality is there blame or anger, only love. As dog, I become aware of the burden of guilt that humans carry, and I try to love it away.

Gradually, awareness withdraws from separate aspects of the dual psyche, and I become myself sitting in a chair in my sitting room.

—

I LOWERED MY HEAD and cried, all the suppressed pain erupting in a torrent of tears when the deeply hidden guilt finally came to the surface, as in a long-festering wound. And I felt rage. How dare Pan trick me like that! He had known I was going to experience something awful. Why hadn't he told me what to expect? Why hadn't he even hinted that I should be prepared. Without doubt, he had known what awaited me. I cried for a long time, tears coming to the surface from some deep source. When I noticed that Pan was back in the room looking at me, I ignored the compassion and love in his eyes.

"You tricked me!" I spoke with controlled vehemence.

"Michael, I love you. Why would I trick you? It was you who determined where in the Nature of animals you would go. You, yourself, connected with your unfinished business. What is unresolved in the past remains unresolved in the present."

"Why didn't you at least warn me? That was a horrendous experience! I suffered from both my human and dog aspects. I loved and died, and killed both dogs — one I tore to death, the other I shot. Do you wonder I feel betrayed? How could you let that happen to me?"

Despite my anger, I knew he had been right — I *had* made the choice. I had felt misgivings when he told me I would choose my own experience. His next words were very unwelcome.

"I am sorry, but it is not yet ended. You had the opportunity to let go of all your guilt feelings concerning your connection with animals, but those feelings continue to fester within you. If I *had* warned you of what to expect, you would have *expected* the experience and therefore rendered it totally valueless. As it is, you can now see the emotional chaos you have been suppressing regarding your role as a dog owner. You must deal with those feelings or there can be no further progress."

Fists clenched, I felt my anger flare. "That suits me fine. I've had enough of this anyway. I got shot out there. I felt it in my consciousness. I got killed. I died — even though I'm not dead."

"And do you remember the feelings within your animal consciousness toward your human self? Do you remember the love that dog felt for you? You were the dog that loved and you were the human with guilt. Why do you cling to the guilt and deny the love? Why are love and peace more difficult to embrace than pain and discord?"

I knew I had become irrational, but I could not stop myself. All I wanted to do was lash out and hurt. "It's easy for you to talk. It wasn't you out there being shot or feeling guilty as hell. I seem to suffer no matter which side I'm on." Lost in anger and confused emotions, I jumped to my feet and stalked out of the room, dismissing Pan.

—

A MONTH PASSED BY and I saw nothing of Pan. Once I had recovered, I realized how silly I had been. He was right. He always was! I told Treenie the whole story. I shared with her all that had happened during my experience as the consciousness of dog and of my angry reaction to Pan immediately afterwards. With her help, I explored my feelings. I knew the experience had not ended. Somewhere out there — in there? — I had to connect with an essence of myself, or of life, that I did not yet comprehend. I had to deal with my guilt. Pan had made this clear and I realized that until I resolved my guilt feelings I could make no further progress in my quest for self-realization. How strange that my relationship with a dog should be the stumbling block. With all my human lives and my multitude of experiences, I had no feelings of guilt that I was aware of. I may well have lied, cheated, slain others in battle, and maybe even committed murder in my various incarnations on Earth, but I felt no guilt. Maybe I had worked it all out, leaving the slate clean. I hoped so! But with the animal connection, I carried this guilt.

With Treenie listening sympathetically, I recounted some of my memories of Spud. During our decade as farmers in Tasmania, cattle dogs had been essential to the easy and efficient movement of the cattle. Spud had been outstanding as a working dog. In keeping with the farmers' tradition, I had not allowed the working dogs to become household pets, but nevertheless I had become very attached to them.

I sighed at the thought of all the changes I would have made had I experienced dog consciousness then. Both Ringo and Spud

had excelled in their skills. I could send them to the farthest paddocks, a mile away, to bring the cows home. I used to boast that
the only thing they could not do was open and close the gates!

The problem began after we finished milking. At this stage, I
no longer needed the dogs to work. To make matters worse, I had
been practicing communicating with our cattle by "thinking"
them to where I wanted them to go, all in accordance with the
inner consciousness of the cattle. This effort had been so successful it had made the cattle dogs practically redundant, so I stopped
using them and put them on long running chains so they could
get plenty of exercise.

"Should I have sold them?" I asked Treenie.

"What do *you* think?" she parried.

"It wouldn't have made any difference." Even as I spoke, I
knew my answer was true. The guilt had merely been brought to
the surface by my experience of shooting Spud. Somewhere in my
past lay other painful encounters.

The sharing and exploration of my feelings helped me understand that I still had work to do, but I continued to feel frustrated
about my reactions to Pan.

"Be patient, my darling," suggested Treenie. "Pan won't desert
you. Allow yourself to remember the actual experience of being
dog. Write it down. Maybe you will learn something that Pan is
waiting for you to learn."

I recaptured in memory the love I had felt as Spud. Even
death had made no difference. Going through the transition from
physical, individual dog to dog spirit had been without trauma. As
dog, I had not clung to the act or the moment of dying. I had
remained dog, loving and generous.

Only in my human self had pettiness been present and, worst
of all, I had directed it at Pan . . . and myself! Perhaps I needed to
learn to treat myself with greater love and respect!

I was concerned that I had driven Pan away forever. "What
should I do?" I asked Treenie. We were having breakfast and the
thought of another day without Pan was disturbing.

"Why don't you apologize to him?"

I stared at her in indignation. "If I could do that, I wouldn't have the problem, would I?"

Treenie is ever patient. "You have told me that Pan is in all Nature. He is in the trees and in the river. Why don't you go down to your favorite place by the river and simply apologize aloud."

"That's a brilliant idea." I smiled in approval, then I frowned. A question that had often niggled me came to the surface of my mind. "Do you resent me having this relationship with Pan? Do you ever feel jealous . . . or threatened?"

Treenie gave me a level look of appraisal. "At the beginning of it all, I thought I might," she said candidly, "but not anymore. I'm your physical and spiritual partner. We are soul mates. So why should I feel threatened by a Being who shares only your meta-physical life? That he is for your ultimate good and inner growth, I don't doubt. I can't resent that. Besides, you spent years attuning with Nature on the farm and then a few more years of more concentrated attunement down by the river. If Nature responds by revealing that there is a mystic dimension to all that only appears physical, and a teacher comes from that other dimension, should I object? It seems to me that you have earned the right to encounter a Being like Pan."

I kissed her!

Later that morning, I went down to the river. Standing on the end of the diving board, I called out. "I don't know if you can hear me Pan, but I apologize. I was overemotional and rude. I'm sorry. I want you back in my life. I miss you."

Two strong hands held me briefly around the middle — and then pushed. I hit the water with the sound of wind chimes ringing in my ears. Surprise! They continued chiming while I swam underwater! I came up laughing.

Together, we sat on the old bridge board. I gazed at his faery beauty with deep appreciation, while his golden eyes regarded me with amusement and affection.

"Nothing has changed, you realize." There was concern in his voice.

"I'll do what I have to do. I guess it's a case of either trust you or quit. And I know I couldn't quit!"

"You have to go back into the experiences of your own connections with animals. It may be rough, but there is no other way. Your path to Beyond requires that you journey into the consciousness of Nature. You must experience Nature's metaphysical perspective and accept it. You must learn to let go of emotional attachments, becoming as free and unencumbered as the breeze." He laughed. "That's all!"

I swallowed in apprehension. "As you probably know, I had another really bad episode with a dog. I had to shoot my much loved Great Dane, Whisky. She was ailing with a cancer. I chose to shoot her rather than call in a vet. Now I wish I hadn't." My eyes misted over at the memory. "When I recall her life, there are so many things I could have done better."

This time, I could see the compassion in Pan's eyes.

"Don't you feel in retrospect that you could have done many things better? Relating to people, for example?"

"Oh yes, I do, but I don't feel guilty about that."

"Why?"

I sat for a while thinking it over. "I think it's because I view people as being responsible for themselves and for their own actions, but domestic animals are the responsibilities of their owner, as is their behavior."

I felt comfortable realizing this, and for a while there was silence as we watched the river sweep past with soft, hesitant gurgles.

"Pan. Do I have to experience the Whisky trauma?"

His voice was level, calming. "Only you can decide. If it is resolved within you, then it is finished; if not..."

"If not, then I'll find it all happening again." I winced at the thought. "And there's nothing I can do to prevent it. What a prospect."

I felt shaky. "Will you be with me when I journey out?"

"Yes, but as Spirit. I cannot help you. I cannot change anything. You are totally responsible. You determine whether you will suffer or not. You are the experience."

"I wonder that you still have patience with me. I have failed in my reconnection with Spud, and I know I'll fail if I relive Whisky's life."

"What nonsense you talk. Failure and success are illusions. As long as you measure yourself in terms of success or failure, you will remain unenlightened."

I thought about that, trying to find a way to rephrase my words. "Well, I didn't succeed with Spud, did I?"

He laughed. "Nor did you fail!"

"Didn't I?"

"You experienced an inner connection. You made a connection with the consciousness of dog, and your emotions were too deeply involved for you to perceive with clarity and insight. You are too harsh on yourself. Acknowledge your capacity and merits. How many people do you think could make such reconnections and come out unscathed?"

That was a line of speculation I had never considered.

"Only you judge yourself," he went on. "Nothing else in life does this except humans. Humans judge themselves and each other. Give it up. You don't need it. Judgment is an unnecessary burden. Did Spud judge you and find you guilty, or was it you who made that judgment? Believe me, Nature makes no judgments."

I knew Spud hadn't. That had been particularly obvious.

Pan moved over to the bank, and I followed. I sat down beside him.

"Are you ready?"

"Oh! No!"

"Good."

For an eternity I encircle the planet. It all seems familiar, a planet I have visited many times. Slowly, without any sense of time, my consciousness becomes more solid, taking on form. In many, many separate bodies, I roam the Earth, but gradually my focus becomes one single animal. I am a dog. I experience my self as separate, yet my awareness of connecting with the All is ever present. There is only Now. Thoughts of soon or late are nonexistent. Within the Now, beyond any need of thought, I am connected. I am a large dog, a Great Dane, and I live on a farm in the foothills of Mount Arthur in Tasmania.

I experience my years of puppyhood by eternally playing with the children who live on the farm. I live in the house with the family, spending the winter evenings on a rug before a blazing fire. I am loved, and that love is part of my connection with life. I need love; I thrive on it. To be stroked and patted is rapture. The vibration of my owners' Being is transmitted by touch. Their love is as vital to my well-being as food.

When I am full grown, something dreadful happens. I am dismissed from the house! I no longer sleep on the rug before the fire. I feel that I am shamed, but no punishment for misdeed is inflicted. Nobody tells me why I am banned from the house and garden, but it happens.

I am given a new bed in the soft hay in the hay barn. I lack nothing in comfort, and if the evenings are more chilly it does not greatly concern me. What festers within me is the lack of stroking and touching on which I thrive. But I cannot reflect on such matters. I live what is. If something is missing, it is missing for all time.

I grow older, less capable, while the children of the farm become stronger and more capable. My special attention is always focused on the master of the farm. A look of love from him lights me up; a frown of anger devastates me. That he loves me is apparent. I can read his energy as easily as I can read any human energy. Humans are an open book. Emotions play out in streams of energy around them, signaling their intentions long before they act. Sometimes, visitors to the farm are deeply repulsive to me, but this is rare. Many fear me because of my size, but fear is their constant companion; I only externalize it. This I know, because in the Now their energy broadcasts their feelings to all Nature. Humans cause me fear and pain, love and joy. A fearful human is fear, transmitting the emotion to me and the other dogs. We snarl in rage, hating the vibration, and the fear grows stronger.

Love is my life. To love and be loved is my purpose, and I know this with every atom of my Being.

The disquiet I feel at being removed from the house is never in my head, but it is *me*. I become that energy. The ruling never has to be enforced. Once removed, I know the rule but never why. I am never tied up. I have freedom. The whole farm is mine to roam, but the house and garden are banned.

As I grow older, an ache develops in one of my front legs. Gradually, it becomes a deep-seated pain, not intense but an endless throbbing. I limp, and this is difficult on my long, rather clumsy legs.

I ail, moving less and less frequently from my snug bed in the hay barn. I see less of the children, and this also becomes a pain. I see far less of my master as well, for his work consumes his time. Only when he feeds me do we physically connect. I deteriorate rapidly in health and condition. One day, my master comes to me, and I know he carries my death. The distress emanating from him is terrible, and my fear for him is paramount.

Suddenly, there is duality. I am dog, suffering from a growth in my leg, and I am master, crying as I hide my gun behind me.

He wraps his arms around my neck, and I feel him shaking in anguish. And I am my master, as, wrapping my arms around Whisky, I cry with what I have to do.

I watch, unresisting, as he levels the gun at me. I know it kills, for I have seen it in action. I know he is going to kill me, but I have no fear. I have no knowledge of death. I am dog. I live, I love, I bark, I die. None of these are separate.

I am the man, shaking with contained grief as I take aim between the eyes of the trusting dog. I see those limpid eyes of devotion gazing into mine, and I can hardly hold steady. Taking a deep breath, I squeeze the trigger.

I gaze into those blue human eyes, and my love pours forth. Abruptly, there is a tremendous shock to my head followed by a far distant explosion. I am no longer in pain, no longer contained by an ungainly body. I am light, free, spirit of dog, loving my human master. I gaze at him as he holds the bloodied head of my dead body. I try to lick the tears from his face. I want him to know that I bear no grudge, but he is unaware of me. I want him to know that I love him, that death is only a movement in life, one I have experienced many, many times. But all he feels is grief... and something else.

I hold the shattered head of Whisky and let the grief pour out of me. My thoughts hold only one phrase: if only, if only! If only I had let her live her life in the house with us. Why did I allow such petty issues to change things? So she knocked the children over with her great size. So what? Did they ever complain? So she left a large pool of saliva on the lounge floor where she slept! How trivial it now seems. I cry, cradling her head in my arms, her blood mingling with my tears. And I feel the guilt of my failure. As a dog owner, I have failed, and my guilt is a pain.

THE CONSCIOUSNESS of dog self and human self merge. As human, I become aware of being Whisky and all I can feel is an overwhelming love for my human self. I become aware of having experienced this connection to resolve all the guilt that has accumulated in my human psyche. I try so hard to let it go... and I open my eyes, staring tearfully up at the sky.

The words of Pan come to me as soon as I open my eyes, soothing, yet powerful. "Let it go, Michael. Focus on the love of

Whisky and the love of Spud. That love is *now*, Michael, not some time in the past. Focus on love... and *go*."

———

I AM HURLED OUT of my physical body with immense energy. The soundless blast of power, though enormous, is totally pain-less. I spin over and over, my mind empty. Space fills my consciousness forever and nothing exists. No form holds me, no physical entity attracts me, and for eternity I am nothing. I am Beingness.

Gradually, with incredible slowness, my consciousness focuses. I run, swift as the wind, over the Earth. I am pure nerv-ous energy in physical form, but I live in exhilaration! I am hare. No, not *a* hare, but *all* hares. When danger threatens, instinct draws forth the required behavior. I become immobile, perfectly camouflaged and blending into the Earth. Or I run, racing over the soil with abundant vitality.

Nothing exists but Now. I live, mate, fight — and die — without a care or worry. Life is exuberance, an endless overflowing cycle of dynamic tension. I fight with other buck hares, experience the breathtaking delight of mating with the does, and as a doe I watch in keen pleasure as other bucks fight for the right to mate with me.

In a cycle of seasons, the fields on which I live are sown by the farmers; they change from bare earth to green oceans of food and then to golden corn. Here I live, safe and secure on a thousand farms. I live also in meadows and wild land, untamed by man, but my focus becomes a number of hares on a particular farm in Eng-land. Each year, huge machines devour the yellow corn in which we live, and each year comes the terror.

I am a young man, riding the combine harvester as it circles the field of ripe, golden wheat again and again. I am excited, for the field is full of hares. Each time I circle the field, it becomes smaller. Now, hares are beginning to rush out, ears laid back as they run for their lives. I pick up the shotgun and with easy familiarity swing it snugly into my shoulder. I fire, and a hare pitches head over heels, screaming its pain and agony. I fire again and again as the hares run the gauntlet for their freedom. I am proud of my ability to shoot.

I am hares, ears back, running in terror from the approaching monster. I comprehend nothing. All is fear... and running. I have no knowledge of what to expect. I run. In a dozen hares, I run like the wind, and pain and oblivion smash into me. Yet I run, leaving behind the struggling forms as they kick out their abundant nervous energy. I am long gone, no longer physically limited as I race across the Earth. I am free. I run from shattered bodies and have no knowledge of death. It has no reality. As *all* hares, I am on the physical Earth, but I also roam the ethers and their etheric structures. There is no difference, no separation.

I am human, I am hare. Our consciousness mixes and merges. I know that as a human I carry the consciousness of all hares within me. Nature and humanity express the same consciousness of One. We are linked, irrevocably. I feel no guilt at my actions as a young man. I knew no better. Hare is hare and I was me.

I am consciousness, a thread connecting all living creatures on Earth. I am briar. I am rock, alive and vital. I am cloud, drifting on the high winds of consciousness. I am cattle dog, living on a farm in Tasmania, and I am Great Dane, loving my master. I am hare, running fleet of foot. I am bird, singing on a branch in a garden. Winter is ended, spring is here, and I sing with the joy of life.

I am a small boy, creeping down to the garden with a brand-new slug gun. I am excited, a great hunter. I see a robin, high in the branches of a tree. I stalk the bird, oblivious to the beauty of its song. Quivering with excitement, I raise the gun to take my first shot at a living creature. I pull the trigger.

In the middle of my song, I am struck in the throat. I fall to the ground, but even before my physical being has landed, I am free, flying to a tree of shimmering light to finish my song of joy.

My joy is even greater now, for here there is no fear. I am *all* robins. I am *all* song.

I pick up the tiny carcass. I feel ashamed. A single drop of blood hangs trembling on the red feathers of the bird's breast and now I remember the beauty of the song. Tears flow from my eyes. I wish desperately that I could change the bird back and hear it singing again from a bursting heart, but I know this is impossible. I bury the robin and erect a tiny gravestone in a secret place. For twenty years, it is a constant reminder never to shoot another robin. I never do.

I am consciousness, connecting all life. I am aware of self and of my connection with Nature. For endless time I move in and out of various animals and birds. I experience a lizard, but it is a time of dull instinct, connecting once more with my childhood.

I am cattle. I am many cattle on the foothills of Mount Arthur. I am aware of a changing relationship between us and the farmer who cares for us. After a time of total separation, we begin to connect. We begin to trust him. We feel his growing love.

I am a single cow. I am sick. As the farmer feeds us hay one winter's day, he notices my distress. He walks me out of the paddock, away from the other cattle, and down the hill. We are on the familiar walk to the cattleyards, but my time has ended. I know this, but the farmer does not. Within me, the new life I carried has ended. I do not know why. At the bottom of the hill, we cross a creek. I turn off the road, and, following instinct, go into the creek. I stand in the icy water and the farmer tries to make me leave it. I will not. I am ready to die. A natural process is taking place. I feel it and trust it. To leave my body is to return to the One. I want this to happen. I am sick. I am in pain.

I am seething with frustration as I try to get the cow out of the creek. She is a cow I have reared on the bucket, and I am very fond of her. I know that she has a dead calf inside her, and I fear she has peritonitis. Everything I do to get her from the creek fails, and after two hours I am exhausted. Finally, as a last resort, I put a halter over her head, and tying the rope end to the Land Rover,

I drag her bodily to a small tree. There, I tie her securely to a branch, before driving up to the house to phone for the vet and to change my soaking clothes.

I go back to the cow. She is a big, well-bred, strong cow, overdue to have her second calf. When I get to her, I find she has broken the branch off the tree and is back in the creek. She is lying down, and the icy water is flowing over her body. I am very distressed. I realize that the water will numb any pain in her body, but I know she is going to die. So many times I have seen cows die. Often, when a cow knows she is going to die, she will arch her head round her back into a classic dying position.

I sit down helplessly. The cow looks at me, making deliberate eye contact. She holds my gaze. I am surprised. Animals rarely hold eye contact with a human. Even a dog will look away after a few moments. She stares into my eyes and I read her knowledge of her own death. There is no fear within her. I am crying. I am bonded to my cows and I do not want this to happen. Into my head comes a thought, a knowing. She does not recognize death as an ending; it is continuation. She has no emotion regarding death, but I am all emotion. I must learn to see life uncluttered, rather than through the clutter of intellect. Misused, emotion and intellect are handicaps. They distort my view of Nature. The knowing ends, and through tear-filled eyes I watch her head arch around her back. Then, calmly, without fear, she places her head underwater and quietly drowns.

I am cow. I stand beside my drowned body in the creek. I am connected with the consciousness of all cattle, but something strange is happening. Something I recognize as a Higher Being is beside me, filling me with a knowing beyond cattle knowing. I had waited with this Being for the farmer to come and witness my death. He understands so little as he weeps out his emotion.

As he quiets, I connect with him. I am able to do this because he has learned to link with our consciousness. His eyes open wide in surprise and, through me, the Higher Being pours forth a golden energy. I see it clearly, shimmering as though a cloud of dust surrounds the farmer. He sits down, his head in his hands. But only for a moment.

Something peculiar is happening. I am sitting beside the dead cow, but I am no longer human. I am consciousness. I am connected with all Nature, all Life. I see beyond the deceit of death, and I know life to be the totality of what is. I know that I am responsible only for myself and that Self connects with All life.

As briefly as a blink, it is finished. I am sitting by the dead cow. My sadness remains, but deep in my psyche there resides a greater knowing. Somehow, sometime, I will connect with that Greater Self.

I am consciousness. I am joy. As a human, I have reconnected with my own inner knowing. Now I know that I know! I spin through the etheric structures of reality and experience a hundred other animals. I become cat, renewing the many times we have come together, and I find immense satisfaction within this union. I become wallaby, playing out the trauma of my years shooting these gentle creatures, and I no longer hold onto guilt and judgment. I allow life to come and go in its endless cycles, no longer deceived by the physical illusions of form. I become an eagle, closely bonded with human self as an Indian in North America, and I am falcon in old England. I become a jackdaw linked with my childhood, and the union is bittersweet. I become magpie and man in a recent encounter, and I have the knowing of bird. Every creature I become is a connection in my life as a human Being. Some of the connections in consciousness last for years, some are a brief moment, but in all-time there is only no-time. An eon, a second — there is no difference.

Tumbling, drifting, no-thing, every-thing, I am back in my human body.

❧

ANOTHER REALITY. I was stiff; I ached! The riverbank had not been kind to me and the small stone under my neck had become a boulder. I groaned, physically exhausted, but inside me there was joy. The breakthrough had come with the death of the cow. Memory took me back to those farming years when her physical death had taken place. She had looked at me with her huge, brown, expressive eyes, and in some way I felt a knowing. Insight had surged within me, revealing my emotional state at the time. Crazy as it had seemed, I had *felt* that some other presence was with us, but as I had stared anxiously around I could see nothing. I remember one logical part of my mind trying to rationalize the feeling by thinking that it could be the vet, yet I also knew that was not possible.

I stood up and stretched, easing away the kinks as I thought about all that had taken place. Going back into my death as a cow and experiencing it from a metaphysical perspective, I had *seen* that other Being. Should I be surprised that it was Pan? All those years ago, Pan had given me an insight that, by defying subjective time, had now assisted me in my battle to go beyond my emotional relationship with animals. Pan had given me a brief but penetrating insight into the totality of life. I had seen that life as one continuum, not a series of beginnings and endings, and, even though at that time I had not been able to take that leap of understanding, the view had helped me.

The joy of my recent triumph was a warm inner glow. Having experienced the dying cow and my emotional self on a spiritual plane, I had somehow experienced a fusion within my consciousness. My emotion had become revealed as if it had been a thick fog obscuring the view of a great valley. That my emotions were still my own was apparent, for tears trickled down my cheeks. But my feelings would no longer cloud my perception of the animal consciousness or block my ability to reach a greater insight. With the emotional attachment ended, I had been able to flow into a whole series of other incidents involving other animals. Each had been without trauma. The experience of shooting wallabies — and of being the shot wallabies — had flowed without hitch. I had laid aside blame and judgment, allowing the continuity of life's expression to be revealed. It was a good feeling!

I walked up the steep steps slowly. Now I had made one more step in my overall journey into a holistic Nature. I had connected with plant, mineral, *and* animal consciousness, resolving all the discord that had inadvertently accrued between myself and Nature. I was aware that this was my particular path, but we each walk the path of our choosing, and I knew that I was not alone in consciousness. We are *one* humanity.

6 Within a Storm

The day had been unpleasantly hot and humid, and we speculated eagerly about when the inevitable thunderstorm would strike. During the afternoon, ominous black clouds had gathered and, although I looked forward to the cool relief of the impending storm, I felt an odd apprehension.

"I don't like the look of this at all," Treenie stated, as she joined me on the lawn. Together, we stared up at the clouds. A slight breeze pulled gently at our hair and stirred the leaves on the trees.

"Neither do I. I reckon we're going to have one hell of a storm. I'll go and make sure the henhouse is secure and check anything else I can think of."

For the next hour or so, I was busy. I laid heavy planks on the henhouse roof, braced the garden shed, and generally prepared for a violent night.

The storm was slow to gather, but this gradual building only heightened my anxiety and increased my apprehension.

Throughout the afternoon and into the evening, the storm slowly gathered power and momentum until the valley was filled with clouds. These seemed different from normal storm clouds. It was as though an inky pigmentation had leaked from some malevolent dimension, staining the clouds with impossible layers of darkness. These clouds met and merged with night, bringing the day to a premature close.

We ate our evening meal in a subdued silence. Even our teenage children were quiet, affected by some outside influence. The racket of television was a welcome distraction, and our choice for comedy was unanimous.

Not until eleven o'clock that night did the storm begin, commencing with a torrential downpour. Anticipating a disturbed night, we straggled off to bed, but sleep was impossible. Around one o'clock in the morning, with the darkness seared and illuminated by almost continuous lightning, the whole household was awake. For quite a while we stood on the verandah, watching in subdued awe, literally overwhelmed by the sheer physical enormity of the storm raging over the valley.

As our family members retreated bleary-eyed back to their beds one by one, my persistent inner anxiety became even more intense. Continual deafening blasts of thunder combined with vivid, twisting flashes of lightning and a powerful gale-force wind that failed to move the storm away. It all induced a deep-seated unease. Staring spellbound into the storm, I became aware of the similarity between this and the forces inside the Guidestone. Yet there were differences. In both cases, power was involved, but the power seemed of two kinds and of different orders.

I am a light sleeper, so I decided to sit in the living room for a while. Our electricity had failed, but in the flickering candlelight I could see our two Abyssinian cats cowering under chairs. Half-heartedly, I tried to evict them, but they resisted strenuously. Owing to the cats' habit of bringing rats, mice, snakes, and other undesirable prey indoors to devour, these two were always shut out at night. This indignity — even during most storms — they had long ago accepted, but not *this* night! With a shrug, I allowed the cats to stay. I blew out the candles and sat back in an easy chair to watch Nature's grand display of fireworks.

For maybe half an hour I watched light flicker and flash around the room. Rain drummed on the tin roof in a heavy roar, while the thunderous sounds of violently released energy raged overhead. My heart thumped with inner tension as I tried unsuccessfully to relax.

Suddenly, during a startling crash of thunder, I saw that Pan was in the room.

His appearance was so completely unexpected, I was shocked. "What are *you* doing here?"

Pan seemed larger and more powerful than I had ever seen him. The energy emanating from him was almost as electric as the storm itself, and suddenly I was chilled with worry. His words rang inside my skull, while he stood back, looking remote and alien.

"The Door to Beyond is not easily entered. So far, you have experienced the inner realms of water, plant, mineral, and animal consciousness. This is the Nature you are comfortable and familiar with. I have told you many times that humanity is of Nature, not separate in consciousness. When humans misuse Nature, the environmental impact soon reveals the effect of that abuse. Equally, if humans physically or mentally abuse each other, the negative effects are quickly revealed in your everyday lives and relationships." He paused, his impassive face turning toward me, his eyes holding mine. I swallowed nervously, unsure of what was coming next.

He continued. "More subtle by far, yet no less powerful, is the effect of negative thinking in the natural world. Nature is affected by negative action *and* negative thoughts. Seldom do humans realize this. Very rarely do humans even consider the possibility that the quality of their thoughts might affect Nature. You have experienced the results of your own negative action in spraying toxic poison onto blackberries. Now you have the opportunity to experience the cumulative effect of negative thinking. You will experience the effect this can have in Nature."

Thunder pealed and crashed around us, but Pan's words were crystal clear — too clear! — in my head.

"But why?"

"Because you are a part of that negativity. With *very* few exceptions, all humanity is involved. If you agree to experience this dimension of negative human power, you will benefit. Because you are not separate in consciousness from other people, they will also benefit, even though they will be unaware of it."

"*If* I agree? You have never given me a choice before!"

Pan shook his head slowly. "You made the choice to journey into the hidden realms of Nature. Thus, each experience and its content has been your choice. You know this. This time, however, you can refuse the experience."

"Why?"

"Your previous encounters have involved your own personal relationship with Nature. This one involves the wider human relationship with Nature. You are only a part of that."

"You've told me I can refuse. But can you tell me what to expect if I agree?"

"No. You will have to go on trust."

"On trust of what?"

"My love for you."

On a reckless impulse, I blurted out, "Okay, I'll do it."

Immediately, Pan dramatically increased in size. This Pan, one I had never seen before, loomed huge, fully fifteen to twenty feet tall. In some inexplicable manner, he stood right up into the roof of the house, and it was as though no house or room existed. His size was horribly intimidating, yet there was no menace in the hand that reached out to me.

Unthinking, I took it.

With appalling strength and power, I was snatched out of my body and hurled like a rag doll up, up into the violence of the storm.

⟋

I AM LOST. Although formless, I am battered and exhausted. For long ages I am tossed and torn within the raging forces and seething energies of incomprehensible turbulence. I sense conflict of a type totally unknown to me, something that surely dwells in dimensions of madness. All around me, an awful blackness tries to engulf shattered, scattered fragments of rainbow-colored light, while pure whiteness of incredible intensity writhes as though in pain among patches of malignant gloom. In some way, I seem to be protected from the maelstrom of violence that engulfs me.

I watch, feel, as segments of whiteness seek to combine and fuse with the rainbow-colored light yet are hindered by the black turbulence. I am helpless. I have no power to assist, although my whole Being cries out for the light. I struggle, feeling like a tiny child held tight in the arms of a giant. For ages I strive ineffectually to help, but I have no form, no way of reaching out. I am exhausted.

Gradually, into my consciousness comes an idea. Within the grayness of my Being, a tiny spark of hope slowly grows into a small, twinkling light. Eventually, responding to this inner light, I do the only thing I can — I visualize the rainbow-colored light and whiteness as One.

The result is catastrophic, for in that instant my protection is gone. Instantly, as no more than a tiny mote of human psyche, I feel the violence and raging fury of the maelstrom enter me. I am shattered, fragmented, torn into a million fragments of rainbow-colored light — but in that moment, a new awareness literally explodes into my psyche.

This storm, of vast and awesome proportions, is of humanity. I recognize it as a manifestation of our collective fear, born from our rapacious greed and appalling negativity. *This* is what Pan meant. The rainbow-colored light is symbolic of our highest human ideals, while the terrible blackness is our own negativity. It hampers our collective endeavor in our struggle to reach the light — pure Love. It is our negativity that hinders our spiritual evolution.

I am torn to pieces, hurtling around in the center of the storm as though I were a million grains of sand in an endless cyclone. But I hold onto my knowing and a faint determination slowly grows stronger, gaining strength from my insight into truth. As my own determination grows, I feel that within my psyche I make a connection with the rainbow-colored light.

Instantly, a rainbow forms, whole, new, invincible, and I know that the human potential has no limits. My determination is no more than a mere echo of all human determination.

Regarding me with stunning indifference, a Being beyond anything in my experience reaches out to embrace me within its formless energy. Its words, which I hear as soundless, crash as thunder into the physical world.

"Just as the suppressed rage of an individual eventually explodes in temper, so also the accumulated fears, spites, and hates of humanity unleash all the forces of a tempest."

I can hear thunder pealing with the words, but I am held in the soundless vise of an unbreakable grip. The words continue, echoing in my consciousness.

"Human beings have the collective potential to create a fine song of harmony in the atmosphere, but instead you create the heavy storms of discord. So divorced are you from your true reality that you do not recognize your negative manifestations. Many of the storms of destruction that rage above you are the reflected storms that rage within the human psyche. As within, so without. A storm of Nature compares with the negativity of humanity in the manner of a snowflake with a drop of acid."

For a long moment, there is nothing. All time, violence, and storm have ended. I hang suspended, contained in a furious hush more frightening than the maelstrom.

Then, into the shocking silence, come the final words.

"Only by surrendering to the storm is it possible for you to conquer it."

This said, the power I sense grows to proportions that are indefinable. I feel that the whole universe is involved, but in a detached manner, like a child prodding a reluctant ant with a big stick. I feel that I am the reluctant ant, being toyed with by powers and forces so far beyond my human comprehension that even to probe with thought is no more than trite insanity.

In a manner I do not understand, I am able to allow self to yield, neither to resist nor invoke. I realize that to surrender is to cease my struggle. By becoming resistless and defenseless I become vulnerable, and I know that I will find peace here in the same way I found peace within the turmoil of our community. Within the collective human consciousness, there is peace as well as negativity, and it is to this peace that I surrender.

Slowly but surely, the peace within me grows stronger. The rainbow is luminosity itself. In this sphere of peace, the storm begins to abate, and I know with a surge of joy that we humans can overcome our negativity.

Abruptly from the roily space, a single, brilliant shaft of lightning blasts from the black clouds to Earth, and my total awareness is centered in a rigid body in a chair. It is my body, that which I call me!

———

I WAS TOTALLY WRUNG OUT! I had to concentrate on relaxing, limb by rigid limb, as I eased the aching, muscle-locking tension from my trembling body. During this time, as I tried to come to terms with what had just taken place, the storm abated, gradually losing its fury.

It was now nearly three o'clock in the morning. Climbing stiffly to my feet, I stumbled into the bedroom and fell exhausted into bed. My last fading thought was never to trust Pan again!

I slept late next morning. By the time I got up for breakfast, Treenie was having a midmorning cup of tea. "Whatever time did you get to bed?" she asked.

I regarded her wearily. Despite a long shower, I felt jaded.

"About three o'clock."

"And what were you doing so late?"

"You wouldn't believe me if I told you."

"Oh. Why should I stop believing you now?"

"Okay, point taken. Pour us both another cuppa; we're going to be here for quite a while." So saying, I launched into the story. Details were etched clearly into my mind, so I took my time. When I had finished, Treenie gave me a strange look of admiration. "You really are something, you know? You really are."

I felt pleased. But I had to be honest. "Don't forget it was that deceitful cosmic clown who did it to me. He tricked me. 'Trust me,' he said, and then he hurled me into the heart of a terrifying storm. If I had had the slightest intimation of what I was getting into, I would have run from the room."

"Which is, of course, why he didn't tell you."

"Maybe so, but that was the last metaphysical experience I want. I came out of it shell-shocked! He literally threw me into it." I scowled at the memory. "Never again! I'm finished with trusting him."

The more I thought about it, the more indignant I became. Treenie got up and made us another cup of tea. For a while she clattered around, and I knew that she had things on her mind.

Sipping on her fresh cup, she began to share her perceptions of my experience. Finally she asked, "Do you think if Pan had politely asked you to enter the heart of a storm you would have considered it? Come to that, would you have thought it possible? What choice did he have?"

"Just whose side are you on? I'm fed up with Pan. He's too cold-hearted."

"You're avoiding the question."

I squirmed.

"I'm waiting. Face up to it and confess. Pan had no choice. I have to lead you by the nose to everything you achieve in life, while you kick and struggle all the way. Look at our journey around Australia. You would have settled for something safe and

234

secure a dozen times if I had agreed. Same with Homeland. If you could have wriggled out of that initially, you would have." She snorted in disgust. "Pan asked you to trust in his love for you. And, I might add, despite the trauma, you are safe and sound!"

"So what happened to all my praise? I'm the one who gets shoved on a hook, dangled into all sorts of weird situations, and has to get out of it. And you're on his side!"

"Gosh, you're a tricky one. As soon as you can't win, you try to make me feel sorry for you. Pan asked you to trust him. Of your own choice, you did. So stop grumbling. He didn't say it would be easy, did he?"

Grudgingly, I surrendered. "Okay, okay. You're right."

"And one more thing," she declared. "While you persist in being reluctant and negative, you are still part of that storm!"

I spent the remainder of the day reading, although speculating on the night's events occupied much of my time. I acknowledged that the mystical whiteness and blackness of the storm had a counterpart in every human Being. The negativity I had encountered was indeed partly my own, magnified and amplified by that of countless other people. But I had not been engulfed. As a surfer would say, I hadn't wiped out!

EARLY THE FOLLOWING MORNING, I headed for the river. As I walked beneath the huge outstretched branches of the Morton Bay fig tree, large, crisp, sun-dried leaves crackled beneath my feet and sunlight burst with tiny explosions of heat onto my shoulders. I had hoped to catch a glimpse of a platypus foraging in the river for a late breakfast, but I was out of luck. The surface of the water was dark; the deep, early-morning shade had subtly altered the mood of the river. Scarcely a ripple broke the water's tranquil surface.

I walked out onto the end of my board and dived. The cool water closed over me. I floated very gently and slowly to the surface, my eyes just clearing the water, and noticed a huge bronze dragonfly perched on a spike of sedge grass only inches from my face. I stayed unmoving, captivated by the beauty of this superb, biologically perfect creature.

I chilled quickly in the water, so I climbed from the river to sit on the board in the warm sun. Impossibly, Pan sat next to me. He wore the same faded greens, and was again a normal size. Looking into his eyes, for the first time I felt comfortable without needing him to make me feel at ease. And I knew what the difference was!

"I suppose you know all about my little outburst to Treenie?" I asked. "I meant it, every single word! Do you know what really bugged me? You asked me to trust your love for me. That gave me confidence, but then I felt betrayed! Going into that storm was the worst nonphysical experience I have ever had. I felt totally lost."

"I know all that, Michael, and I do love you. I consider you a most courageous person. Once thrown in, you respond magnificently. One thing, however — you do not know what *lost* is."

I ignored the last remark; it did not seem important.

"Tell me, did you listen to my altercation with Treenie?"

"Of course. I hope you heed what she said. I even prompted her with a few suggestions." His mouth curved into a sly smile, tiny shards of light flashing from his eyes.

Despite my indignation, I had to laugh. "You're absolutely impossible."

"Only if you believe in impossibilities, Michael. And luckily, despite all your truculence, you do not!"

"What was the point of throwing me into that storm?"

"Michael! I have told you before, I know you better than you know yourself. You *know* the purpose. Suppose you tell me!"

I frowned in thought, seeking to sum up the essence of what I had learned. "The strongest impression I have now — having had a chance to simmer down — is that human negativity is a creative force. I had always assumed that anger, bitterness, greed, and our other negative feelings merely dissipated when they left us, somehow dispersed into nothingness. It's a real eye-opener to learn that such energy builds into a destructive force that is eventually expressed in violence."

"What else?"

"Well, it's rather shocking to learn that that negative energy can only be expressed by returning to its point of origin. I had no idea that cause and effect worked within atmospheric levels. Knowing that our mental garbage can accumulate in the atmosphere and then be dumped back on us in the destructive fury of a storm is rather frightening. It's the sow-and-reap effect! Just imagine the effect if we could create that much love and joy!"

"That is the human potential. And?"

"By yielding to my own inner negative fears, I conquered them. Without doubt, negativity is born from all our many little fears, and those fears destroy the quality of our lives. Yet I'm not really aware of surrendering. I don't feel I did anything."

"That is the whole essence. You did nothing. If you had tried to surrender, you would have created resistance, for surrender is a 'letting go,' not something you can force. By 'giving in,' you give to your inner self."

We sat in silence. I wanted to digest what he had said, while Pan was happy playing with blue wrens.

I was so lost in thought that Pan's next words caught me by surprise. "You have made many journeys out of your body, but each time it is I who have taken you out."

"Taken! *Blasted* is the operative word," I said laughing. "You rip me out of my physical body."

"Yes, well, I'll teach you a rather unique method. You can exit the body by certain excellent meditation techniques, but I have a method that you may enjoy. Maybe then you will not need my assistance."

"I'm all for that. Your last effort nearly dislocated my neck."

Pan laughed in delight. "Yes, it was a mighty snatch, even if I do say so. Now, to business. You are about to learn the Pan method of leaving your physical body."

He pointed to the base of the old bridge board where it was lodged under a small shelf of rock. "Sit on the board so that your feet are firmly on the ground."

I did so.

"When I say one, you stand up, two, you sit down, three up, four down, and so on. When I reach eleven, your physical body remains seated, but your inner consciousness leaps up ... and out! Ready?"

"One!"

I stood up.

"Two!"

I sat down.

"Three!"

I stood up.

"No. No. When I say stand, I mean leap up with total abandon. Up, up, as though reaching for the sky. And sit down with a heavy thud. Right. Try it again."

"One!"

I leaped up energetically.

"Two!"

I collapsed back.

"Three!"

I leaped up enthusiastically.

"Four!"

I thudded back onto the board. This continued until ...

"Eleven!"

MY SPIRITUAL SELF LEAPS UPWARDS, soaring out of my physical body with ease. I am up and out!

"That was easy enough. You did well. The Pan technique seldom fails, once mastered!"

He is mocking, but it is a thrill to be walking in a body that although appearing normal, is made of light, is weightless. And to be walking along the surface of the river with Pan — is something else!

Because I am wide awake, I am aware of both physical self and nonphysical self. The former remains calm and relaxed, while the latter moves into a different mode of experience. Both aspects of self are integrated into a single conscious experience.

I am lighter than mist as I move down the river, and my visual impressions come from an all-embracing inner seeing. Moving rainbows of light cling to trees, bushes, and every blade of grass. Everything is transformed by light and color into a subtle vibration. I am aware that this kaleidoscope of color and light somehow lives, is part of Nature, blending and exchanging energies in the endless movement we call life and death. All the living creatures of the riverside are contained in this fluid light, some individually, some as a group.

The water on which my light self hovers no longer clings to the riverbed. No longer is it controlled by physical laws. Instead, it flows in multidimensional layers of visual sound, a stream in which I can faintly perceive other Beings. Some of them see Pan, and when they do their light presence glows brighter, as though influenced by some powerful energy source. Briefly they look at me, and I feel there is a registering of surprise among them. To perceive other Beings that are composed of light and to try to decipher them in human terms is not easy, especially when a feeling of otherness accompanies their obvious intelligence.

—

How long Pan and I flowed in total harmony with the life of that multidimensional river reality, I have no idea. In human terms, the experience lasted no more than thirty minutes.

Under Pan's direction, we returned to the board on which I sat. I felt my physical body take a long, deep breath as my light, nonphysical body merged with it. I felt dense! After an experience of such lightness, my body felt heavy and cumbersome. I actually felt that I was resuming a nonreal state, that this was not my natural body or my natural state of Beingness.

Pan glanced at me in approval. "Your perception is correct. The total time you spend in a physical body is only a fraction of your experience of Being. You spend far more time outside the human reality as you understand it than in it. Of course, in reality there is only no-time."

I looked into his golden eyes. "Pan, how did I get into the Guidestone in my original experience? My physical body locked, while my nonphysical body was literally drawn out. Were you involved in that?"

"I helped. Let us say that your Greater Self set up the timing and the situation, while I assisted. I switched off one reality, and switched on another. You did the rest. You put your self into the Guidestone, not me."

I could accept that. After all I had since experienced, I was beginning to realize that my human potential was very considerable. But I had another question. "What is the Guidestone? It certainly isn't just an average stone."

"No, far from it. The Guidestone is a stone of power. Some are natural in Nature, but some are primed by Beings. The Guidestone was one of the latter."

My mind boggled.

Pan jumped onto the end of the board in one bound. Again, he leaped high into the air, the board whipping him up as though it had flexed under half a ton of weight. As he vanished, his words, in total conflict with all logic and reason, continued to emanate from where he had been sitting.

"You have done well, Michael. Be happy."

I swam again, but I no longer felt the magic in the river. Still I stayed, knowing I had to accept physical reality as the major part of my daily life. Whatever my mission was on Earth, it required my physical self. I thought about Pan's last words: be happy. Yes, I felt happy. Despite a bumpy journey, I had experienced the inner realms of plant, mineral, and animal consciousness. I had been within the essence of water and had entered a storm. And I had emerged from all of it unscathed, even if badly shaken. Each mystical experience connected with the previous one, rather like the beads on a necklace. By commencing with water, I had gained an overall impression of the whole, for water is in all life forms, even rock! The plant kingdom had revealed that a physical act, such as the spraying of toxins, in one small place has an effect on the whole. The mineral kingdom revealed both how we have each become concretized in our separation from one another and the potential of the whole. The animal kingdom revealed my inability to love myself and how I judged myself. It also showed that none of the animals involved judged me. Nature does not judge.

I stared up river, wondering what awaited me. Each experience revealed to me a greater view of myself and the way I and every other human fitted into the overall pattern of life. Pan was showing me that the nonphysical aspect of Nature and humanity had many hidden ramifications. I was learning that to find out "who I am" required that I embrace not only the me I *think* I know, but also my mystical self. The unknown outweighed the known, but paradoxically I could not make the unknown known. I could only experience, learn, and accept. This was the path into the Beyond, and I knew now that the membrane at the Door to Beyond would never yield until I knew who I was.

Pan had often told me that he knew me better than I knew myself. I believed him now. Even though I had chosen the mystic path of Nature, Pan was designing this journey. I realized, with some irony, that I now trusted him implicitly.

When a yellow and gold butterfly settled on my towel only seconds before I reached for it, its wings opening and closing in flashing golden winks, I knew that Pan was still nearby.

7 Becoming Dolphin

"You will have to leave all this."

I stared upriver, my eyes moist. That I was attached to the river was acutely obvious. A week had passed since Pan had taught me how to leap out of my physical body, and each day I had spent hours on my old bridge board. Evening shadows were stretching dark, elongated fingers across the water when Pan made his appearance. We chatted for a while before Pan dropped his bombshell.

"Why? Why do I have to move from here?"

"Having acknowledged your fixation, the reason should be obvious. You must withdraw your roots from dear old Mother Earth. You must become a free spirit on this planet, not attached to it. You cannot remain fixed and go Beyond."

"So where do Treenie and I go from here?"

"Life will present your next home at the perfect time. All you need for assisting the process is trust."

"Will you be able to find me if we move from here?" I asked rather anxiously.

Pan tilted his head back, laughing uproariously. When he turned those golden eyes on me and blinked, I noticed that the light in them illuminated his eyelids. The evening dusk made the effect quite startling, rather Halloweenish.

"Michael, I could find you anywhere."

"That's comforting to know."

He only smiled, while my fascination with his illumined eyes took my thoughts elsewhere.

"It may surprise you to learn that your next connection is with an intelligent species."

"But humans are the only intelligent species on Earth," I began, and then I realized my error. "You mean the dolphins, don't you?"

"That is exactly who I mean."

"But I have tried to connect with dolphins dozens of times. Treenie and I sometimes see them on our beach walks, and, no matter how hard I try to communicate, nothing happens!"

Pan dismissed my comments with an elegant wave of his hand. "As always, it's simply a matter of timing!"

ONLY A FEW DAYS LATER, Lance Rose, our landlord, told Treenie and me that he had been offered a good price for the riverside property we'd been living on. He had not even considered selling, so the offer came as a surprise. Because of a prior agreement, he offered the property to us first. He was keen for us to buy it, for we had become good friends and he enjoyed paying visits to the place where he and his wife, Enid, had spent much of their lives.

"You go ahead and sell," I said with some reluctance. "Treenie and I feel it's time we moved out of the valley. Given the choice, we would like a place with some elevation."

Treenie and I realized that life was indeed saying, "move on," so a few weeks later we set out on a journey into southern Queensland. At this stage, we decided to look not for a home but simply for an area where the vibrations were right for us. Staying with friends on each leg of the journey, we moved from one place to another, finally deciding on a particularly exotic and pleasing location. Feeling happy with the results of our search, we drove homewards, calling on our good friends Mike and Rosemary Nicholas in Brisbane to stay the night and share our news.

"Did you go and have a look on Kiel Mountain?" asked Mike. "It's very close to the place you like and really beautiful. You'd love it."

I looked at Treenie uncertainly. "The name's familiar. Have we ever been there?"

"We were there about six years ago, very briefly."

I have a bad memory for places, and couldn't remember the place at all. Also, I had no intention of going back to look at any mountain. We were very satisfied with the area we had chosen.

Next day we drove home.

During our trip away, the expected sale had fallen flat. Nevertheless, we felt that life was prompting us to make the move. Still, with the pressure off, we decided to take our time. A few days later, a man I was talking with casually of our trip said, "Ah! I know that area very well. Did you go and have a look at Kiel Mountain while you were there? It's a really beautiful place to live."

I looked at him in surprise. "Funny you should say that. Someone else also suggested we should have looked up there."

Three weeks later, Russell, our youngest son phoned to say he'd met the daughter of a friend of ours. The girl asked about us, and in the course of the conversation she mentioned a house for sale — a house on top of Kiel Mountain!

"I think you'd better give me that phone number, Russ. And thanks," I said.

I told Treenie about the conversation. "Life is saying Kiel Mountain loud and clear. Three times should be enough for anybody!" I was enthusiastic.

"I think you'd better phone and get some details," she suggested.

I did. I was told that Kiel Mountain was reputed to be a power point on a ley line. Ley lines are to the planet what meridian lines are to our bodies. Many old European churches, cathedrals, and monasteries were built on ley lines, and it is said that power accumulates at certain points. I was also told that the small mountain was only a few minutes' drive from the sea and that the climate was mild, without extremes in heat or humidity. The unnamed property was two acres of open forest right on top of the mountain. All in all, the place sounded like paradise, and the photographs that arrived by post a few days later appeared to confirm it.

When we visited the property, we found it to be simply perfect. From the moment Treenie and I first set foot on the drive leading down to the house tucked in among the gum trees — by mutual consent — it was ours.

The transaction went without a hitch. We were due to take possession in one month.

Packing made the month pass quickly. On the last day, I could not leave without saying farewell to my beloved river. I had a heavy heart as I went slowly and carefully down the steep steps. They were wet and slippery from recent heavy rains.

I was in for a shock! My bridge board was gone! A week of heavy rain had produced a flood; at its peak, flowing fast and very powerfully, the river had taken my old bridge board ... my old and faithful friend. How strange life is. Shortly after we had moved to this place six years earlier, a flood had deposited the old, washed-out bridge board onto the rocks where I now sat. Now, in the manner it had brought the huge, heavy board to me, the river had as easily removed it. What uncanny timing! I felt, then, that the

246

river had welcomed me with the board and now it was saying farewell.

As I watched, gently undulating shoals of tiny brown fish clustered near the rocks where I sat. A fantail flew from a twig above my head, swooping to the water's surface to catch an insect before flying onto a drooping frond of wild palm grass. The vivid splash of black and white bird on dark green foliage was the perfect art of Nature. Despite the bird's tiny weight, the slender stem dipped alarmingly toward the river, down and down in response to its diminutive burden. I watched the fantail's antics with a feeling akin to envy. The bird was so free, so sure of each movement, so totally in the moment. The fantail's only concern was food — and in that it was certainly not alone! Beneath the bird, a small rock dragon scampered over the drying remains of flood debris, its jaws snapping as it pounced on first one March fly, then another. Smaller and skinnier than its water dragon cousin, its head twisted as though on an endless swivel, the rock dragon kept watch on me while pursuing its prey.

Another fantail flew in on a nervous blur of wings, and for a few breathless seconds the pair of birds sat close to each other, beaks almost touching in a moment's intimacy, before their fluttering, uncontainable energy took them deeper into the wild palm grass.

I dived, frolicked, and swam, coming to terms with my leave-taking. When I emerged from the cold water, a twig fell from the treetops and splashed into the water before me. I looked up to see a pair of pale gray herons on long, stilt legs perched on a high branch of a river oak.

This was one of those moments of natural elegance when everything comes together with serendipitous grace. The great bronze dragonfly, by no means a common visitor, zoomed past with an aura of majesty, while the river formed small, gasping whirlpools as it flowed powerfully over the submerged rocks.

A lonely gray feather riding high on the water had completed several ineffectual circuits from the rippled edge of the open flow back into an inlet when a slight gust of breeze took it skimming across the surface onto the current of the main stream. I watched as it began its journey downriver, a single gray feather facing the unknown, no longer part of a heron's plumage. The message was clear. Time to go!

OUR FIRST WEEK on Kiel Mountain was all frenzied activity. Treenie, who had shed her tears as we departed our home by the river, was a bundle of organized energy. I had departed in high spirits but was feeling totally misplaced. I had looked forward to living in the house but now found it impersonal, like a motel. And the mountain was achingly devoid of a river — my river!

It was not until I realized I was looking for the river each day that I finally came to terms with our parting. Deliberately, I turned my attention to accepting and appreciating the particular beauty of our new home. And there was beauty in abundance. Gray gums, which shed their bark each year, astounded us with the deep ochre-orange coloring of their new trunks when wet. Also, there was a great peace on the mountain, perfect for a writer, and if Nature was less flamboyant than by the river, it was no less active. While we now had no platypus to grace a river, we had the echidna, a marsupial spiny anteater, to wander our garden of trees. Still, it wasn't until a yellow and gold butterfly slowly winked its delicate wings from the edge of our swimming pool one sunny morning that I knew I had made the adjustment!

ONE DAY OUR MAIL produced a letter from the west coast of Australia. Christine Olsen and Keith Nightingale had purchased and read *Talking With Nature* and, having felt a great affinity with it, invited Treenie and me to do a series of workshops in their area. With uncanny foresight, they offered me the perfect bait — if we wished, they would take us to Monkey Mia for a few days! I did not know Christine or Keith, but I did know of Monkey

Becoming Dolphin

Mia! I had been wanting to go there for years and had been waiting for the right opportunity. This was surely it! We accepted the invitation, and at the appointed time flew to Perth.

A sign on a bag carrier read, "Welcome Michael and Treenie," and in no time we were firm friends with Jack and Barbara Bailey, our hosts in Perth. Workshops and talks came and went, and the time to visit Monkey Mia arrived. Monkey Mia is no more than an isolated caravan park in Shark Bay. Situated hundreds of miles from anywhere in a bleak, inhospitable landscape that could easily belong to another planet, its one redeeming factor is the group of wild dolphins that voluntarily meets there with hundreds of people every day.

Our group consisted of Christine, Keith, and their delightful eighteen-month-old baby, Amy, a couple of their friends, Marie and Sonia, and Treenie and me. We took a car, plus their Land Rover and caravan. The two-day drive north of Perth is an unrelieved, straight coast road that seems endless, but thoughts of the dolphins interspersed with flashes of color from Western Australia's incredible and strange native wildflowers made the trip pass very quickly. Unfortunately, we were too early for the full wildflower display, and only caught mere hints of the glory to unfold in another couple of months.

At the appropriate junction, we left the main coast road to drive another hundred miles or so along the peninsula on which Monkey Mia is located. Finally, in a cloud of red dust, we pulled into the overcrowded caravan park to find our prebooked site.

There are only two reasons for visiting Monkey Mia: to fish and to see the dolphins! Of course, without fish there would be no dolphins, and the fishing is famed for its excellence. Because of its sheltered position, the bay is predominantly calm, the water seldom disturbed by large waves. Golden sand, unlike the usual white sand of our shoreline, stretches endlessly along the lonely beaches. Seen from one of the nearby low hillocks, the caravan park is an ugly sprawl of caravans intruding into the natural sweep of beauty. Stark, dry, and desertlike, the vista of Shark Bay is outstanding. But the visitors are required to accept this area on its own terms, not imposing their own. When they do, the beauty shines through, overwhelming the initial impression that this is a barren land. It is indeed a place of contrasts, harsh and hot, of prickles, burrs, and thorns, yet the flowers that grace these well-defended plants are soft, delicate, and unique.

A flotilla of small fishing boats bobs gently on the undulating sea, while pelicans fly among them in a stately grace. Along the shoreline there are people, old and young, wealthy and poor, fat and thin — people who appear to have nothing in common. There are probably as many visitors from overseas as from our own fair land, yet despite the obvious diversity one common factor unifies them all: they are here for the dolphins.

After setting up our tent and caravan, we had our meal and retired for the night. It was midwinter, so it was cold despite the midday warmth. Next morning I arrived on the beach just before 7 A.M., eager for my first physical contact with the dolphins. I was alone; the beach and sea were cold and deserted. Minutes later the sun appeared, rising blood red over a low bank of clouds. A snort among the fishing boats announced the arrival of the dolphins. I waded in, calling softly. Five dolphins came cruising up from the greenish depths to the knee-deep shallows. The leading female offered me a small wisp of sea grass. As I took the gift from her, she rolled slightly to one side, making deliberate visual contact with me with a pinkish-red eye. I was instantly aware that this was an intelligent species, and Pan's words came flooding back: "Your next connection is with an intelligent species." I stared at her, awed by the obvious intelligence of her appraisal. She showed none of the normal discomfort an animal exhibits when held by a prolonged stare, only a keen curiosity and hints of deep awareness. By placing the wisp of sea grass in my hand, she had thrilled me beyond measure. I felt the keen pleasure of a child handed an unexpected gift.

Having learned from our eye contact all she needed to know, the dolphin rolled onto her side, presenting herself in a mute invitation I could not ignore. Wonder coursed through me as I stroked her warm, wet-rubber skin. What a privilege. The connection was a thrill far beyond anything I had anticipated. I would have walked all those miles from Perth for a moment such as this!

Within minutes, other early dolphin lovers had spotted our little group, children and adults jostling for attention. Every day people come in the hundreds, some for a few hours, others for days, weeks, and even months. From daybreak to dusk, from fifty to several hundred people throng the beach and shallows, hands reaching out to the dolphins, eager to connect with these amicable and patient creatures from the sea. And every person who approaches the dolphins is given careful scrutiny, as though the dolphins can see into each individual's inner being. Even where a hundred people compete for the attention of half a dozen dolphins, when a stranger walks down to the edge of the sea, a dolphin will look over the newcomer.

Later in the morning, I carried a folding chair onto the small jetty close by the stretch of dolphin beach. I was ready now for a deeper connection — if it happened! — a linking of consciousness on the level of Spirit.

For a while I watched the scene before me: people reaching and stroking, and squealing with excitement, their faces smiling, cameras clicking, a ranger patrolling the water to ensure the dolphins' safety. On the dolphins' side were the permanent smiles, gray hides, and flashing tails. The creatures cruised up and down along a hundred-yard stretch of beach in water no more than knee-deep to a human; it was a startling demonstration of trust.

The jetty was thronged with people, so I decided against Pan's method of exiting the body! Instead, I allowed my awareness of self to expand slowly past my physical senses. Even as the process unfolded, I was, surprisingly, aware of a definite surge of assistance from Pan, causing a spiritual reality to emerge as my physical reality receded.

———

I BECOME AWARE of being engulfed by ocean. Somewhere, a lone dolphin, an elderly female, is dying. I know this clearly for I can feel her — I *am* her, though only partly. I know she is aware of me, and even in her final moments she willingly shares her reality with me. It is almost as though she has expected me! I feel her lungs expand one last time as she takes a final deep breath of air, and I see through her eyes as she takes a last look at the blue, cloud-scudded sky, curiously close and solid, before her body slides smooth and slick beneath the waves as she dives her last dive. No cold forbidding ocean this, but a warm embrace of comfort and great familiarity.

My self is locked with the dolphin as she slides with abandon and grace into the beckoning depths. She is calm and totally purposeful. There is no pain, nothing obviously wrong. Shocked, I feel seawater flood her lungs after she violently expels her last breath, a rush of huge bubbles hastening to the surface far above. Her calmness controls my panic as her physical body, now vacated, slides gently toward the ocean floor.

Confusion overwhelms me. At the precise moment when her consciousness leaves the dolphin body, somewhere else in the vast ocean a powerful ejaculation forces a baby dolphin from its mother's womb into the waiting waters. Immediately, a nurse dolphin ushers it to the surface, where its first breath gushes into its blowhole.

As the death and birth coincide, I feel some essence of the exiting dolphin mix and merge with the newly born one. I feel other dolphin identities in the new dolphin, yet somehow they instantly integrate into a single sense of One. I am bewildered.

Now, consciously linked with the dolphin that has departed its body, I seem to expand swiftly into a faintly golden light, swimming with a freedom and grace akin to flight. The sensation of free flight deepens. I have a feeling of falling but no fear, and we burst through something into an ocean of richly golden, liquid light.

On the jetty, I am flooded with joy. Tears fall from my physical eyes and love washes over and through me in wave after exquisite wave. It is an exultation. With a dolphin, I dive in a body of light into a liquid of no more substance than an early morning vapor.

"Where am I?" The words, though silent, are spoken in my mind.

"No place. No place in human terms, but a place of substance. Call it a different layer of reality than the one you've been used to."

I feel shock as I recognize the silent voice. "Pan?" I ask in astonishment.

Only the laughter of wind chimes answers me, a sound strangely at home in this place of wonder.

"That was Pan, yes, but I am not it." There is reverence contained in the dolphin's words.

"Do you know Pan?"

"Why not? We know the Being, but not by that name. The name is an identity tag, meaningless — except for the meaning you humans give it, and that is generally false."

"But how can you know him?"

"Why not?" the dolphin counters. "A Being that moves through realities with total ease is not exclusive to the human experience. We know this Being, but we give it a different name."

"What is that?"

I sense a soft, curious whistle, which rises slightly to curl, hesitate, and end with a sigh. The very sound produces joy. For all its beauty and simplicity, I know the word Pan will never again be totally adequate.

For a while there is silence as we absorb the movement of the golden liquid light in which we bathe. Curiously, we are not moving through it; rather, it seems to flow through and around us. I feel that this life, so different from my usual one, is living me, that I am being experienced just as I am experiencing!

I remember the simultaneous death and birth I had witnessed. "How did that happen?" I ask.

Only as the dolphin begins to answer do I realize that I have not defined my question. But the dolphin and I, although separate, are One! Thought is not private.

"A dolphin is different from a human in a way you might find incomprehensible. Humans experience only a single self in each lifetime, while we experience a number of identities in each life."

"I don't understand."

The dolphin continued. "Humans experience life through intellectual processes. Your sense perceptions are relatively undeveloped. But we experience life through heightened, multiple-sense perception, and our intellectual capacity is far less developed."

A light dawned. "So our environment has basically determined the way we have developed?"

"True, except that we *choose* the environment we live in so we can develop what we consider important. The choice is not random."

"Are you suggesting that my presence here now might mean that I was a dolphin once?"

"I am saying you have a spiritual connection, as do all humans. We are not separate in consciousness."

There is a long, slow, no-time pause while I digest the implications of what I have learned. I have a feeling that the dolphin's reference to the experiencing of several identities is important, but the *why* of it eludes me. I feel I have something very important to learn here, but I cannot quite grasp it. It has to do with *identity*, possibly my own identity, of knowing "who I am."

The dolphin's next words could be my own thoughts. "There is a truth here that you must find. Consider your method of searching. Humans must reason to know, but we know simply by perceiving. Perception reveals no error even if it reveals only a fraction of truth, but reason can be in error, can misinterpret its fractional glimpse."

Another long, no-time pause! Without help, without words, I know that this dolphin and human experience combines to be something far greater than each alone. I know that I am here to learn more about myself, for each step along my path to self-realization seems to involve a higher order in Nature's expressions of conscious form. I have been water, mineral, plant, and animal; now, briefly, I am dolphin, an animal with an unmeasured intelligence. Each experience until now felt familiar, but this dolphin shares knowledge with me of which I have no concept.

I have the feeling that identity is the big lesson here, plus the ability to learn by perception rather than by reason alone.

"Humans are an immortal expression of Divine Love; identities are a brief expression of human individuality. Perceive the truth in this and you will realize the truth of Self for which you search." The dolphin's words are within me. We are dual, combined, yet very individual. I am neither overwhelmed nor overpowered, and I can leave any time I choose. However, although I share her words, sadly, much of their meaning I hold as knowledge that I cannot interpret. It is beyond me. A scale of Beingness is involved that I cannot fathom. I am acutely aware that my intuitive perception is slight compared with the dolphin's — yet I feel we are equal.

Without any awareness of change, my self has separated from the dolphin's. I see her light body shimmering like silver as she swims in the golden liquid light. Her eyes are on mine and in them I see a clear promise.

⟶

SUDDENLY, I was gazing out of physical eyes at a sleek dolphin swimming among the jostling people. Oddly, the dolphin turned away from all the outstretched hands, and with an incredible burst of speed approached the jetty. For a long moment, our eyes met; then, with surging strength, the dolphin headed out toward the open sea. I wondered if she, or any of the other nearby dolphins, had any knowledge of what had just taken place.

Later that day, I went for a long walk along the curving bay. Shell rock lay in large slabs on the glistening sand, and the fossilized shells stuck out in a profusion of varieties. As the tide receded, huge stretches of sand were revealed. Oyster catchers sporting black and white plumage and glossy orange beaks pecked them over. A few dozen large pelicans eyed me suspiciously as I strolled past, but I was not enough of a threat to prevent their frenzied preening and cleaning of their flight and chest feathers. Like leaves blowing before a mischievous breeze, sandpipers scuttled over the beach, moving in a thin, ragged wave before me.

I watched Nature as she unveiled her west coast beauty, but my thoughts were elsewhere. I was remembering the ease with which the dolphin had let go of her body at the moment of death. This ease attested to a greater-than-human knowing. There was no choking on that great lungful of water, just a smooth exit. She had surrendered her body with the same ease with which I would emerge from the driving seat of a car — and with no more attachment! It was apparent that death was no mystery to a dolphin.

I marveled then at the simultaneous birth and death. How extraordinary! That any life form could experience more than a single identity at once had never even occurred to me. This was not a group soul; it was an individuality that encompassed more than one. What a contradiction! The dying dolphin had retained its particular identity, while at the same time projecting some part of its consciousness into the baby. I had felt other dolphin identities — as many as six — enter and merge. Were they dying?

"Embrace the reality without too much analysis."

"Pan!" I was so pleased to see him at my side, I turned to embrace him, but — how strange! He was at my side, but then again he was not! I could see him, but he had no physical substance. Even before I reached out to hold him physically, I knew his solidity was an illusion. "Pan?"

He chuckled, a human sound mingled with distant wind chimes. "This will suffice. I am with you. Disengage your reasoning and allow the essence of your experience to filter across your senses. Allow what is to simply be. Not knowing allows access to *knowing*. Reason that!" Wind chimes and laughter drifted from silence into reality.

He continued to walk — or drift — at my side, and it was clear he expected me to stop thinking and...to feel? Clarity emerged. Without knowing how I knew, I came to understand how a number of dolphins could share a reality within one physical body. They share a perception of life, experiencing without conclusions. Conclusions do not exist for them. Humans, though, *reason* with life, drawing conclusions. If a number of human psyches were to inhabit a body and reason with life, the result would be chaos, madness. For the dolphins, a shared perception increases the experience and somehow magnifies it. There is no conflict, no confusion.

"You see, all things are possible when you allow the possibility of impossibilities!" Again the laughter, not mocking, but so filled with joy and love that tears filled my eyes.

"But, Pan, what about those things the dolphin told me?"

"What do you...feel?"

"I don't know. I really don't. The meaning is so far beyond my experience. I just don't know."

"Wonderful. Another opportunity for knowing through not knowing."

I sighed, releasing the problem. It would just have to wait for some other...and again came clarity!

The death and exit had been smooth and familiar, the dolphin totally at ease, in control. She "knew" what to expect. The golden sea of light had been as much — or more — home than the physical ocean that housed her physical body. Generally, we humans do not know what to expect of death, and the death experience therefore varies according to our spiritual development. By sharing perception through an individual, the dolphins shared a spiritual evolvement. As *one* knew, they *all* knew.

The ocean of golden mist existed on another level of reality. It seemed to be a place of deliberate synthesis, where the merging of two streams of consciousness created a greater wholeness in each individual stream than the single experience did, or could.

The number of individual dolphins and humans involved was comparatively small, but it felt deliberate. I was aware that it was not an experience exclusive to me, for in the ocean of light I could feel other participants. In terms of Wholeness, the experience of the few became the experience of the All, even if not every individual was conscious of it. Consciousness is One. As humans, our individuality separates us from each other. Dolphins experience the individual on a shared basis: thus, individuality is synthesized into a holistic experience. Oneness!

The differences between dolphins and humans loomed large to me . . . and then receded. We were as different as earth and water, and yet as close as brothers and sisters.

Later that evening, I shared my experience with the others in our group. They accepted it easily. Still, I felt the need for confirmation. My experience was so outrageous alongside the little dolphin literature I had read, I was very hesitant to share it any further.

Early on our fifth morning at Monkey Mia, Treenie and I went for a walk along the beach. We talked of our time with the dolphins. After about three-quarters of an hour, Treenie turned back, but I continued to walk. As I strolled on, I tried to communicate my need for confirmation to the dolphins, but I heard and felt nothing. Some two and a half hours later, I arrived back at the caravan park to be met on the beach by an excited Treenie.

"What do you think?" she called out as I approached. "A mother dolphin came in about an hour ago with a new baby." She paused, her eyes sparkling. "The rangers estimate that it is five days old."

"Oh," I said blankly. "That's nice."

"Don't you see?" exploded Treenie. "You had the experience of the dolphin's death and birth five days ago. This confirms it for you. If the mother dolphin had come in tomorrow, it would have been too late."

Treenie beamed at me while it all slowly registered.

"Wake up. We leave first thing tomorrow. The dolphin has met your need," she said patiently.

While Treenie went to make me some coffee, I walked over to the crowds, excitedly pointing at the new baby. I stared in wonder as mother and baby swam among the people in total trust. The baby was maybe four feet long, a perfect replica of its mother. As they cruised close, I reached out, stroking the baby as it briefly detached itself from its mother's side. Instantly, I knew that this was the baby whose birth I had experienced. In that moment, I felt the familiar presence of a female dolphin swimming with a body of light in a golden ocean of mist — and swimming in the baby body in a physical ocean by the mother's side.

"It gives us joy to meet your need of confirmation. We acknowledge that it was neither doubt nor lack of acceptance that created your need, but a sincere desire to represent us in a truthful manner." Fleetingly swift, the words flowed through my mind, highlighted by the presence of the dolphin of light. Then the words faded into the "oooh's" and "aaah's" of human admiration as the little dolphin bobbed in the sea beside its mother's sleek body. And within a few minutes, the two had gone, heading out to join the large school of dolphins playing offshore.

I sighed with pleasure. When Treenie and I had come to Monkey Mia, I had had no expectations of any exceptional happenings. I had come content to see and stroke wild dolphins; anything else was a bonus. The last thing I had expected was Pan — and that the dolphins knew him seemed extraordinary. As always, my experience had been another step along my path, but the reality of self-realization and stepping through the membrane into Beyond seemed remote. I had learned from the animal consciousness to cease judging myself, and I had experienced the dogs' unconditional love for me, but, alas, perfect self-acceptance defeated me. Knowing about the need for unconditional love was important, but to actualize this knowledge was vital to my progress. Now I had learned that individuality in a dolphin can include a number of separate identities. Wow! I was aware of being locked into my present identity, but how could I possibly break free? This identity is me, but it's only my personal self. I wanted the Greater Self. Is that some other me? The dolphin had given me a clue where it — I? — was, but I was helpless to pursue it. I sighed, perplexed. All I could do was allow Pan to teach me in his mystical way. I had once said he was my guru; well, I would trust him. That, at least, I had learned!

8 Entering Another Realm

"Am I ready to enter the Guidestone again and walk through the Door?"

Pan shook his head absently, his eyes cast up into the branches high above.

"But why? I've experienced all the realms of Nature you said I needed to explore. I've learned many lessons, so what's stopping me?"

He pointed up into the branches of the tree against which I was leaning. "That is so beautiful," he murmured. Curious, I stared up into the tree, following the line of each branch and limb and looking in vain for the creature that was evoking his admiration and attention. Systematically, my eyes searched the tree, but I could find nothing. Defeated, I asked, "What is?"

He turned toward me, his golden dome of a head seeming to reflect the rising golden sun. "Look at the leaves outlined against the sky. Watch the play of their movement. They live."

I gazed up into the tree again. Ah, yes! He was right. Now I could see and appreciate the movement of beautifully sculptured gray-green leaves set against the clear blue sky. Maybe it was a breeze in the upper branches, but each leaf was moving as though separately animated, engaging in active conversation with its neighbor.

"*That's* why."

"Uh! Why what?"

"Why you are not yet ready."

"What! Just because I didn't notice the leaves in the way you did?"

"No. Because you are so preoccupied with form you do not perceive the formless. The leaves you so glibly dismiss as waving in the breeze are, in fact, animated by other forces that you should have remembered."

I frowned in perplexity.

"Relive. Remember."

Starting with the dolphin encounter, I fumblingly worked my way back through the range of extraordinary experiences that Pan had opened for me. When I eventually recalled the blackberry experience, reliving the relationship between blackberry and tiny Beings, I understood the connection. "So what happens now?"

"You have connected with another form of intelligent physical life. Now you must renew and expand your connections with metaphysical intelligence on this planet."

"Gee! Is there no end to this?"

"That is for you to decide."

"I didn't mean it."

Pan chuckled mischievously. "Are you ready?"

In my haste, words tumbled out. "Hang-on-a-minute-before-you-do-one-of-your-snatches. Let me jump out." I was breathless.

His smile was a delight. "I planned to."

Vigorously, I jumped up and sat down heavily a few times. Then suddenly I was up and out.

RATHER TO MY ASTONISHMENT, I am balancing on the slender twigs of a fallen branch. Whereas they would normally be crushed flat by my weight, I am easily supported a couple of feet above the ground. I am aware of light around my body, which is glowing from some inner source. It occurs to me that I am that light.

When I step off the twigs, my weightlessness opens up a whole new experience. I lift up my arms and float gently upward, hovering as I hold my arms out at shoulder level. Timelessness is obvious; I can feel it. No aging mars this wondrous realm. There's no hurry to do, no hurry to finish, just a timeless sense of Being.

I look at the tree through eyes that are undoubtedly my own but that must normally be closed. Imagine my dilemma. I am trying to describe something that is metaphysical with words that have been created for a physical reality. The tree on which I feast my eyes is both physical and more than physical. To say it is beautiful is trite. It is something beyond our classification of beauty; it is *alive* in a way far beyond our understanding of that word. Take the fallen branch on which I am standing as an example. By normal definitions, it is dead, a lifeless branch, yet I now see it as seething with energy. Although it is no longer animated by the life sap of the tree, it is nevertheless vibrant with a life not dependent on the growing tree. Despite a process of decay, the "dead" wood is a force field within itself, host to an incredible array of tiny, almost transparent Beings.

And the tree from which it fell! In normal terms, the tree is just another gum tree, without any particular beauty of shape or foliage. But in this realm it is breathtaking. It is a living rainbow moving as a column from the Earth, flowing into the shape of the physical tree. The rainbow of energy is enclosed in a sheath of vibrant, white, motionless motion.

"Nice, huh?"

"Nice! *Nice* doesn't get close." I turn expectantly toward Pan, but he is not with me. Instead, I am gazing upon an elf, a classic elf of the type I read of as a child, except for one thing: it is easily three feet tall!

"No good looking for Pan. I am your guide in this realm."

"Oh, er... thank you."

"You are not frightened, are you?"

"No. I don't think I am. Just a bit disconcerted."

"Oh. Why?"

"Several reasons. For one thing, I didn't know elves could be so tall. Also, while Pan is nothing like I ever imagined, you're a classic fairy tale elf. That's odd, to put it mildly. Even your clothes are classic elf costume." I have to smile. "You're a nonsurprising surprise!"

The elf laughs, a sound startlingly reminiscent of wind chimes, and I feel suspicious. "You're not Pan having me on, are you?"

More laughter, echoed by a myriad of tiny Beings smaller than damsel flies. They fly around my head, diving into my aura of light with obvious enjoyment. I have the impression that they are swimming in my Being in much the same way that I swam in the river.

"Really! I am not Pan. He is an entity unto himself."

Bemused, I gaze again at the elf. My impression is of neither male nor female. The elf is of both sexes while being neither! It is wearing a small green skull cap set on fine yellow curls. A dark green, skin-tight tunic encloses it from neck to wrists and ankles. On its tiny, slender feet are pointed brown boots. The face now regarding me with amused tolerance is beautiful — the features are delicate yet stamped with strength. The nose is tiny, exquisitely molded above small, clearly defined lips. Blue eyes of great intensity meet my own, and I feel connected to this Being in a way I do not understand. The most ridiculous question surfaces in my mind. How did it get those clothes on? No zips, no buttons! The elf and the clothes are not separate. Odd.

My thoughts must be as transparent as ever!

"I do not put these clothes on, I draw them to me. I can draw any form to me I wish...within certain limits. I do not put clothes on; they just *are*. I drew this form from you, from your impression of elves."

Aha! That explains a lot. "So you can be something else if you wish?"

Instantly, the elf disappears, but in a blink a faun about the same height and build is standing in its place. This is another delightful Being. Its head combines that of a child and a kid; it is blended in an utterly natural way. I can see why children are called kids, so completely natural is this faun. Again, it is a classic. The body is that of a boy; the legs and feet are a kid's.

"Do you like me?"

"I think you are wonderful. I *love* you." I am surprised, but it is the simple truth.

The faun vanishes, to be replaced by the elf. "Which do you prefer?"

"Do you mean I have a choice?"

"If you need to choose."

"I don't. Any form you want to take suits me. Even though you change form, your energy remains the same. I'm not sure how I do it, but I recognize the essential you."

In a blink, the elf vanishes once more, to be replaced by a twinkling light about the size of a ping-pong ball. "Are you comfortable with me now?" The words come in the same manner of inner hearing, and I can feel the Beingness of the light.

"Yes, absolutely. But do you have a name?"

"Not in humanese. You give me one."

"How about Ping?"

"I like it. Any more questions?"

"No."

"Then you are ready."

"Ready for the Door?" I ask excitedly.

"Oh, good heavens, no. Ready for our realm, is what I mean."

"But aren't I in your realm?"

A thin chuckle comes from Ping. "To coin a phrase from your own mind, you ain't seen nothing yet!"

"Oh! So where do we go from here?"

Ping is flying around me, a flashing circle of twinkling light. "We are only on the periphery of my realm, sort of half in yours and half in mine. Follow me and do as I tell you."

I notice a huge orb of pale silver light not far away. How it got there or where it came from I do not know. It looks rather as though the moon has fallen to Earth, and though it is opaque, it is verging on transparent. Ping is already flying toward it and, after only a moment's hesitation, I follow. I am half floating, half flying. I realize that when Pan took me onto the river he must have helped me move around without my knowing it. I feel a bit wobbly as I follow Ping, but my control rapidly improves.

As I pass through the silver orb, I feel a brief chill penetrate my Beingness; then it is gone. What I see, feel, am, is sheer wonder. Although it is still daylight, the light is silver, rather than sunlight. Soft, subtle shades of glowing light cast shadows unlike normal shadows. The shadows here are somehow transparent and wraithlike, highlighting rather than subduing whatever they fall upon. The light is fascinating — it comes from within rather than without, and is clearly an energy. I am aware that normal Earth light is energy, but this is different — you can *feel* this light. My whole body is tingling with light. Light is my substance, my food, my drink, even my breath.

I am not breathing; there is no need. This light is everything I need, everything I am. I can feel this light as my Beingness and, even more wonderfully, I can feel my Beingness in the light. Where this light shines and illuminates this ethereal realm, I am.

I am Ping, an experience of Being that is extraordinarily different from humanness, yet it contains the same notes of a cosmic song. Our inner melody is One, but the singer and the song are very different.

Before me is a small, radiant-green hill. I could say illumined-green or living-green and each term would be accurate. Beyond the hill, everything is shrouded in silver light; there is no distant vision. All is here and now. What I see is what I am involved in; there is nothing else. Small trees, amazing trees, are growing on the hill. The physical tree is clearly apparent, yet within and without are other dimensions of tree. Within is a similar flowing, spreading stretch of rainbow light permeated by countless numbers of bee-sized Beings of intense light. I cannot see any form to them, just light...and energy. But, oh, what energy! Simply standing near these myriad Beings is rather like taking a blast of heatless energy, as in the chamber in the Guidestone.

"Without their assistance, there could be no trees." Ping's voice is with me, his own light body close by. Of course, what I am seeing is not really seen! It is a totality of spiritual absorption. In some inexplicable manner, I am all that is happening in this realm. I do not see it — I *am* it. Beyond that, I cannot explain.

The tiny specks of energy, Nature Spirits, are zipping in and out of the tree. Obviously, to them the physical tree is of a substance no denser than the rainbow light. But there is more to this. I see another Being that both contains and is contained in the tree. I am aware that to separate them is to cause the tree's death, yet the Spirit of the tree is eternal, immortal. And so also is the tree. Whether the tree is physically cut down or dies of old age, the physical tree and the Spirit of tree are one and the same. Death is the great illusion of physical reality. This Being, often called a Deva, has an influence stretching beyond the physical reach of the tree. I can feel it. All trees of a species are contained within the ethereal body of a Deva spirit, no matter how physically separated they may be.

I feel approval from Ping as I and the Deva merge in consciousness. In this realm, there is only here and now; all else is shrouded in a silver nothingness. The same is true of the reality of Deva Spirit. With respect to the Spirit, distance and time do not exist. The Earth is no more than the palm of my hand, the beginning and end no more or less than Now. This is the Deva's reality. Even the hill contains and is contained by a Spirit Being, one that differs from that of the tree inasmuch as Deva connects tree with air while the Rock Spirit connects tree with Earth. And the trees? They are a pipeline of Energy connecting the stars with Earth, essential to our well-being, our balance, and universal vision.

Ping moves to the hill, pausing at its summit. As I follow, a whole new scenario opens before me. Different types of Nature Spirits are massed upon the hilltop. There are many hundreds of elves all moving around with a purpose and order that is somehow both poetic and confusing. All have an overriding quality of gentleness and fairness. Hovering above the elves are tiny patterns of light weaving in and out of a self-contained spiral. As I watch, I see they are minute, transparent forms as elegant as...fairies! Enthralled, I watch them winking — they are tiny transparent fairies. Then they are intense specks of light. Then they are fairies. They have all the ease and grace of butterflies delicately opening and closing their wings in the sunlight.

Ping is hovering close by, taking care of me rather than becoming involved with the activity on the hill. I watch, utterly bewitched by the magic of this other realm, which is both within and outside our own.

Gradually, the elves begin to fade away, becoming light, only to reappear as though nothing has happened. The effect is disconcerting, but it does not seem unnatural. By now, my impression is that most of the elves are consumed in light, and they begin an intricate dance, weaving among each other in an ever-changing pattern of flexible lines. No longer following the contours of the hill, they create the impression of a multidimensional dance of light. A line of light simply winks away to appear at some other point, continuing the beautiful pattern of dance. Above this structured dance of total freedom, myriad tiny fairy lights are swirling at tremendous speed in an ordered part of this complex interweaving of energies.

Ten of the elves have retained their classic elf shape, and now, in front of Ping and me, they clasp hands to form a ring. "They want you to stand in the circle," says Ping encouragingly.

"Do I have to do anything?" I whisper.

Ping chuckles. "Not really. Being involved is doing."

Light as a feather, I step forward. The circle opens to allow me entry and then closes around me. Gradually, the bodies of the elves brighten, becoming lighter and lighter until their forms are lost to some powerful inner illumination. Slowly yet steadily, the circle of light is closing in on me until it touches . . . and I see anew.

A faint shimmering ray of violet-pink light is pouring down from the sky, bathing the hill on which I stand. In some strange way, I can see that this light is composed of minute particles of color, infinitely tiny. They swirl ceaselessly, involved in the same order of movement that is the Nature Spirits' dance. I am aware that this outpouring is endlessly absorbed by the Earth, a source of continuous energy.

I have the impression of tiny, random flakes of snow in the center of this swirling light, caught as though by some inner breeze at odds with the ordered pattern of natural energy. Faintly, the haunting sound of distant wind chimes rings across the hill. Then, in a manner defying all logic and reason, the flakes of snow-light come together as Pan.

He looks at me and smiles, and within that smile is more love than I ever knew was possible. Love beyond human comprehension washes over me, bathing me in sheer goodness. Only in essence is he the same Pan who visits me in our physical reality. He is the violet-pink light, the energy of Earth, the Spirit of Nature.

"Do you recognize your surroundings?" His voice is within me, crystal clear and unmistakably Pan.

"No, I don't. Should I?"

"This is the little mountain on which you live. A far more in-depth view to be sure, but the same locality expressing the same energies."

"Good heavens!"

Pan gives a hollow laugh. "I like that. Heaven it is, providing you can see it. Equally, Earth is heaven, here and now, if you can accept that reality."

"How do I do that?"

"Know who you are."

"Oh! Who am I?"

"No one can be told who they are. It is an experience, a shift in reality, a change in consciousness. The dolphin told you who you are, but until you are that Greater Self you cannot know it." He chuckled. "The irony of truth. Who you are encompasses all you are now experiencing, but this is under my influence. When you become that Greater Self, you will know this is who you have always been."

"Is this why Treenie and I moved here? Because of the mountain?"

"There is no single factor. This is *your* place to be at this time. There is no more a single *reason* for anything than there is a single reality. Life is like the multifaceted crystal you experienced in the plateau. Each facet comprises the whole, yet the human view of life is but a single facet. Know the crystal as a whole, and you know who you are."

"It's very difficult. I have been through the experiences of Nature as you required of me, but I still don't know who I am in the way you speak of. What more is there?"

"The facets of Self."

"How am I supposed to come to grips with...me?"

Wind chimes peal delightful laughter into the silence.

"In your inimitable manner, I am sure you will manage."

Sadly, wind chimes are the only sound remaining as the whole scene around me slowly fades away. Only as it fades do I realize that a faint, hauntingly beautiful sound has been permeating everything I have experienced. It is so alien a sound, yet so familiar, that I hear it only as it ceases to be — or, to be accurate, when I am no longer able to encompass it. As I am compelled toward a dense physical reality, so I lose the sound of foreverness.

Everything disappears. All too soon only Ping remains, and I feel desperately sad — sad because nothing has changed. All that unheralded wonder is continuing forever, but I am expelled by the nature of my physical reality. It is beyond my reach.

"And there you have it!"

Even as Ping speaks into my mind, I realize my own thoughts. I am not really expelled, even though the reality is nonphysical. One of the purposes of this journey into Nature is for me to learn of other realities and be comfortable with them. "Is all this what life is really about?' I ask Ping.

"Yes and no. This is one reality of life, not *the* reality. And incidentally, it is not beyond your reach. Your purpose on Earth embraces what you just experienced."

"What *is* my purpose on Earth?"

Ping materializes as the classic elf, hovering a few inches above the ground. "It will only have meaning or value if you find your purpose."

I give up on the subject!

Ping accompanies me, and again I perceive the forest of trees as I first had, as a column of light and color both containing and contained by the physical tree.

"Can I give you some advice?" asks Ping.

I turn to him eagerly. "You most certainly can."

"Try to hold the realization in your mind that everything you can see around you is *you*. Nothing is not you. Nothing is separate from you. When you plant a shrub, or pick a flower, it is you — totally, absolutely you. You in a different form, another disguise, but you."

I am impressed by Ping's sincerity and power. Each *you* is laced with emphasis, as though to punch the ideas into my psyche.

———

PING VANISHED, and with him went all metaphysical reality. Tears trickled down my cheeks as I stared blindly at the stark physical beauty of the surrounding trees. I had never in my life felt so blind, so numb, so entombed, so dense.

I sat for a long time, trying to come to terms with my normal reality. Gazing at the area where I had so recently experienced euphoria, I tried in vain to recapture the images. I got unsteadily to my feet and walked my heavy body on heavy legs to the very place where violet-pink light had poured — was pouring — into the Earth. I sank to the ground and lay flat, hoping to absorb some of the energy I knew was there.

I gazed up into the sky. This was the most incredible of all that I had experienced. Ping's last words remained with me: "Everything you see around you is *you*." I could believe and understand that now, after all I had experienced in the consciousness of Nature, but Ping's words summed it up. The human consciousness *is* in all life.

Why had Pan propelled me into the realm of Nature Spirits? It could only be to show me, through experience, that this world of ours is not quite as it appears. He wanted to expand my vision, my inner knowing. And, as before, my experience of it became an experience in the whole human consciousness. I also learned that this world of ours is not *only* ours. We not only share it with Nature, we share it with Beings on a dimension out of our physical sight. Then I remembered my artistic friend Kinsley and his drawings of the Nature Spirits. Clearly, some humans can see these dimensions. Where was it all leading? Surely there was nothing left in Nature to experience — except humanity itself!

9 Lost

I t took several weeks for me to recover my equilibrium. Each day seemed to be shrouded in clouds. Not even the sun could disperse my sense of loss. The weightiness of physicality was a drag, but normality prevailed, everyday life continued, and gradually the metaphysical impact faded.

Pan was not to be seen, but I had the feeling that he was never very far away. I would have welcomed Ping with open arms, but that little Being was now unavailable.

I spent quite a while discussing the latest "happening" with Treenie. While she was a good listener, as ever, she could not bring the experience back.

Still, her advice was practical. "It seems that a central theme of your experience has been a total involvement in here and now. And it seems very clear that while you are fretting and thinking about it, you are not here and now."

"Yes, I realize that. It's just that — oh, what's the good?"

Time resolved the problem. A few weeks of compulsory involvement in the regular mundane realities of life, and my balance was restored. Once again I could appreciate Nature on her physical terms, but now there was a difference. There's no way I could have lived through that metaphysical experience without my ways of seeing and relating to physical life being changed. My ability to perceive the invisible beyond the visible was becoming activated and enhanced. I now knew that when I listened to the silent voices of Nature, the intelligence I sensed was not abstract. Beings of another reality were the architects of form, the builders of our physical Nature. One of the insights I had gained came with hindsight. When I had witnessed the supernatural dance of the Nature Beings, I had felt the vaguest twinge of familiarity. Later, when thinking about it, the association became clear. The dance had taken the shape and form of the double-spiraled helix of the DNA. I now knew that beyond DNA there was intelligence of an order that would never submit to a physical inquiry. I would have to use more than my intellect. In my journey toward true Self, I would have to learn through doing and being, by knowing through not knowing, as the dolphins did!

PLANNING AND PLANTING a new garden on top of our small mountain near the ocean was pure pleasure. For the next few months, I buried myself in it, lugging ironstone boulders around to suit Treenie's and my taste in landscaping. The open forest I left strictly alone, complete with undergrowth, fallen trees, and rotten hollow logs. There were also several species of native orchids and wildflowers to enjoy where we found them.

Gradually, I grew to love our new home. I now felt connected with the Spirit of the mountain, at ease within some extrasensory aspect of Nature that increasingly imbued me. Despite our intuition that this was *our* place when Treenie and I first set foot on this mountain, it had taken me several months to release the river and embrace the mountain. Although I felt a greater connection with Nature than ever before, I was now far less attached.

Lost

My relationship with the land was deeper, yet without the roots, and balanced.

Still, during Pan's prolonged absence, I felt an ever-growing sense that I was not doing something I should be doing. I began to feel restless, longing for the kind of action he had made available to me. But the months passed, and nothing! Finally, I decided to go it alone. I gave the matter a lot of thought, trying to determine just where, how, and when I could go. Under Pan's guidance, there had always been a destination and a purpose, plus the security of knowing — or hoping — he would bail me out if things got too rough. Now I was on my own.

But I could come up with no goal that seemed like an inner imperative. Finally, I pushed myself to my limit, and a new idea dawned. Suppose I was now ready for the Guidestone. Suppose I tried to discover my Greater Self on my own. Surely then I could pass through the Door into Beyond. Suppose I initiated my own initiation.

The idea excited me. There were no answers to my suppositions. I simply had to try to find out for myself.

I had to admit that the prospect of going it alone frightened me. My only journey into the Guidestone had been nerve-wracking, and I did not want to repeat it. I procrastinated for another month, hoping that Pan would appear and take control. He did not. I then spent a week trying to convince myself not to experiment with things I didn't understand, but I remained unconvinced. During this time, I immersed the Guidestone in a bucket of fresh rainwater for a couple of days and set it in the full sun to get charged as I had before. I even looked for the little mustard-seed hole, but in vain. Physically, it did not exist.

The inevitable moment arrived. I waited until Treenie was out shopping, took the Guidestone onto the point where I had seen violet-pink light pour into the Earth (I figured I might as well choose a safe place), and sat down comfortably with my back resting against a friendly boulder.

For a while I stared at the Guidestone, half hoping I would get switched off and drawn out as before, but not really believing or even wanting that to happen. The stone sat on a tiny mound about a yard in front of me, as innocent as any of the many rocks scattered about the mountain, but distinguished by its honey color and egg shape. Half an hour passed, and nothing happened. Determined that it was now or never, I jumped up vigorously and leaped skyward before collapsing back to my seat. I leaped up and down until I was exhausted, and still remained totally earthbound, so I gave up in sheer disgust. After ten minutes of frantic leaping, my lungs were panting and wheezing like a pair of ancient bellows.

Soon, when I was breathing at a normal rate, I lay back on the grass, deliberately dismissing the problem and relaxing. I simply watched the leaves on the gum trees gently swaying in a caressing breeze and became blank, emptied of thought, as I relaxed. Without any intent, my mind's eye conjured up the inner chamber of the Guidestone...and, with a total absence of effort, I was again in that vast interior.

I AM SURROUNDED by the flames without heat and, as a whispering background chant, the endless litany of *"run, run, run."* This time, I am unafraid. Walking forward with a firm tread, I move deeper into the colossal chamber, seeking the massive Doors that previously challenged me. I can feel the presence of the Keeper of the Door, but it is no longer a threat. I feel no menace, only a keen awareness of my presence. After what seems a long time, during which I walk farther into the chamber, I begin to wonder if the Doors still exist. I stop several times, peering into the softly illuminated chamber immediately around me. The flames, which are continual, provide the light, but they also block from my vision anything else that might be of interest. I have no choice but to persevere. The uncomfortable thought that I do not know how to get out of here assails me, but I dismiss it, intending only to go forward into Beyond.

It seems I walk forever, yet I feel no fatigue. Despite the paradox, I am aware of the passing of an enormous amount of time in this state of timelessness. I cannot explain this; it just is! It feels as if years could be passing while I walk, but the time may have been mere seconds.

As I continue doggedly on, the flames grow taller around me. For some reason, I feel encouraged by this, and it is without surprise that I eventually see the vast Doors looming before me.

They are closed, but, as before, I place one hand on each Door at the center and push. They open as softly and smoothly as the passing of a dragonfly.

Before me, in pristine beauty, I see another Earth spinning in orbit — our planet Earth. I have only to pass through the open Doors to go Beyond.

Gingerly, I put one hand out before me, and, as before, I encounter resistance. Although I do not have a physical heart in this mystic place, I can feel my heart pounding. I push hard against the resistance, but it is useless. The harder I push, the greater is the resistance. This gives me an idea. Turning around to face into the chamber, I stand nonchalantly for a while, before casually leaning back against the invisible membrane. "Grrr! Scrap one good idea!"

I try everything I can think of to get through that open Door. I try crawling, jumping, wriggling, even an apprehensive rush to bash my way through, but nothing works.

I'm beaten, and that insidious, unwanted thought comes creeping back into my mind like a horrid worm: how do I get out of here? I do not know where or how I came in at the back, and I cannot get out the front Door!

As I mull this over, I become aware of a malignant energy close by, and a chill of anxiety sweeps over me. I peer around, trying to see beyond the flames, when with devastating abruptness the flames die down to a few flickering inches. My anxiety climbs higher.

Following a new thrust of hope, I begin to walk alongside one of the huge Doors, hoping to find some salvation where it meets the wall of the chamber. I have an uncomfortable feeling that my reasoning is faulty, but doing something, anything, is better than doing nothing.

Within a few paces, the malignant chill intensifies, and I peer cautiously ahead. Wrapped in living gloom, I see an old witch, and she is staring at me. Her eyes are cold fire, utterly evil. Horrified, I gasp in sheer terror and, turning, I run blindly, frantic to get away.

A sudden blast of cold heat washes over me and I am spinning over and over in utter blackness, sobbing in horror. I float, aware of the evil presence of the crone, but I am no longer able to run. I drift in no-place, lost in some awful dimension of desolation and isolation.

Centuries or seconds pass, I have no way of knowing, but the terrifying, unrelieved darkness is giving way to a gray-white gloom. Much of my terror has been sobbed away and, although I am frightened by the presence of the old crone, she is no longer in my immediate vicinity.

Gradually at first, and then with a rapidly increasing and undeniable strength, I am gathered up and hurled into a large, elegantly furnished room.

I am a sixteen-year-old girl, tall for my age, with long blonde tresses reaching down my back. I am unhappy, in pain, and dying. My name is Jandine, and I was born with a deep and passionate desire to sing. Singing is my love and my life, my one ambition. Can you imagine the devastation I faced on my fifteenth birthday when my father forbade me to sing? He gave me a long lecture on how a family of our wealth and social standing could not possibly tolerate such a low-bred activity. He told me he would lose his position and standing of favor with the king if I so demeaned myself. He forbade me on threat of banning me not only from my family but from my country as well. That I could not face. I appealed to my mother for help, but she is weak. He dominates her ruthlessly and, much as I hate to admit it, she is no more than his pampered lady in court.

At one stage, I even threatened to ask the king's permission to sing at court, but my father beat me and kept me locked up until I promised I would not disgrace him so. He has always been a remote figure, seldom giving, mostly denying, yet until this I loved my father. Now I hate him. My mother I despise. How could such weakness be so greatly rewarded in life? She is a despicable creature, and I know she dislikes me intensely. I think it is because I am so much stronger than she. She avoids me, although her reason for avoiding me has changed. Once it was because she feared my anger when we clashed, which was often; now it is because she cannot face me.

I slowly draw aside the silk scarf that is wrapped around my neck, and I look again at the terrible growth that is revealed. It is as though a clenched fist is being forced through my neck, pushing out from my throat. It is red, angry, and malignant. I fear it, for I know that I am dying. I do not fear death too badly; I have had time to come to terms with it. But I am sad because many of my hopes and dreams will remain unfulfilled. When I used to sing, lost in an inner joy, I would feel a deep inner knowing, almost as though an inner me was trying to tell me something. I have the feeling that I am more than merely mortal, but I do not know with whom I can safely discuss such sacrilegious thoughts. Such speculation has long interested me. It is ironic that I will soon have the opportunity to learn if I have an immortal Self that can survive beyond death. Sometimes in my deepest, most disturbed dreams, I see an old woman coming toward me. She has terrible eyes that sear my very soul, and I wake up screaming. I know that she is death.

One day, feeling sick and shaky, I decide to go to the temple and pray for help. When the carriage comes around to my door, I notice that the footman cringes back, as though afraid I may contaminate him. I can forgive him, for, much as I hate it, my breath is becoming putrid as the growth eats deeper into my flesh.

Entering the tall, fluted doors of the temple, I feel, along with guilt at my long absence, a breath of cool freshness. Since the growth took hold, my sanctuary has been a dell in the thick oak woods of my father's estate. There, I used to sing, unheard and unhindered, with only the birds and beasts of the woods to hear me. I say used to, for I can no longer sing at all. As my voice fades, so does my health. I am sad; I have many regrets. If only my mother had been able to give me a sister or brother, things might have been different, but she could not. When I was younger I overheard one of the servants describe her as barren as a clay bat. It took years before I understood her remark.

I walk deeper into the coolness of the temple, approaching the altar. There is no one else present, and I feel grateful as I kneel down to pray. I am so thin now, my knees are little more than bone. For months I have lived on a thin gruel, unable to swallow anything of substance. I have felt the presence of that woman of death lately, but I am no longer frightened. Death is inevitable, and I accept that...even welcome it, though I do not know what to expect. I can only hope that my thoughts and deepest feelings may be based on truth. If I have a Self that can survive death, then it is possible that I could live again in some other body. This is what I pray for.

The walk to the altar has drained what little energy I have, and I feel shaky on my knees. A hand gently grips my shoulder, startling me, and the robed figure of a traveling sage kneels at my side, supporting me. I am weary and grateful, and my head rests on his shoulder, my hand automatically fluttering toward my silk scarf to ensure that my throat is covered.

With a gentleness I have never before encountered, the sage takes my hand in one of his, and with his other hand draws my scarf from my throat. He ignores my weak protests, and, to my shocked astonishment, he bows his head and kisses me on my throat. He kisses me directly on the growth.

Something wonderful is happening. I can feel a warmth spreading through my body, delicious relaxation and peace far beyond anything in my experience — and I am floating, floating, floating.

I am aware of my self floating, slightly shaken by the way I have just died. How I love that unknown sage as I drift in no-place, nowhere at all, in no-time. I realize with an inner glow that I *have* survived death.

I am floating, drifting in timeless space, surrounded and contained in pale light. Drifting, falling, turning over and over... frightened... falling... toward trees... a man...

I hurry through the deep woods toward my home feeling rather pleased. My name is Joaquín. Beneath my arm, in a bundle of moist sacking, I carry six new plants, all unknown to science. I am scowling and automatically clutch at my neck. Scientists! What do they know? Pompous, stuffed-up idiots standing together in an elite, ignorant group. I seethe with rage as my thoughts follow a familiar track, my fingers tightening their grip on my neck. I was born with a twisted neck and distorted features. A large hump of gristly flesh straddles my shoulders and, I confess, I am not pretty to see.

My parents were not deterred by my physical problem, and the tutor they employed declared that I was a brilliant scholar. Since then, I have advanced the study of botany immensely, yet I remain unacknowledged, unrecognized. Instead, I am considered a freak!

During the past few years, I pushed back the limits on human knowledge of Nature. I have discovered that I contain the ability to communicate with Nature. It has crossed my mind that God may have wished to compensate me for my handicap. Recently, thoughts, ideas, and concepts regarding Nature have flowed into my mind, and my experiments have confirmed them. That Nature is an expression of intelligence I no longer doubt, yet such speculation is considered blasphemy. Nature has taught me that I am immortal, as is all humanity. Sometimes when I am being ridiculed I wish immortality were mine exclusively! I am now embarking on studies to find a way to prove that each separate human is part of one whole consciousness, including Nature, yet I suspect it will be a waste of time. It will gain me even more ridicule. I am almost certain that we each have — or are — a Greater Self, but to discover this part of our normal everyday self requires total dedication. This is why I probably will never prove my theory.

I have shared my insights with a few friends, and the meetings I now attend to discuss my ideas have become quite crowded. This pleases me, for it is a measure of acceptance.

Passing from beneath the huge trees that surround my home, I enter my house. Shock! Half a dozen soldiers are waiting, and they roughly seize me. The contents of my house are smashed and scattered, my botanical experiments strewn about and wrecked.

———

I HAVE BEEN IMPRISONED for more than a month, and there is no hope. I have been tortured into confessing that I am a sorcerer, and I am bleeding and broken. My legs have been disjointed, my arms broken, and my face mutilated. Today I face the prospect of one last session of torture, designed to implicate my very few friends, but this I will not do. This session will be the last because today I will die. My deformity has brought me a life of ridicule and rejection. The few dear friends I have shall not suffer for their love and acceptance.

I lie secured on a rack and slowly I am being stretched. Intense pain is searing my body like fire. Amazingly, an old crone stands in the corner watching the torture. She frightens me more than anything they can do. They engender pain; she engenders fear. She alone threatens my feelings of life after death — and no physical torture could be worse than *nothing* after death. Her eyes blaze with an unholy fire and, as the pain reaches an unendurable crescendo, I fall, spinning slowly, into pale, gray light.

Floating, drifting, pain ending, healing…I have survived. I was right, there is life after death, but who am I? I am

Jandine...No, I am Joaquín...or...am I? Floating, drifting, hovering in a mist of subdued light, images flicker and flash in my mind. I am falling, falling toward those images that I see... falling...

I cry weakly, fatigued and distressed as I stare up at the palm fronds waving from the tops of long, supple trunks. I am a tiny black child, helpless, abandoned before I can even walk. I am exhausted, thirsty, and hungry, my stomach distended. I have lain for three days beneath the palms, and my time is ending. Maggots are crawling and spilling from the huge weeping sores that cover my body, and I ache from shivering.

I stare up into the palm fronds, and, as I gaze at them, they gradually fade away and I am falling into light. I am floating, floating, wondering who the child was? Was that me? Who is me? I am confused. Am I Joaquín? Who is Jandine? I am lost. Where am I? Who am I? I *must* be someone, but who?

I am drifting. Images flicker before me; I see an image of a man...

This time, the crowds listen. Turning them from their pious and piteous belief about God is not easy, but they listen. They listen to my passion as much as to my words, and that is good. People do not want to release their concept of God. They cling, unreasoning, blind but unrelenting.

It terrifies them that God is judgmental, to be feared, yet this is their belief. I speak of a God of love, a God of compassion, and they murmur of heresy. Do I not teach what Jesus taught? I sigh. Look what happened to him! If there is anything I fear, it is torture — and yet each day I court the possibility.

I wish I could speak of God in total truth, instead of behind veils of insinuation. God is in *all* life, in *all* things. This I know. Heaven is a state of Being, not a place for so-called good people to go. I am a pantheist, but pantheism is considered devil worship, so I speak half-truths and disguise the issue. How I would like to speak of my quest for the Greater Immortal Self and urge others to join me. Then we could quench our natural thirst for Truth.

But sadly, very few humans have this thirst. I try to awaken this in others, but they hunger for more and more possessions, more money, more status. Seldom is there a hunger to seek the God within.

My talk is ended, and I step down from the box from which I have addressed the crowd. The people move back as I pass, for a wandering sage is a figure of mystery. My close friends and traveling companions surround me, offering gentle blessings to those we push through as we make our way back to our inn.

I pass through a hundred small towns and villages, speaking, with an ever-growing passion, of God. Discontent with blind faith and the fear of God are spreading, for people are weakened by fear. I offer the strength of love and the forgiveness of God, and the crowds respond. Increasingly, I am hounded and harried by the churches, for their hold on the people is threatened. Often I weep, for those who want freedom, who want love, are punished. We are controlled by fear, separated and isolated from true faith.

In another town, larger this time, people gather in the hundreds. I am warned that there might be trouble. There is an undercurrent of resistance engendered by the churches. There are arrests, and this frightens me, but I cannot stop. I dreamed last night of arrest and torture. In my dream a voice said, "Michael, Michael, do not break. Your time is drawing to a close and you will be tested. Know your own faith. Whatever wounds you suffer, I will heal. If you will endure, I am truly your God."

It is inevitable. I have no wife or children to mourn me, but I am sad. I have a haunting fear, beyond all normal fear, of torture.

Before I finish speaking to the crowds, I am approached by some priests and denounced as being in league with the devil. I am arrested and imprisoned for heresy.

It crosses my mind that these prison walls are not dissimilar to the walls men build around themselves. I can see mine and know that I am forcibly contained. Am I worse off than those who do not see their constraints and do not know they are imprisoned?

Tomorrow I am to be placed on the rack. I have a choice. I can denounce my teachings, confessing a relationship with the devil, and die, or I can hold to my love, confessing nothing — and die! That death is inevitable I do not question, but my fear threatens to choke me. Why should my fear be so great? Do I fear they will break my spirit? Some of the angel's words come back to me: "Michael, do not break. You will be tested. Know your own faith. Whatever wounds you suffer, I will heal. You will endure." I give thanks for such blessed comfort, but it does not allay my fear. I will try to hold out. Is God testing my own faith? Have I been tortured to death in some previous life? Is this why my fear is a tangible force? I am sweating as, one by one, the last hours of my mortal life pass by.

I am strapped into the rack. I have the crazy feeling I have been here before, that I have died on the rack, but it must be that fear is causing hallucinations. My mind is wandering from the pressure of fear.

As the tension on my limbs is increased, the pain in my lower spine grows steadily greater. I am blinded by sweat, while every pore of my naked body is running water. Urine is splashing my thighs, and my bowels erupt as a blinding bolt of agony lances through my body. My brain is boiling, but clearly I feel and hear the parting of my spine. Through an open, agonized, distended jaw, I scream, *"God is looooove,"* and collapse into a smothering white light of total peace.

No pain. I am healed. I live. I see images leaping from the subdued light in which I drift. I see a prison cell, the huge blocks of stone remorseless and implacable, and I am falling with dread toward pain...

Sweat is stinging my eyes, caked into the filth congealed on my body. The throbbing pulse in my hands is beyond belief, my groan prolonged and feral. I am a small, lithe, young man; my clothes are in tatters. There is blood smeared over my face and on my garments. I am sitting on a heap of filthy, lice-infested straw. The gloom around me is malignant.

I rock back and forth, holding my fingers in my mouth while I moan.

I am a pickpocket, and the judge ordered that my tools of trade be removed. They tore out my fingernails, one by one, laughing! Only my thumbnails were spared.

A couple of days pass in a blur of utter misery, I cannot eat, and the sickening offal that is thrown into my cell would offend a dog. Suddenly, there is a voice, and the cell door opens with a creak. "You're free. Get out."

I wander the streets of London, and the cobbles that were once so friendly now jar my body with each uneven step I take. Unintentionally, I blunder into a dockside area, a foul and dangerous place I have always avoided. I look at my blood-caked hands and decide to wash them at the water's edge. I need to see how badly damaged they are, although I know that they will never again settle light as a fly on a lady's purse.

With some effort, I reach the boarded edge of a rotting quay, and I kneel down, stretching my hands to the water. God! It is cold. I lean out further when, soundlessly, a rotten plank gives way.

I am in the water, struggling weakly in the numbing cold. I grab for the boards, crying out in fresh agony as my mutilated fingers strike against the wood. I cannot grip. Within a few minutes, water floods my mouth as I ineffectually cry out for help. There is no one, but for one brief moment I see again the old crone with eyes of death. It was she who called out as I lifted that last purse.

All is rapidly fading into the awful dreams that plague me so often. I dream that I am a young woman with a terrible growth, that I am dying. Then she is replaced by a hunchback. He is a horrible sight and runs toward me, but as I flee I become a holy man in a prison cell.

I make a last ineffectual grasp at the edge of the jetty, sobbing. As I sink into the water, I realize that the dream came true. My prison cell was the cell in the dream, imprisoning the holy man.

Lost

Who...? I am drunk as I gulp water, laughing as my body sinks, thick and heavy, in the Thames.

I am drifting. Now I know who I am. I am Darfred. I have just drowned, but who is Michael? Drifting, drifting. Who is Darfred? Who am I? Drifting. Another young man walking along the streets...I don't want to be this person...No.

Whistling a happy tune, I amble away from the trade houses where my father is doing business. I wander downtown, away from the affluence and wealth into the poorer quarters where there are many beggars. I muse on this odd fact. Beggars gain more in the slums from the poor than they do in the wealthy part of town. Compassion must surely be born from pain and need!

What draws me to these undesirable quarters I am not sure, but I often come here. I seem to have a fascination with beggars. To amuse myself, I sometimes put money in a purse and fasten it to my belt. When I walk the streets of a slum, I wait for that feather-light touch of the pickpocket. Strangely, I can always detect it. I pretend that I do not know, so the thief gets the purse. I don't mind. I am wealthy, and they are poor. I feed many families in this way, and it pleases me. I also give to the children. They know I am a soft touch, but I feel so much compassion for starving children. I cannot bear to see the bloated tummy of a hungry child.

People smile at me in the slum quarter. I am no longer resented as though I insult their poverty with my wealth. They know my game, and we play it with skill and dignity. I once saw a young girl with a growth on her throat. Without warning, I burst into tears and she ran into the hovel where she lived. Several days later, I dropped a silver coin onto the street when I knew she was looking. I hid around the next corner and waited for her to claim it. She did, and I felt a rush of pleasure.

I cease my aimless whistling when I see a beggar approach whom I have never seen before. Most are familiar to me. He comes directly to me, which is very unusual. He is particularly filthy, yet he is unstooped. There is something very odd about this man, and I watch him with keen interest as he reaches me.

He holds out both hands and, looking me in the eyes, asks, "A coin, D'avid?"

But his eyes! Never have I seen such eyes. The eyes of a beggar are furtive at best and usually they are diseased. But this man's eyes are direct and somehow free. They are the eyes of God, of immortality peering into a mortal world.

I reel back from his eyes, staggered, when he turns, and within moments he is lost among the throngs.

For the following two years, I visit the slums, endlessly searching for this man; I know him to be God. Why he should dress in such a way I do not know. I know nothing about him, but his eyes have ignited me, and my search for God will never, never cease until I find him. Although I am a young man, I have always had a feeling of continuity. I have always felt that life is all One, and that each individual is part of the Whole. I have a strong sense of having lived before, a feeling heightened during moments of great stress.

My parents are distraught by my ceaseless search for the godman, and they resent the time I spend in the slums. How could they understand? They are wealthy from trading in this large town in northern France. They want to leave the business to me now that I am twenty-one, but this means nothing to me anymore. Once the business was all I lived for, but that was before I saw the man. They reason, they threaten, they plead, but nothing can deter me. I must see the beggar who is God again, so I continue to haunt the slums.

Many think I am mad, and no one (except the little girl with the growth on her throat) has seen the man I describe. I find the girl collapsed in a narrow lane, and as I carry her home, she raves in delirium. But she raves of a beggar with stars in his head . . . and I know.

She dies the next day, but I cannot feel sad. I somehow know she is with her starman.

I am walking once more on my mission of hope when I see a human bundle of rags lying in the gutter. People pass it by, but I cannot. I must help. I kneel beside the body, and it is a man. He looks at me, and it is the one I have been seeking. His eyes have never known nor will they ever know death.

"Why?" I gasp. "Why are you like this? Aren't you God?"

His voice is soft but clear. "I am God as mortal. I am a mirror. To find me, look within yourself. Do this, for it is your destiny."

"But how is it no one else has ever seen you?" I ask in tearful anguish.

"They do not see life. I am life."

His head falls back and he is dead, a clear denial of his words!

Even as I gaze at his peaceful face, I see my error. This is not death; this is withdrawal. He has stepped from his body in the same way I step from my carriage — and with the same ease!

A week later, I enter a monastery. This is known to be the place of God. Here I will find him.

TWENTY-FOUR YEARS HAVE PASSED, and I have never once left this monastery. I have tuberculosis and I am dying. I am not afraid of death, for it is only now, in the last few hours of my life, that I realize the depth of my mistake. God is not contained within monastic walls, nor in any church or dogmatic institution. All those years ago, I saw freedom in a man who demonstrated life, not death or poverty. He appeared to me in a way that contained a message, but I was unable to interpret it. I offered compassion to the poor, and within that I found God. Not knowing I had found God, I dismissed that state of Being that God is and went looking for that which I already was. By looking, I denied the having!

During my years here, I have become certain of the continuity of life. I am aware of having searched for God for many lifetimes. In deep meditation, I have connected with some of those past selves. I was a young woman who died from a tumor in her throat. I have been a scholarly hunchback with a passion divided between botany and the search for Oneness. I have been many people who died miserably, and it seems that this death will not be much of an improvement. But at least I am spared pain. I have detected a common thread among the lives I've lived — the endless search for Self, the search to know the truth of who I am.

Phlegm is hot in my throat and I cough. Despite all those years in a monastic order, I have followed my own path. Yes, I mouthed the words of a monk, but in my heart I spoke to God in my own way. During those long hours of silence, I learned to reach the deepest parts of myself, and it was here I found Michael. He had been a holy man. He — I — lived with and will die in truth. During those moments of profound meditation, I learned that I shall live again as another, different Michael, reincarnating once more into this world. I look forward to my next life, for I have learned much that I can bring to a new physical existence. I now know that the Greater Self is not to be found in separate identities but in the Whole. This knowing will emerge in my next life, and I will know *who I am.*

Coughing shakes my body, and I wipe bloody phlegm from my lips. Weakly, I laugh. What a joke that I looked for God in a grim, austere, loveless monastery! God is *love!*

I lay on a thin straw mattress on a solid board bed. My cell is doorless, one cell in a long, bare corridor of empty, lonely cells. Even when occupied they are bare, for without love a human being has nothing, less than nothing. Coughing out my last few breaths, alone in this bleak place, I am feeling a joy such as I never imagined possible. I am thrilled. For the last hour or so, faintly, as if from a far distant angel, I hear a voice calling, "Miiicchhaaeell, Micchhaaeell," over and over. It confirms all I learned of a future me. I am responding. D'avid seems to have receded, and I am attracted to this ethereal, other Michael.

Without any fear or trauma, I feel myself float gently from my body. I am filled with joy. As I float in pure, shimmering light, the arms of a little girl go around me and I look into her eyes. No growth mars her throat, but her eyes are the eyes of God, and I laugh at the joke. No wonder I could never learn her name! No wonder He could not be found. God reaches us through...us!

I float, drifting in peace. Who or where I am I do not know. I am lost but I no longer fear. Am I Jandine, Darfred, or D'avid? I am lost in identities, and I laugh, for I am not afraid. I *am* love...and this I know.

"Miicchhaaeell"...."Michael."

⟶

MY BODY JERKED CONVULSIVELY and I opened my eyes. Treenie knelt at my side, concern and love showing in her face. I opened my arms and engulfed her, holding her for long, long minutes while I cried softly. She said nothing — time enough for that later. She simply held me tight, knowing that was my need.

I cried with the memory of suffering and pain I had endured in other lifetimes. I cried for all my suffering as a whole, and I cried for the suffering of each individual identity as he or she struggled to understand. And I cried because I knew that in every other human Being a similar story of pain and suffering was being endlessly enacted. And my crying was a healing.

Dkdlxl 1234

10 Going Beyond

We lay together in the soft kangaroo grass. All the identities I had experienced tumbled through my mind.

"Why didn't you shake me out of it?" I whispered unsteadily.

"I didn't dare. It was obvious you were somewhere else and I thought it might be dangerous. I could only call you."

"How long were you calling?"

"Long enough to frighten me."

"How long?" I persisted.

"Oh, nearly ten minutes."

"Only minutes!" I echoed in astonishment. "I lived a life in those minutes. I lived a long, boring life of chanting, praying, meditating, and misery. I was cold, forever cold, except in mid-summer. Ugh! The coldness of stone is incredible. The only relief was meditation. Only in meditation could I enter states of love ...and discovery."

I told her about David and his meeting with the beggar who was God and about all the years following.

She listened gravely. "Well, it explains your easy ability to meditate, and your intense dislike of cold. Even your love of conversation."

"Of *course*. All those years of strict, imposed silence. We could speak for only an hour each day. And do you know the greatest tragedy? After a while there was nothing to talk about, nothing to share!"

We walked indoors, and over a succession of cups of tea I told Treenie my story. Each detail was etched with such intensity I flinched as I recalled and told it.

"So many people," she said. "Jandine, Joaquín, a poor little black child, another Michael, poor Darfred, and then D'avid...and yet all were you."

I smiled ruefully. "It's rather like a litany of pain. Pain and suffering are the only real connections."

"You know better than that. The real connection is the spiritual one. You *were* those other people. Every one of us shares the same truth. Every human being on this planet is an individual who in some way is the total, or an aspect, of all the identities he has ever been. And within all that is the Greater Self, that part of us that is the total, the Whole of who we are." She became excited. "Don't you see! The Greater Self can't be found in a single identity, so looking within must mean looking within the whole, not at a single collection of thoughts." She stared at me expectantly.

"You're right. I know that my search for the Greater Self has lasted many lifetimes. I've just experienced a few of them. Some of the connections are startling, yet they shouldn't be. That other Michael, the wandering holy man, he was a pantheist. So am I. We share the belief that God is within *All*, rather than being a separate deity. But beliefs aren't all that are shared. The very place where that other Michael felt his spine break is where I get my lower back pain. And poor Darfred's fingers. I have bitten my fingernails since I was a child, and even when I stopped my fingers just go to my mouth — but never my thumbnails! There's more than habit involved. It would seem that my fingers need to be loved and reassured that they are safe. Our consciousness is even within the cellular structure of our bodies, and it carries its own memories. Can you imagine how many people are crippled or deformed as a result of something so shocking in their past that it impressed itself into their bodily consciousness? I seem to remember Pan telling me that anything unresolved in the past remains unresolved in the present."

"Give me a summary of the main connections of your various experiences," Treenie said. "Perhaps then we might find a vital clue that will help reveal the truth of Self. I'm interested in this for me, because _the Truth_ is true for everybody. We may differ in our beliefs as individuals, but the Truth of Self is universal."

"That's a tall order." I gave it some thought. "Well, the first thing that comes to mind involves the dolphin experience. I learned that the dolphin experiences a number of identities in each life, while we humans, of course, experience only one. But we do experience a number of identities in a series of lives. The only trouble is, the lives _appear_ separate. In truth, the total is one _whole_ life. So our way is different from the dolphin way, but it achieves the same result. We try to sort through those many identities and learn who we are. The joke is that we're none of them but we're _all_ of them. That much I learned. I knew all this intellectually, but it wasn't my reality.

"The dolphin also told me that while humans are an immortal expression of Divine Love, our identities are brief expressions of human individuality." My eyebrows arched. "Well, at least I know the reality of that now. I've just lived it!"

I did another spell of thinking. "Except for my experiences in the Guidestone, the Door to Beyond hasn't featured in what I have been learning. The Door obviously has a key, like any other door. However, the key to this Door is unique. I'm certain that the key to the Door is the consciousness of self-realization, of knowing _who I am_. In other words, the key is a state of Being. Anything less, and that membrane will not yield. It's not what we know that's required, it's what we _are!_"

"I agree with all that," Treenie replied. "When you consider that the Door is the threshold to other realities, it would seem likely that consciousness is the key. A certain vibration of human love probably vibrates with that invisible membrane."

I nodded, "Beautifully put."

"What else comes to mind?" Treenie asked.

"I think each experience in the mystical realm of Nature is a lesson in the way life works on Earth. Each of my experiences seems to have been a preparation for the next step. Is it possible that I am now at a stage where I can realize that Greater Self and penetrate the membrane of the Door? I suspect that going Beyond is only now a possibility. Other lives and other times have been a preparation.

"What Pan has in store for me next I can't imagine. One thing that's apparent is that each and every experience connects with the Whole. For example, when Pan took me down from the top of the plateau into the center of the huge crystal, I saw each flickering light as separate. It was only when I allowed my perception to emerge that I knew each light was part of One vast Light. Perhaps that is another way to experience everyday life — to allow reason, intuition, and perception to merge. Maybe these faculties together will create a greater view of our reality than we presently enjoy."

"Anything else?" Treenie encouraged me.

"Yes. The consciousness of water gave me an experience of Oneness, while blackberry consciousness revealed that although physical forms of a single species are separate, they are One in spirit. The blackberry reinforced the water's lesson and extended it into a physical reality. And then there was Ping! Ping's words about seeing myself in all the plant life around me indicated that I am also in every *person*. We all are. Talk about Oneness! Nature and humanity *are* One. We cannot learn about a holistic Nature by excluding humanity, nor about humans by omitting Nature. To find the true Self, we must obviously embrace *all* life."

My thoughts had turned back to that night of the terrible storm, and to the storm Being's final words: "Only by surrendering to the storm may you conquer it."

I felt a surge of exciting insight. I gazed at Treenie, my eyes shining. "The Being in the storm was telling me how to become free. It said, 'Only by surrendering may you conquer.' *Now* I get it! I finally understand. The answer is — let my Greater Self emerge. Let it appear within me by surrendering all attachment to identity. We must become individuals *aware* of the All. We have to *be* the One in All, the All in One." Now I was really excited. "Don't you see? We already *are* what we are looking for! We...we..."

I looked beseechingly at Treenie. "I can feel it in my heart, I almost know it, but something is blocking that final leap." I sighed in defeat. "Pan also told me that surrender is a letting go, not something you can force. By giving in, you give to the inner Self. Maybe I need to give in. Not give up, but give in!"

Before I went to bed that night, I had the feeling I would soon be seeing Pan again. I mentioned this to Treenie.

"I felt that also," she said. "I feel that a culmination of events is imminent. I wonder how it will happen."

"Does it worry you?"

"It concerns me, but I don't really worry. I trust the process and I *know* you are in good hands. How about you?"

"No, I'm not worried, although if I thought I had to go through some of the experiences again...I would rather not think about it."

A week later, I saw Pan sitting on the rock where an invisible violet-pink ray penetrates the Earth. He looked so physical and solid it was difficult to grasp that this was the same ethereal Being I had encountered there several months earlier.

"I welcome you, Michael."

Was it respect I saw in those golden eyes? I could now gaze into them without threat or fear. God, he was so beautiful! For the first time I actually understood those people of an earlier time who may have encountered him. If one could not accept such unearthly beauty and feel at ease within its aura, then one would have to experience fear and distortion. The demarcations between beauty and beast, love and fear, are within our personal consciousness.

"Hello, Pan. I'm really glad to see you." I hesitated only briefly. "May I hug you?"

Pan came to me, his arms open. Hugging him took my breath away. In hugging him I hugged the sky, the open universe. I hugged the woods of my youth and a wilderness I have yet to encounter. I hugged light and a nonhuman Being within the light. He was both solid and without substance, formed and nebulous. But more than anything he was Love!

"You have done very well."

"I thought you might be angry. I didn't know whether I should go alone or wait for you, but I know now. You maneuvered me, didn't you? You knew what I would try?"

"Of course. I told you once that I know you better than you know yourself. I know the Self you are looking for! What was I supposed to do? Ask you to get lost? Only recently I warned that you did not know what lost was. You chose to ignore my warning. Only by becoming truly lost can you find yourself. Don't you remember the question I once asked you? If you lose yourself, how do you find yourself if you do not know who you are?"

"But I haven't found the Self I'm looking for."

"You did exceptionally well. You found the thread of seeking Self and Wholeness within each identity, and you followed it."

"But if Treenie had not drawn me out, I might have drifted forever in that other place."

"Ah, but she *did* draw you out. This was known. I love you, Michael. I wouldn't abandon you. Although I could not be with you — that is Law — your soul mate could not be denied. Without her, you could never have entered that other place."

His eyes danced like twin reflections of the sun. Mischief shone from them as transparently as from the eyes of a child.

"And you are not angry at being tricked again!"

I smiled at him. "I seem to have lost my anger — and my fear. When D'avid lost his fear, I lost mine, which isn't surprising considering we are both the same Being. Losing my fear has been rather like losing the dragging weight of a huge anchor. I feel *lighter!* But, one last question. Who is the old witch? She was an evil presence in so many lives. Who is she?"

"I have only one answer to that. We must enter the Guidestone together."

"I don't have the Guidestone out here. It's indoors."

"We don't need its physical presence. Your consciousness contains the Guidestone, just as you are contained by it. You need only relax, visualize the interior, and we are there."

"Relax! That's funny. Did you see me jumping up and down trying to get into the stone? It must have looked like I was throwing a fit." I laughed at the memory.

"No, I didn't see you. I was in another reality."

"Well," I continued, "it was only when I stopped trying that it happened. An image of the chamber in the Guidestone came into my mind, and without struggle I was there!"

"Michael, you have just summarized the art of life. Humans can achieve many of the things they struggle for merely by relaxing. We are talking again about surrender. Focus on what you want to achieve, and then relax. This does not mean that you do nothing; it means you allow the achieving to unfold as a result of your focusing ability. Focus creates the result."

"That's exactly what happened! I take it that you can find your own way into the Guidestone. Or do I visualize us both in?"

Pan laughed, wind chimes and happiness.

"Whichever."

I lay back on the soft grass and relaxed, eyes closed. I felt no sense of urgency. Pan lived in no-time, so there could be no wait. What luxury! For a while I concentrated on the harsh calls of some distant currawongs, relaxing, letting go.

Once again, without effort, an image of the chamber in the Guidestone flowed easily into my mind, and I was there.

⸺

I LOOK AROUND, very pleased. I am standing before the Doors, and they are open. Pan is waiting on the other side — in the Beyond — and, walking on air, he comes through the Doors toward me.

"Can I walk through the Doors?"

"Try it."

With my hands out before me, I advance a step, only to meet the familiar resistance. I shrug. "Nothing's changed."

"In reality, much has changed."

"I still cannot enter Beyond."

"Are you sure you really want to?"

"Very sure. After all I've been through? Definitely!"

"Nervous?"

"You know I'm not. Well, just a bit apprehensive. I've had some pretty scary times in here. Come to that, nothing nice has happened to me here at all except meeting you! But I guess that makes up for it."

"If you have any residual fear, tell me now. It's important,"

Concentrating on my past states of fear, I grope as deeply as I can into my psyche.

"I am not frightened."

"Why not? It is stupid not to be frightened."

Pan's voice is loud and menacing. I can feel a threat, an unknown power, in his energy. But I am certain. "Because no matter what happens to me, I continue. I don't know who I am, but I do know that my identity is not physical. No matter how bad, how agonizing, physical life may be, I am something more than that — and I will endure."

His voice is a roar, a blast of power. And his face has altered, becoming longer. His horns now embody menace and an aura of evil enshrouds him.

"Are you so sure? Is it not possible that I am the Devil? Humans are so gullible. I may have tricked you!"

It is only now that I really know.

Laughing in his face, I say, "Do your worst, Devil. Gobble me up and spit out all my separate identities."

A naked, sexless, golden Pan regards me. Love and purity radiate with such intensity it seems impossible that evil could ever have existed. Even as the thought comes, I know the truth. Evil does *not* exist. It never has. Ignorance conjures evil from our consciousness and gives it power through our fear.

"You have passed, and I rejoice."

He beckons to me. "Come. Take a look at your old witch woman."

The chamber is illuminated by those white, heatless flames, and I see. Alongside the Door, where I had tried to find a way around it, stands a huge mirror. Looking in, I see my own reflection.

I gasp. What I see is more than a reflection, far more. It is holographic reflection, a perfect three-dimensional image.

"A physical mirror reflects physical reality, but this metaphysical mirror reflects states of consciousness. If your state of consciousness contains fear, fear will be reflected. The old crone was your own fear. It took that form because of an incident in a life long past in subjective time."

"But how? Where did I run?"

Pan points in the opposite direction, to another flawless mirror alongside the other Door. "You ran through the other mirror. A physical mirror can only reflect, but a metaphysical mirror can reflect and absorb."

"Where? Where was I?"

"Exactly where you believed yourself to be. You were in no-time, the space between realities, the all-time."

I turn back to the first mirror, regarding my reflected image with affection. It is only then I realize that the mirror reflects nothing else around me. No flames, not even Pan. Pan?

I spin around, searching, but he is not to be seen. He has soundlessly vanished.

"Paaan. PAAAAAANNNNN." Nothing!

But I am not afraid.

I turn back to the mirror, intrigued by the concept of meta-physical reflection. The perfect flawlessness of the mirror is stunning. I reach out and touch the surface of my reflection, snatching my hand away. It is warm, as though alive! In faithful duplication, the mirror reflects my every move, the reflection seeming almost more real than me. I reach out to touch the sur-face without the imprint of reflection, and there is nothing!

I draw back cautiously. With or without fear, I have no wish to get lost in the mirror again!

I walk to the side of my image, hoping to peer around it and, faithfully, it walks to one side, peering around me. Most perplex-ing, but why? What is the purpose of this? I turn around, searching once more for Pan, but he is not to be seen. Turning back to the mirror, I recoil in shock. A short, dark-haired girl wearing a dark green dress of some heavy material is staring back at me, her face reflecting astonishment as she recoils from me. Intrigued, I step closer to the mirror, peering into its mysterious depths, and she steps closer to me, peering intently.

I smile and she smiles. I raise my right arm and her right arm is raised. I wriggle my neck and shrug in resignation and she per-fectly reflects my actions.

Wow! What a mirror. But who is she? If she is my reflection, is she the *real* me? I am shocked, and my shock registers on her face!

I turn around, facing away from the mirror as I once again look for Pan. "PAAAANN." My shout is smothered by silence. No echoes bounce in this chamber. "Gee, Pan, it just isn't fair. Now what am I supposed to do? Anyway, who is the girl? I've never met her before."

Nothing! No sight or sound of Pan. No response to my attempted conversation.

I turn back to the mirror, deciding to ask the girl who she is. Perhaps this mirror will allow conversation.

Tall and blonde, Jandine stares back at me, her mouth open in astonishment. Another involuntary step back. "Good grief! Jandine!" Her mouth opens and closes soundlessly. Pity. I cannot talk to her... me? Stepping closer, I peer at her intently, while she peers at me with equal intensity.

Only slowly, and with great difficulty, am I able to accept the idea that the reflection is myself, not someone else. I am the reflection, no matter what reflects.

I gaze pensively at my reflected Jandine, when, with the faintest wisp of movement, the outlines blur, fade, and reform to reveal the exceptional ugliness of Joaquín.

The impact of contrast is considerable. I stand straight, while Joaquín's stance is stooped and twisted. Jandine's throat was unblemished, but poor Joaquín looks as though his neck was twisted by some giant hand when he was a child and he failed to die.

I gaze at him through tear-filled eyes while he stares back with compassion and love.

I ache to hold that broad, squat figure with its unmistakably intelligent eyes, but even as I step helplessly forward, he is changing... and a very tall, lean Egyptian is revealed.

Another smart step back! This me looks fierce and arrogant, even ruthless. I feel uncomfortable. I have no recollection of this other me, but I realize that he must be one of the many identities I have forgotten. I step closer, gasping as I see just how tall he is compared to my present body.

I watch and wait. Sure enough, he fades and is replaced by Darfred. I feel I know Darfred well. Looking with interest at his fingers, I see to my surprise that they are healing. This can only mean that my own healing has affected him.

Darfred fades, to be replaced by a small urchin girl, who in turn is replaced by a tiny, helpless black child. Other identities come and go. A Native American stands before me, proud and with immense dignity. My recall is powerful and immediate. After a long life of spiritual development with Nature, I went into the hills to die. By choice I remained bodiless on Earth, moving over the familiar hills and valleys for another century of Earth time. My wisdom and insight into Nature from another dimensional perception revealed the truth of human and Nature as One. Such was the depth of spiritual insight among my people that they knew of me, and I was given a name symbolizing great love and respect. They knew when I passed through their villages, when I helped their dying, and though unseen they would greet me. Never was I feared, for they knew me to be not dead but merely living without a body.

The reflection had faded to be replaced by others, forming and in turn fading. I stare at them, mesmerized. The images are coming faster now. Some cause an immediate emotional response; others are unknown and I cannot respond at all.

Faster and faster, the rapid appearance, consolidation, and fade-outs occur, until I am overwhelmed by identities.

I must get away from this bewildering mirror. I try to turn away but cannot. As long as I watch, neither turning away nor trying to depart, I can move freely, but I am compelled to watch.

A change is taking place within me as, with remorseless purpose, the images come and go. I no longer resist or accept the characters conjured up. I cannot. I am overwhelmed. I cling with despairing energy to the one identity I know I am — Michael, or was it D'avid? No, of course, I am Michael, the heretic sage. No! Who am I really? Abruptly, the images cease. I gaze at . . . nothing. Nothing. *Nothing*! I recoil. Shrinking, shrinking into blackness, endless black density. Dark. Forever, never-ending . . . silence. *All is dark.*

Daaaaaaaaaarrrrrrrrrkkkk.

A speck of light. In all this total darkness, a minute speck of light. Tiny light, growing... growing rapidly. Expanding. *Light. Expanding.* Consuming all dark, devouring black until all is light. All light.

Liiiiiiiiiigggggghhhhhttt.

Mirror. Metaphysical mirror. Reflection. Human is light! Light of Being. Light of beauty. All light. I... I am.

I am *light!* I see light reflected. I see the light of consciousness. This is human consciousness and I realize I am *all* consciousness. I am *all* human. I am One in All, All in One, All in All. Now, finally, I know who I am.

Before me, the mirror is alive with reflected radiance. A light, vaguely shaped in human form, fills the surface. Within this light of consciousness is *all* I am. I see blackberries creeping over the steep hillsides and hares nibbling the new growth of spring barley. I see a great bronze dragonfly hovering over the cool water of a fresh, clear river, and I see the fish in the river's depths. I see a platypus, my ancient self, and an eagle, hovering against the backcloth of an endless blue sky. I see beyond the deceptive sky into another familiar world, spinning with silent orbit in a far-distant galaxy.

And there are human Beings. All the identities I have ever believed myself to be gaze back at me. And they smile. I gaze upon my reflected truth. No longer do I see the physical body containing consciousness; it does not. The mirror reveals that consciousness contains the body. In the way a cloud contains the water that will become individual drops of rain, so consciousness enfolds each one of us. And when we become individual, we are still contained within consciousness. Consciousness knows no boundaries; there are none. The consciousness of you and me is One consciousness. We are individuals, not separate, within it. If we are hit hard upon the head, we are no longer conscious of consciousness. But there is no unconscious! It is a lie, a hoax. All is consciousness. As we treat each other, so we treat our self. We are

One Self. Consciousness is *all*, never separated, never fragmented. Consciousness is *Whole*, forever One.

"Could any Being be told this? It is an experience."

Pan is beside me, radiance sparkling from those golden eyes. I turn to him and find there is nothing to say!

"It can only be an experience. By knowing all selves, you become free of the illusion of self and all with which it identifies. Know also that within this change all the selves you have ever been are changed, for they are not separate from you. The past and the future are a grand illusion."

I smile at him, my heart filled with love. "They are changed because I am changed. We are One. Also, all humanity is affected, for there is no separation between us. Deep within each human psyche, a flame grows brighter, for what affects a part affects the Whole. That is the truth of spirit."

A whole new understanding of life opens before me as I consider it from my new perspective. I like the thought of my past identities experiencing change, however subtle it may be. What a joke! The past is not past. Pan's words of truth have many levels: anything of the past that was unresolved is unresolved now! Equally, what is resolved now is resolved in the past.

My anxieties have vanished. The subconscious imprint that programs our worries is no more. I know that I am not a random collection of genes but an "inspired person." Becoming awake is the birth of purpose.

Glancing pensively at the Door, I am aware that it will now yield to me.

Softly, as though echoing eternally, the words of the Keeper of the Door catch my attention. "To open the Door is to invoke an awesome responsibility. Do not open the Door unless you are prepared to accept this."

Well, I had already opened the Door, even though I had not yet entered.

I accepted the responsibility.

The Keeper's words continue. "If you step into the Beyond, the full force of Nature shall pivot in your Being. Can you accept this enormous responsibility?"

The full force of Nature shall pivot in my Being. Powerful words! I consider them carefully. I am Nature. Nature is within the consciousness that I am. I am changed; I myself am a pivot of change. I accept this!

"Misused . . . it will destroy you."

Even though I am a mortal human being, I am far, far more. I am consciousness. I span the Earth, the universe. And as I am, so is every human Being, but now I know this *profoundly*, not merely intellectually. I cannot misuse the power of Nature. I am that consciousness.

"Well, that takes care of the preliminaries. Now we can wrap up the action." Pan's words are a breath of light, of never-ending humor.

"I'm ready, too." So saying, Treenie stands at my side and reaches out to take my hand.

For long moments, I am speechless. Then I laugh. I ask no questions — after all, this angel does it her way! Together, Pan, Treenie, and I walk through the Door into the waiting mystery of Beyond.

Epilogue

Some considerable time later, after I had written this book of my experiences, I asked Pan if there was anything I could share with you, the reader, that would empower you, or enable you to find the truth of who you are. He smiled at my seriousness. "Within the pages of your book are many truths that apply to all. I am sure they will be recognized."

"Yes, I know that. But I want to offer something that can be used daily, something with tangible value."

"Then I suggest you search your own memory and draw from your own experiences. You, more than I, should be able to encapsulate the knowledge you have gained and make it available."

I walked alone among the tall trees, listening as the breeze whispered among the leaves overhead. Ah! Yes! Here lay one tangible reality. Here was a part of life that eluded most people, as it had me. The art of *listening*, of being in the moment. If we listen, totally, we cannot think, for thinking moves us away from the moment. We can think and hear, but hearing is not listening. Listening brings us into the moment, the only place of life, of God.

Practice listening to the sounds of Nature around you, or, if you live in a city, listen to your favorite music played softly enough that you really have to listen to hear it. When thoughts intrude on your listening, just accept it and, without resistance, let them go. You cannot force listening; you can only surrender your resistance to listening!

As I gazed up at the leaves moving above me, I remembered Pan having asked me if I could see what he was seeing when he and I gazed up into a similar tree. And I had looked in vain. That incident taught me that we are very practiced at "looking at," but not at seeing. We look at Nature and people through yesterday's eyes, just as we hear with yesterday's ears. We have forgotten how to see anew, the way a child sees, everything brimming with the excitement of discovery. We have labeled and categorized everything, and we have lost the newness of seeing. Practice seeing your relatives, your family, your life partner, and your closest friends as totally new people every day. Put aside yesterday's images and concepts of who they are, and experience them anew, each day.

Once again, this brings you into the moment, the *isness* of now. See each familiar flower, tree, and plant as though you were seeing it for the first time. Really *see*. You will find that your relationship with your life partner, your parents, your children, your friends, and Nature will change. It will become more creative, more open, allowing far more room for love. But even more than this, your relationship with yourself will change, for as you see others anew, so will the newness of yourself emerge within you. And within this newness lies the potential of you experiencing who you are.

I sat down, my back against the smooth, comforting trunk of a small gum tree. What else? What other simple, overlooked reality is lost in the claw and rush of daily living? What we see and hear is by far the greatest part of our sensory input, but what other aspect of life lies hidden under separation, habit, and illusion?

Memory conjured up the lesson from Ping. Ah yes! How to practice connecting with life by deliberately defying the illusion of separation. Practice seeing everything around you that has life as you in disguise. Again, this means you within your friends, family, loved ones, even those people you dislike, all trees, animals, in fact, all aspects of Nature. If you truly practice pretending that you are everything around you in disguise, eventually you will experience the overwhelming exultation of *knowing* that this is not pretense. Your relationship with life will change positively and dramatically.

I lay back, staring up at the few pale gray clouds scudding across the vast backdrop of space.

It's not much, I thought, and it all seems far too simple, but it is something that can be practiced in everyday life. Simple it may well be; easy it is not! Nevertheless, I know that if these few basic realities are practiced with a focus on becoming aware and awake, then in perfect timing these realities will help to overwhelm the illusions that enfold you. I know that if you accept that "knowing who you are" is possible, and if you have the courage to follow wherever the journey takes you, then nothing can stop you.